Praise for *Aging in Stride*

"Excellent! Of all the books I have seen, none is as comprehensive as this one. I particularly appreciate how it captures information on relevant topics and allows readers to use its tools, materials, and research to plan for their own future by making their own decisions. The basic premise—and I agree with it—is that successful aging calls for a thoughtful blend of information, planning, partnership, and the right attitude."

Robert W. Littke, Ph.D., President and CEO
Senior Services, Inc.
Kalamazoo, MI

"Every family needs a few carefully chosen books for its bookshelf. This is one of those books. The issue discussions, more resources, forms, and online reader support center are practical and easy to use. What you have here is a roadmap, compass, and words of encouragement, all rolled into one."

Pamela Piering, Director
Seattle/King County
Area Agency on Aging

"Congratulations on a wonderfully organized, refreshingly straightforward guide to healthy, successful aging. As a case manager, I found the forms section invaluable. The links to more resources and the online Reader Support Center will also be of significant benefit to readers."

Ellen Aliberti, B.S.N., M.S., C.C.M.
Director of Continuity of Care
Health Plan of Nevada

"A remarkably clear roadmap to healthy aging. Of course, it won't answer every question. And it won't make the smart choices that often need to be made. But it can help in a wonderful way by giving the reader both the big picture and a better understanding of the many forks in the road that may come along."

Nina Tumosa, Ph.D.
Co-Director, Gateway Geriatric Education Center of Missouri and Illinois
Education Officer, Veterans Affairs Medical Center/Saint Louis

"This is a wonderful book—respectful and thoughtful, yet direct and to the point. Its great strength is that it takes into account the whole person: mind, body, and spirit."

Robert G. Peirce, President and CEO
Ocadian Hospitals and Care Centers
San Francisco, CA

"The families and friends of older clients we work with often ask: 'How can we help?' *Aging in Stride* helps them answer that simple question in so many ways. The book's 'you-can-do-this' approach to healthy aging and eldercare is reassuring and absolutely on target."

Mary Lynn Pannen, R.N., B.S.N., C.C.M.
President, Sound Options, Inc.
Tacoma, WA

"*Aging in Stride* is an essential first step towards successful aging. It features excellent resources, including 'quicklinks' that give the reader a whole clearinghouse of valuable information. The concepts are well defined and presented from a perspective that is positive, yet realistic."

Bonnie Cashin Farmer, Ph.D., R.N.
Assistant Professor, University of Maine
College of Nursing and Health Professions

"I finished *Aging in Stride* and I LOVE it. I think this will be such a valuable resource for people. Straight talk, but presented in a friendly, upbeat, positive way. Definitely recommended."

Carol Santalucia, Ombudsman
The Cleveland Clinic Foundation
Past-President, Society for Healthcare Consumer Advocacy

"*Aging in Stride* will be an excellent guide for three groups: older adults; concerned family members; and health care professionals who work with older people. A 'must have' book for anyone interested in practical advice on aging and eldercare."

Cheryl Hopkins, Patient Representative
Borgess Medical Center
Kalamazoo, MI

Aging *in* Stride

PLAN AHEAD • STAY CONNECTED • KEEP MOVING

Christine Himes, M.D.

Elizabeth N. Oettinger, M.Div.

Dennis E. Kenny, J.D.

Please remember . . .

Aging in Stride has been written to help you better understand what it means to age well and what many people like you are doing to promote healthy aging for themselves and their loved ones. It is not intended and should in no way be used as a substitute for the advice and assistance of a qualified professional—medical, legal, financial, or other—in dealing with symptoms, legal and financial issues, and other facts and circumstances unique to you or your loved one.

Library of Congress Cataloging-in-Publication Data

Himes, Christine L.
  Aging in stride : plan ahead, stay connected, keep moving / by
Christine Himes, Elizabeth N. Oettinger, and Dennis E. Kenny.
    p. cm.
  ISBN 1-878866-24-9 (pbk.)
 1. Aged—Social conditions—United States. 2. Aged—Health and
hygiene—United States. I. Oettinger, Elizabeth N. II. Kenny, Dennis E.
III. Title.
HQ1064.U5H56 2004
305.26'0973—dc22

305.26
Himes

                        2003025757

Cover design and illustrations: Cathy Tousley and Flashcat Design, *www.flashcatdesign.com*

Distributed in cooperation with Conifer Publishing Group, 800-353-2930, *www.coniferpublishing.com*

CARESOURCE
HEALTHCARE COMMUNICATIONS

Caresource Healthcare Communications, Inc.
426 Yale Avenue North • Seattle, WA 98109
Phone: 800-448-5213 • Fax: 206-682-2901
www.caresource.com

About the Authors

Christine Himes, M.D.

Dr. Chris Himes is a family physician and geriatrician at Group Health Cooperative in Seattle, Washington, where she is a clinician and the Director of Geriatrics. She has worked and lectured extensively in the areas of preventive care for seniors, the management of chronic conditions, and the field of exercise physiology in aging.

As a member of the Steering Committee for the National Blueprint for Increasing Physical Activity sponsored by the Centers for Disease Control and Prevention, Dr. Himes is currently leading work to develop a national training tool for physicians for writing exercise prescriptions and has developed, with her patients, an exercise video for the frail elderly. Her interests have focused on healthy aging; since testifying before Congress in 2002 on appropriate preventive care strategies for the Medicare population, she has worked extensively with Congressional staffers on developing a national preventive care bill to improve the quality of care for all seniors.

Elizabeth N. Oettinger, M. Div.

Elizabeth Oettinger is Senior Minister at First Congregational United Church of Christ, Corvallis, Oregon, with her Master of Divinity from Yale University. She previously served churches in Seattle, and Duluth, Minnesota. Ms. Oettinger also holds a Master's degree in Medical Ethics and has extensive experience in patient and family counseling in hospitals, hospices and other care settings. She has served as a board member of Hospice of Duluth, Providence Hospice of Seattle, and Benton Hospice Service in Corvallis.

Prior to becoming a minister, Ms. Oettinger was a member of the Board of Editors, *American Heritage Magazine*. She also co-edited *The Family Carebook: A Comprehensive Guide for Families of Older Adults.*

Dennis E. Kenny, J.D.

Dennis Kenny is co-founder and president of Caresource Healthcare Communications, Inc., in Seattle, Washington. Created in 1989, Caresource specializes in helping health care and senior service providers fulfill their patient, client, family, and community education responsibilities. In partnership with clients nationwide, he has authored or supervised the development of hundreds of healthy aging booklets, brochures, newsletters, videos, and websites.

Mr. Kenny's interest and expertise in the legal and financial aspects of aging and eldercare began prior to establishing Caresource. From 1976 to 1989, he practiced law with the national law firm Davis Wright Tremaine, where he was a partner, chairman of the firm's Health Law Practice Group, and Managing Partner. He is a graduate of the University of Notre Dame and the University of Washington School of Law, and is a current board member and past board president of Providence Hospice of Seattle.

Editorial Review Board

Thanks to the following professionals for reading the manuscript of this book and making so many helpful suggestions for improving it.

Sharon McIntyre, A.C.C.
Director
Resident Councils of Washington

Mary Lynn Pannen, R.N.
Geriatric Care Manager
President, Sound Options, Inc.

Robert G. Peirce
President and CEO
Ocadian Hospitals and Care Centers

Lee Peterson, R.N., M.S., F.N.P.
Geriatric Consultant
Alaska Longevity Programs

Pamela Piering
Director
Seattle/King County
Area Agency on Aging

Carol Santalucia
Ombudsman
The Cleveland Clinic Foundation
Past-President, Society for Healthcare
    Consumer Advocacy

Rodney Smith, M.S.W.
Author
Lessons from the Dying

Beverley Soble
Vice-President Regulatory Affairs
Virginia Health Care Association

Nina Tumosa, Ph.D.
Co-Director
Gateway Geriatric Education Center of
    Missouri and Illinois
Education Officer
VA Medical Center, Saint Louis

T. Franklin Williams, M.D.
Professor of Medicine Emeritus
University of Rochester

Publishing Partners

Aging in Stride is co-published by a coalition of leaders in the fields of aging services, senior living, and health care. Through December 2003, the list of participating organizations includes:

The SPRY (Setting Priorities for Retirement Years) Foundation is a nonprofit research foundation with a mission to promote successful aging in the domains of financial security, physical health and wellness, mental health and social environment, and intellectual pursuits. It partners with organizations to develop and test modules, curricula, training programs, and guides that inform and empower older adults in these four areas. For more on SPRY's current projects and other publications, visit *www.spry.org*.

The **American Academy of Physician Assistants** is the only national organization that represents physician assistants (PAs) in all specialties and all employment settings. Its mission is to promote quality, cost-effective, accessible health care, and to promote the professional and personal development of physician assistants. For more on AAPA, visit *www.aapa.org*.

The **Society for Healthcare Consumer Advocacy** leads the advancement of healthcare consumer advocacy by supporting the role of professionals who represent and advocate for consumers across the healthcare continuum. It pursues its mission, in part, by promoting quality consumer education, especially on issues such as patients' rights, patient-provider communication, and advance directives. For more on SHCA, visit *www.shca-aha.org*.

Easter Seals serves over one million Americans, many of them older adults, and their families through a nationwide network of more than 450 service sites. Easter Seals provides choices when a spouse, parent, or grandparent needs assistance with daily living, but is not ready for full-time nursing home care. Services for older adults include *adult day programs* and *in-home care services*. For more on Easter Seals and the services it provides to older adults and their families, visit *www.easterseals.com*.

New York State Health Facilities Association serves the sub-acute care and long term care providers of New York. NYSHFA members care for approximately 50,000 New Yorkers. The association and its members are dedicated to creating an environment which enables members to provide accessible, efficient, quality long term health care and a continuum of reliable services. For more on NYSHFA, visit *www.nyshfa.org*.

Health Care Association of New Jersey promotes the highest quality of long term health care in New Jersey. Its members are nursing, sub-acute care, adult medical day care, assisted living, comprehensive personal care and residential health facilities. Together, they serve nearly 35,000 patients and residents, and their families. The association's mission includes providing consumer information and education on aging issues, options for senior living, and long term care. For more on HCANJ, visit *www.hcanj.org*.

California Association of Health Facilities is dedicated to improving the quality of long term health care in California through professional and consumer education and legislative advocacy. Its online Consumer Information Center features a *Guide to Long Term Care*, a checklist for selecting a nursing facility, a searchable database of nursing facilities in California, and information on a variety of other related topics. For more on CAHF, visit *www.cahf.org*.

Virginia Health Care Association's mission is to promote the delivery of quality extended health care services through leadership, information, education, and advocacy. Its members serve individuals who need traditional long term residential nursing home care, sub-acute or short-term care, rehabilitative care, or assisted living services. For more on VHCA, visit *www.vhca.org*.

Care Providers of Minnesota represents a diverse membership of senior care and senior living providers in Minnesota. It supports quality consumer and community education through its online Consumer Information Center. It also offers *CARELINKUSA*®, an online, interactive database of long term care providers. For more information, including links to both these resources, visit *www.careproviders.org*.

Wisconsin Health Care Association represents proprietary, non-profit, and government-operated nursing facilities in Wisconsin. Its members employ some 28,000 employees and serve approximately the same number of residents and their families. For more on WHCA, visit *www.whca.com*.

Health Facilities Association of Maryland is a membership organization serving health facilities licensed to provide comprehensive nursing care, assisted living, and sub-acute care. Part of its mission is to be an information and support source to ensure that residents receive comprehensive care and services and an enhanced quality of life. HFAM assists consumers on issues relating to senior care and senior living. For more on HFAM, visit *www.hfam.org*.

The Fountains Foundation is a tax-exempt, not-for-profit organization whose mission includes funding research and education programs for people of all ages that foster respect for and a better understanding of the human aging process. It is committed to developing a positive image of aging and promoting positive aging opportunities. For more on the work of the Fountains Foundation, visit *www.thefountains.com/foundation*.

Acknowledgments

If you've guessed that the contribution the three of us have made to this book is only part of a much bigger picture, you're right. The *Aging in Stride* creative team includes scores of people without whose talent, dedication, and good humor this book would simply not exist. Acknowledgment and thanks go especially to:

- The Caresource team—**Joyce Remy**, senior editor; **Colleen Schlonga**, design and layout; **Aaron Howard**, website design; **Connie Parsons**, marketing; **Sue Morgan**, **Sachka Alexandria**, **Judy Thompson**, and **Jessica Bookwalter**— you never wavered in your support.

- **Diane Kenny**, the book's official godmother and marshal at arms.

- **Verlynn Phillips**, **Janice Engle**, **Connie Wentzel**, **Amy Mayes**, **Astrid Berg**, **Margaret Kenny**, **Wanda Dray** and the many other friends and colleagues who read and commented on various iterations of the manuscript.

- Chris's "Dancing Ladies" exercise group, for your hospitality and the many helpful suggestions you provided.

- The members of our Editorial Review Board, for taking time out of your busy schedules to read and comment on our work.

- The association and foundation leaders who gave their early, enthusiastic support to this project, including **Russell Morgan, Ph.D.**, **Ann Benbow, Ph.D.**, and **Jeff Allum** at The SPRY Foundation; **Jim Emerman** and **Susan Markey** at the American Society on Aging; **Paul Langevin** and **Tom Dorner** at the Health Care Association of New Jersey; **Steve Morrisette** and **Berverley Soble** at the Virginia Health Care Association; **Rick Carter** and **Paula Forte, Ph.D., RN**, at Care Providers of Minnesota; and **Richard Herrick** and **Nancy Leveille, RN**, at the New York State Health Facilities Association.

Our thanks to all of you.

Chris Himes
Liz Oettinger
Dennis Kenny

January 2004

Reader Support Center

You'll find *Aging in Stride's* online **Reader Support Center** at *www.aginginstride.org*.

Readers are invited to use the **Reader Support Center** in two ways:

- **For direct "click-through" access to more resources.** You'll notice the *Quick Links* icon near the More Resources list at the end of each issue discussion. Our *Quick Links* program just means that all the web links we refer you to are also listed online, where they are regularly tested and updated so they'll stay current. The online links will include the exact web locations of the resources you're interested in, so you won't have to type a long web address or search whole sites to find them.

Quick Links

>>> These web-based resources may be accessed through our website:

www.aginginstride.org

- **To print an extra copy of the forms for personal use.** Suppose you want to do a home safety inspection using *Aging in Stride's* Form 6-A. You probably prefer not to write in your book; and getting to a photocopy machine may be a hassle. We encourage you to visit *www.aginginstride.org*, select the form you need, and print a copy at home.

Table of Contents

Introduction

What does it mean to age successfully? As you look around, you have undoubtedly noticed a wide variation both in the challenges that come with later life and how individuals meet those challenges. Does it all come down to good genes? Is aging well just a matter of luck? How much control do we have over our experience of getting older?

While the authors of this book represent very different professional disciplines, we share a common perspective on aging. We believe that no matter what your individual challenges, no matter where you are in the aging process, there are almost always steps you can take to improve your life, helping you feel better, stronger, more confident.

Both research and anecdotal evidence support the conclusion that our response to life events is usually more important to our sense of well-being than the events themselves. In other words, our attitude, our willingness to make healthy choices, and our investment of effort to follow through with a plan of action are all major factors in aging well. Though each of us has limited control over the challenges that come our way, we can maintain and even improve our quality of life by the choices we make and the spirit we bring to those choices.

There is no denying the difficult issues that often come with getting older. But as one looks ahead into the future, knowledge is power! In *Aging in Stride*, the authors have identified a wide range of issues that older people may face, and then have outlined practical strategies for addressing each issue. We want to be of help to you as you make the very best possible choices for yourself in this time of life. As you read on in this book, you will find information, decision-making tools, and encouragement. We hope you will take advantage of them all.

And remember: there is good news about aging. It is too easy to focus just on the challenges of growing older. The good news about aging is that maturity brings certain gifts. These gifts are effective tools—in fact, we would argue that they are the best tools you can have—to approach the work of aging well. As you face the concerns of your own aging, or the aging of someone you love, it is good to recognize these gifts in yourself and put them to work for you.

The gifts we are talking about are these:

- Older people know themselves and their values. More than younger people, seniors are often clear about what is important to them.

- Older people have a wealth of life and work experience to draw on and share. Usually the lessons of a long life teach patience, problem solving, and working cooperatively with others.

- Finally, older people often possess a reflective candor and honesty. They are less likely than younger people to shy away from telling or facing the truth.

At a time of life when one has no choice but to make adjustments and to respond to both internal and external change, these qualities and life lessons become important tools for decision-making. They will be your best helpers as you:

- **Evaluate** honestly where you are in your life and what options are open to you.

- **Plan** carefully, and in advance of events if possible, what is to happen.

- **Act** positively to improve and sustain your quality of life.

So, you have the gifts you need to do the work you have to do; you have the simple formula above to help you structure how you're going to do that work; and you have this book. *Aging in Stride* is a clearinghouse of information on a wide variety of issues concerning successful aging, a starting place for you and your family and friends as you walk that road. It will give you:

- Information on a variety of helpful topics.

- Tools to help you make decisions; simple forms to gather and store your personal data.

- Suggestions of people who can be of assistance to you as you face particular issues.

- Access to other resources with more specific and detailed information than we can provide in this book.

The resources in this book are also supplemented online by a reader support center at *www.aginginstride.org*. For example, each reference to more resources available through the Internet is also listed at *www.aginginstride.org*, where the links are continually updated so you may simply "click through" to any you wish to access. Likewise, each of the forms at the back of the book is also included for your convenience at the reader support center, so you may print additional copies.

We hope that all this, plus our belief that you can make the very best decisions possible for your life, will help you on your way.

There are several ways you may choose to use this book. You might want to read it all the way through as a road map of this terrain called "successful aging." You might decide to consult just one or two issue discussions as you face a particular situation or challenge. You may use one or more of the forms at the back of the book to help you organize information. You may wish to share this book with family and friends. You may even decide to come back to the book to read this introduction over again when you need to be reminded that you have the tools and abilities you need to move successfully through the challenges of this part of your life!

You have paid your dues. Now, if you are willing to use the special gifts of your maturity, along with the information and resources available to you, and take action, then you have the best possible chance to age well. From whatever point you begin, you can take an active role in charting your future and making sure it reflects the values and life choices most important to you.

Aging is not all bad news. You create the good news. We believe that you can do it, and we want to help. Taking aging in stride is . . .

- One part attitude.
- One part resolve and, sometimes, hard work.
- One part information.
- One part teamwork.

Welcome to the road!

Four Building Blocks

INTRODUCTION

Life is constantly changing and challenging, isn't it? Early on we have to learn to walk and talk—no small feat! Soon we're sent off to the unknown world of school, and just when we get the lower grades figured out, feeling comfortable and confident at last, we're sent to high school. Freshmen! Suddenly, once again, much is unknown, confidence is shaky, and there is so much to learn and do in order to succeed. So it goes throughout life. Our life's work, relationships, parenting, finances, physical and mental health—even our very sense of who we are or want to be—all are unknown roads we need to travel.

We manage these changes—take them "in stride"—by learning new things, making choices about how we want to live our lives, planning, being willing to work for what we want, and accepting that life is always changing. The older we get, the more wisdom and knowledge about the world and ourselves we have to help us. But from time to time, we feel like freshmen again, needing to learn new things and develop new strategies to successfully navigate the next stage of our lives.

This chapter looks at the four building blocks that will be useful to you as you chart your own unique journey.

In Issue 1, you'll learn how planning and teamwork can make a difference down the road. Talking with others about your vision for your future can help you define your core goals and needs and give you additional ideas on how to accomplish them. In Issue 2, we focus on staying physically active and the major ways that activity can contribute to a long, happy, and healthy life. Enjoying the companionship of others, examined in Issue 3, expands this vital theme. Finally, in Issue 4, we look at spiritual questions and spiritual life, and how spirituality contributes to successful aging.

As you assess these four building blocks in your life, you may wish to use the following worksheet, which can be found in the forms section at the end of this book.

- Form 1: *Successful Aging Checkup*

ISSUE 1: PLANNING AND TEAMWORK

One of the gifts of growing older is the wealth of life experience you have accumulated. By the time you face the challenges of later life, you have most likely raised children, held several jobs, organized everything from church potlucks to Boy Scout camping trips, garden club fundraisers to family reunions. You have dealt with medical crises and financial crises, times of emotional upheaval and family stress. Though you may not have looked at it from this perspective, all of those life events have taught you the essential skills of planning and teamwork that you can now use in taking control of this stage of your life. You have what you need to consider the options open to you, to come up with a realistic and workable plan, and to live out these later decades of your life in a manner that makes sense to you.

There are always unknowns as we face the future, more so as we grow older. It's impossible to predict when challenges to our health and well-being will appear. However, that does not mean that we are helpless. Any plan for our senior years has to be flexible. It has to take into account the potential of change or of increasing disability. If you begin early, you have a good chance to put in place the outlines of a life that has meaning for you, a life that allows you to pursue your interests and reflects your priorities.

It All Begins With Planning

As you look to the future, what is most important to you? Suppose for a moment you can't have everything you want. What are the conditions that are most essential to your quality of life? Does being close to family make it to the top of the list? Or putting aside resources to allow you to travel? As you look at where you want to live, is it important to you to have a garden, or a workshop, or a good kitchen, or to be located near a variety of cultural resources? It's time to make a plan! The elements that make up your plan should include:

Where Do I Want to Live?

- Where do I want to be geographically?

- With whom and near whom do I want to live?

- What size and configuration of home makes most sense—long-time family home, one-story condominium, mobile home, seasonal residence?

- What activities or interests should my home allow—cooking, gardening, woodworking, quilting, space for children and grandchildren to visit?

- How would my proposed home function if I were to become ill or disabled?

- Will a move eventually be necessary, or can my home environment be adapted to new life circumstances?

What Do I Want to Do?

- What long-time interests do I want to continue?

- What have I always wanted to do, but didn't have the time for?

- Do I want to work for pay part-time, and what are the opportunities?

- What volunteer opportunities would I like to pursue?

- What do I want to do for myself?

- What do I want to do for my family?

- What do I want to do for my community?

How Do I Envision the Rest of My Life?

- Do I want to live in one place forever? What are the tradeoffs in that strategy?

- Do I want to make a plan for the present and assume I will move to a different home or care setting when I get older? What will trigger the decision to make that move?

- What are my priorities to accomplish now, when I am at my healthiest and most active?

- When I slow down a bit, what activities will continue to be important?

- Do I have a spouse, sibling, or other relative for whom I will probably need to provide care at some point? How does that impact my life plan?

As you can see, answering these questions involves a lot of thought. It is best to begin thinking about many of these issues early, well before retirement. It's also helpful to do your initial thinking with the help of others. If you are married or in a committed relationship, obviously your partner needs to be part of your conversation. But it shouldn't end there. Look around you. Who are the people you know who model where and who you want to be in 10 years? Talk to them. Find out how they went about making the life choices that put them where they are. If you have children, it's good to let them know what you are thinking. Their plans for your retirement might be quite different from your own! It's probably best to have all family members working under the same assumptions.

Once you think you know what you want to do, then you need to honestly and realistically gauge the feasibility of your plan. Initial conversations with your financial advisor, attorney, and health care provider will be important at this stage. What are your financial resources and how do they impact your choices? Do you already have health considerations to take into account as you plan your future? Are your legal affairs in order?

Along with these conversations, remember that there are a variety of resources on the market, from purely philosophical reflections on later life to how-to workbooks for retirees. Planning seminars and workshops are offered by insurance companies, health care facilities, senior centers, and community colleges. Take advantage of the opportunities that present themselves to you. They may nudge you to think in ways you would not have considered by yourself.

Once you've done all this background investigation, you can truly evaluate your initial strategy. If you now see that your plan is not going to work, figure out how it might be changed, then check through the feasibility again. Keep at it until you think you have a plan that works for you and is realistic. Congratulations! Abundant research shows those who plan for retirement and later life enjoy life more and make better choices.

Adjusting the Plan

Until this point, we've talked about planning for the future as something done well in advance, in a fairly leisurely manner. As you live out your plan, you will find that life sometimes has a way of altering even the most careful calculations. You already knew that; it has happened before in your life. When life does not turn out as you hoped it would, then it's time to revise your plan based on new information and considerations.

The steps are not very different from making your original plan. You are just working with different information. Given the new knowledge of your situation, you still have choices to make based on what is most important to you, who you want to be close to, what life goals are most important to you.

It is easy to get discouraged when we think we're heading one way and life points us in another direction. When that first set of choices is taken away from us, often we feel like we have no choices left. That is rarely the case. The choices left to you may be different and more limited in scope than you would like; however, the people who achieve the maximum quality of life are those who continue to work realistically with the options they have, choosing what is best for them. This is where the gifts of being older pay off. People who reach their 70s, 80s and beyond have experienced disappointment and change of plans before. Most older adults have the wisdom and maturity to make hard choices based on their knowledge of themselves and their values. So make the choices that are yours to make, and live the best life you can live!

Planning is a Team Sport

As we went through the steps in planning, you probably noticed that making a plan is not best done as a solitary occupation. The best plans are made with the consultation and help of a variety of people.

The Professional Team

As you go about planning for later life, you will have a lot of questions that are best answered by experts. How much money will I have to live on? Are there health concerns that affect where and how I live? Will careful estate planning help me and my heirs? These kinds of questions should be answered by your health care provider, your attorney, and the person you trust to give financial advice. It is important both to seek guidance as you start the planning process and to review any draft of a plan with these professionals. Not only do they have expertise, but most professionals who work with older adults work with *many* older adults. They have a wide base of experience and might suggest options you might not have considered on your own. If your plan involves hiring in-home help, or contracting with a bill-paying service, again, your professional network can often point you in the right direction to get the help you need. Though professionals charge for their consulting services, it is usually money well spent, an investment in your future.

The Family and Friends Network

Professionals provide one kind of support for planning your life. Equally important are the input and support of family and friends. You know who the members of that network are for you. They are the people you already count on for love, friendship, and advice. They're the people you call when you have news or want to chat. As you are trying to decide where you want to live and what you want to do, the people in your personal network often have good advice or can act as sounding boards as you try out ideas. Sometimes your plan will directly involve these people in helping you live the way you would like. Your next-door neighbor might be willing to help with your grocery shopping; your son or daughter might come over twice a week to drive you to appointments, help you clean the house, get your laundry done. Especially if you need help with the basic activities of living, the family and friends network can be an important element in a successful plan.

Beyond the concrete help they provide, your family and friends care about you. Remember that one of the keys to successful aging is staying involved with other people. Sharing your challenges and solutions with those closest to you builds the bonds of relationship. It provides opportunity for significant conversation and closeness. Don't feel you have to do this alone. Those closest to you deserve to know what you are thinking, and they can offer help at many levels. You can't build your team without them.

To Sum Up . . .

Plan your future! Don't just let things drift along. Planning is your best strategy for choosing and maintaining control of a life that makes sense to you. Developing a positive, realistic, flexible plan takes time, thought, and the involvement of your professional and personal "teammates." The goal is living the best life you can live. Your tools in meeting that goal are your wisdom, your maturity, your knowledge of yourself and your values, and again, the help of your teammates. So go ahead, and plan the best possible future for yourself!

More Resources

- The **American Society on Aging** website offers information and resources for retirement planning. (*www.asaging.org*)

- The **U.S. FirstGov for Seniors** site is a portal to government senior programs. The website includes information on a wide variety of topics on retirement planning. (*www.seniors.gov*)

- The **U.S. Administration on Aging** site features useful fact sheets and resources for planning in later life. (*www.aoa.dhhs.gov*)

- The website of **AARP** (previously named the American Association of Retired People) has an extensive "Life Answers" section with information about housing, travel, volunteer work, and more. (*www.aarp.org*)

Quick Links

>>> These web-based resources may be accessed through our website:

www.aginginstride.org

ISSUE 2: STAYING PHYSICALLY ACTIVE

Exercising regularly is important. We've all heard it before. From vitamin ads to insurance newsletters to the proliferation of senior fitness programs, we are bombarded with the exercise message. Why do people keep belaboring the point? Because research in aging over the past 20 years has shown conclusively that regular physical activity is *the* most important contributor to healthy aging. Exercise can prevent or control many medical problems, reduce pain, and promote a feeling of well-being. This is true no matter what your physical or mental capabilities, whether you are robust and healthy, frail, or disabled. Every single person can reap the benefits; and everyone can do it, no matter what their particular challenges.

Despite everything we know, the Public Health Department reports that physical inactivity is one of the most important public health problems in the United States. Lack of exercise gets worse as people get older, making it a high-priority health risk that needs to be addressed. It is so important that the Surgeon General has recommended that everyone get at least 30 minutes of regular physical activity at least five days per week. It doesn't sound like a lot, and yet most people aren't doing it.

The reasons are easy to understand, especially as we grow older. Chronic medical conditions make people worry they may hurt themselves. Physical disabilities make it harder to be active in the ways we used to be. Pain, or the fear of it, often makes people shy away from an active lifestyle. When we are no longer working, we tend to be less active in general.

Then, when we become less active, we lose muscle tone, can't breathe as well, and are more tired in general, all leading to a downward spiral of less and less physical activity, leading to more and more disability. The single most important thing you can do for yourself is to break that spiral and get moving. Be creative—it's fun! Physical activity can make you feel better about yourself and life in general than you have in years.

Breaking the Cycle of Inactivity

Studies show that all older adults can safely do some form of regular exercise, no matter what medical problems or disabilities they face. In fact, frail or disabled persons have the most to gain! You don't have to exercise for hours to gain health benefits. As the Surgeon General recommends, 30 minutes of moderate activity on most days of the week will give you tremendous health benefits. Moderate activity is defined here as exercise that gets your heart rate up a bit and makes you breathe a little harder.

There are many simple ways to add exercise to your days; here are some examples...but be creative and always check with your doctor first.

- Ride a stationary bicycle while watching a TV program.
- Do arm circles and ankle rolls while you are sitting talking to friends.
- Park a little farther from the store when you're out shopping.
- Take the stairs instead of the elevator.
- Work in the garden.
- Play actively with your grandchildren.
- Use a pedometer to count the number of steps you take in a day.
- Dance!

It's Never Too Late to Start!

Did you know that lack of exercise can cause or worsen the most chronic diseases, such as diabetes and heart disease (the primary cause of death in the United States)? Whether you've been an active person all your life or have been a "couch potato" to age 90, beginning an exercise program now will give you great results. A study done with nursing home patients 90 years old and older showed that after three months of muscle strengthening exercises three times a week, everyone in the study showed at least a 200 percent increase in strength!

Sometimes it seems difficult to know where to start, and even harder to keep exercising faithfully. Exercise takes time and commitment. Here are some tips to help you out:

- Set goals for yourself and stick with them.

- Record your progress; it's fun to see!

- Start slowly and build up gradually.

- Create an action plan for yourself.

- Surround yourself with other people, if you are able, who will support and exercise with you.

- Reward yourself for great work!

Developing an Activity Plan

Once researchers determined the importance of physical activity as we age, they tried to figure out the most effective exercise programs. Older adults need to have several major components in their exercise routine: aerobic activity, muscle strengthening and flexibility exercises, and balance training. Be sure to check first with your doctor before starting any new exercise program. Then, try to combine all of the elements in an exercise program your doctor recommends as right for you.

Aerobic Activity

Aerobic exercise simply means exercise in which your activity increases your heart rate and breathing. It expands your lung capacity, allowing you to breathe better and more easily when you are exerting yourself. This is especially important for those with lung disease. When the heart pumps harder, the muscles of the blood vessel walls get stronger and more flexible, reducing blood pressure and improving blood flow to the brain and all other vital organs. The heart, a simple muscle itself, becomes stronger and stronger.

Anything that makes your heart pump faster and makes you breathe a little harder is aerobic activity, like walking quickly or dancing. What's important is to continue the exercise for at least 10 minutes at a time, for a total of at least 30 minutes per day. You'll be surprised at how quickly you are able to pick up the intensity of the exercise and do it for longer. Keep a record of your progress and reward yourself for sticking to your program!

Muscle Strengthening and Flexibility Exercises

The old cliché "use it or lose it" is really true, isn't it? In a study done in the 1960s, members of a national football team were recruited to "go to bed for a week" in a hospital after the last game of the year, when they were presumably in their best physical shape. They weren't allowed out of bed except to use a bedside commode. After only one week of bed rest, not one of them was able to stand up alone initially! Each had lost significant muscle mass. Anyone who has been on bed rest can relate to that story.

The same thing happens to all of us when we aren't using our muscles. They slowly "atrophy," becoming small and weak. We find we are gradually able to do less and less. Very often we are not even aware of our increasing disability until one day we fall and we aren't strong enough to get up off the floor.

A similar process occurs with the ligaments that hold our joints together. When they are not stretched to their fullest length regularly, they shorten, and soon we find that we are unable to touch our toes, or tie our shoes, or turn our necks to see behind us.

The good news is that you can get back much of your muscle strength and flexibility, no matter how weak or stiff you've become! We told you the story of the 90-plus-year-old nursing home patients and their incredible 200-percent increase in strength after only three months. Did you know that is exactly the same increase a 30 year old would expect with similar training? Exactly the same benefits are gained in increased flexibility with three months of stretching!

Many strengthening programs for older people are offered at community centers, senior centers, and health clubs. If you have such a program close to you, take advantage of it; it's much more fun to exercise with others! Or invite a friend to your home and exercise together.

The key is strengthening every muscle in your body and stretching every ligament or joint. This can even be done while you're watching television. You don't need to buy expensive equipment or join a gym to do it. Simply start with your head and work your way down to your toes and you'll feel better and better each time.

Balance Training

Balance problems are very common as we age. And very frustrating! They result from a combination of factors: loss of muscle strength, decreased flexibility, and loss of sensation in the feet. The loss of *proprioception*, or sense of position, can happen to anyone. For people with diabetes and heart disease, it often happens at a younger age.

Proprioception is the ability of the nerves in the feet to feel or "sense" where we are in space, and to make automatic corrections when we get a little off balance. When those nerves are damaged or not working well, we don't get the automatic corrections we're used to and feel off balance much of the time.

Doctors used to think that there was nothing that could be done to improve the nerve damage in feet. Researchers in the 1990s proved that this wasn't true. In fact, regularly stimulating the nerves in the feet can often make sensation return.

We've talked about how to begin a muscle strengthening and flexibility program. It's important to understand that *all* the muscles of the lower leg need to be strengthened to improve balance. If we just concentrate on some, they will be stronger than their opposing muscles and actually make us even more prone to falling. Be sure to work all the muscles in your legs, focusing on the weakest.

Additional Benefits of Physical Activity

We feel better physically and emotionally after we've exercised. Several studies have shown that for people with memory loss or dementia, exercise has the benefit of clearing the mind and improving memory for about 24 hours.

Virtually all medical problems that cause pain are also helped by regular exercise. Increased strength and flexibility bring a better blood supply to the muscles and joints. Exercise is the most important treatment for controlling pain and preventing disability in persons with conditions such as arthritis. Additional benefit comes from the release of endorphins in the brain in response to exercise. Endorphins are the body's natural pain killers and energizers.

To Sum Up . . .

Increasing regular physical activity is the most important prescription your doctor can give you to improve overall health and well being. Pay attention. Follow your doctor's recommendations and be the best you can be, in body, mind and heart.

More Resources

- **The 50-Plus Fitness Association** is a nonprofit organization dedicated to promoting fitness in older adults. Its website includes a library of information about a wide range of topics pertaining to senior fitness. (*www.50plus.org*)

- The **American Academy of Orthopaedic Surgeons** offers information about senior exercise programs on their website, "Your Orthopaedic Connection." (*http://orthoinfo.aaos.org*)

- The **National Institute of Health** offers information targeted toward senior fitness on the Senior Health section of their website. (*http:// nihseniorhealth.gov*)

- The **Federal Highway Administration's Highway Research Center** includes information about safe walking and pedestrian safety. (*www.tfhrc.gov*)

Quick Links

>>> These web-based resources may be accessed through our website:

www.aginginstride.org

ISSUE 3: RELATIONSHIPS WITH OTHERS

You will read over and over again in this book: along with staying physically active, the most important thing you can do to maintain or improve your quality of life as you age is to stay involved in relationships with other people. This is crucial to both your physical health and your emotional well-being.

As they grow older, many people tend to withdraw from their social networks and the activities they once enjoyed. You know how it goes. Failing health or just feeling less energetic makes getting out of the house seem like more trouble than it's worth. Hearing problems can make large-group interactions awkward and discouraging. You've given up driving and don't want to bother someone for a ride. You know all the reasons why it's easy to become increasingly isolated as you get older. You've seen it happen to others. Maybe you've started down that road yourself. If you have, it's time to turn around and head in the opposite direction.

Here is a list of reasons why you *should* stay active and involved in activities and relationships with others:

- It will increase your mental alertness.
- It will improve emotional well-being.
- It will maintain your network of support for a time when you may need it.
- It will help you stay physically healthier.
- You will have fun.
- You have much to give.

Are you convinced yet? We hope you are. We take this seriously and hope you will, too. Yes, as you get older it takes more effort and more planning to stay engaged in life, but the rewards are great.

So Where Do I Begin?

You have decided that you want to become more involved with other people in activities that you enjoy and that are meaningful to you. One of the gifts of being older is that you have more time to spend developing relationships and doing the things that bring you pleasure. So make a list of the activities you already know you enjoy, as well as interests you've always wanted to pursue. What's on your list? Do you like to play cards, do needlework, or arrange flowers? Are you a birdwatcher or a fly fisherman or a bowler? Do you enjoy cooking, or art, or going to the theater? Have you always wanted to learn to ballroom dance, to quilt, to do woodworking, carpentry, or remodeling projects?

As you look at your list, you will see that some of the activities you have listed are naturally social activities, such as square dancing or playing bridge. Other activities such as reading novels, cooking, or gardening may seem like solitary occupations, but there are ways to make them interactive. Join a book group. Take a cooking class. Check out your local garden club.

As you look for ways to translate your interests into activities with other people, the following resources will be helpful to you:

- **Your local senior center** probably offers a variety of classes and interest groups. See what they have to offer. If you're interested in an activity that is not listed, let the senior center personnel know. They plan their activities based on interest. You might not be the first to express an interest in your area.

- **Community colleges** offer a wide variety of courses, many of them designed specifically for seniors and scheduled during the day rather than in the evening. You can take classes in everything from computer basics to genealogy to ancient history to swing dancing. Many community colleges offer one-day workshops and two-week mini-classes as well as quarter- or semester-long courses.

- **Community parks and recreation departments** also try to tailor some of their programming to meet the needs of the older population. They offer everything from senior hiking groups to modified exercise programs for those with physical disabilities. Often they sponsor bowling leagues and one-day excursions to local sites of interest. If you haven't looked recently, you'll be surprised by how much comes under the umbrella of "Parks and Recreation." It's not just softball leagues anymore!

- **Churches, synagogues, and other religious communities** provide a different kind of possibility for involvement. You can sing in the choir, join a Bible study or other class, or be part of the women's association or the sewing group for the church bazaar. Religious organizations are a good place to find community, and most large congregations offer a variety of activities and ways to become involved.

- **Your friends, neighbors, and acquaintances** are good sources of information about possible activities. Maybe your friend down the street belongs to a quilting group and would be willing to give you a ride. Maybe your acquaintance from work who retired the same time as you knows if there's an opening in his bowling league. The word-of-mouth network is often the best way to find new opportunities for involvement.

It's Easier With a Friend

Most of us have some degree of shyness or reticence when beginning a new activity or going to a strange place. If you really want to get involved in something new, convince a friend to join with you. That way you won't change your mind at the last minute, you'll know at least one person where you are going, you'll give each other courage, and you'll have someone with whom to laugh and celebrate when you're done. Who knows? Maybe your friend needs a push to get out of the house as much as you do!

Friendships are important at any age, but crucial as we grow older, especially when family members are not close by. To develop and maintain friendships takes commitment and work, but as you know, the rewards of having a good friend are priceless. As well as finding structured activities for yourself, make sure you save time for your friends. Plan to eat dinner with a friend once or twice a week. It's something to look forward to; you'll probably eat a better meal; and you get to be with your friend. Maybe another friend has been ill or is losing his vision. Why not go and read to that friend one afternoon a week, help around the house, or just stop by for a visit?

When you can't visit in person, the phone is a convenient and, increasingly, an inexpensive way of staying in touch. Even long-distance calls are affordable for most people these days. And with e-mail and instant messaging, there's a whole new world out there for those who can use computers. For those who are not computer-savvy, there's still no substitute for cards and letters from a friend.

What's important here is that you make the effort to stay connected. Personal bonds to family and friends benefit you and benefit them. Maybe now is the time to really get to know your grandchildren or great-grandchildren. Maybe now is the time to develop a relationship with your next-door neighbor. Maybe now is the time to ...

you fill in the rest of the sentence. It's almost a sure bet that your efforts in that direction will be rewarded.

Volunteering: A Special Kind of Involvement

As you think about creating a life for yourself that is full of meaningful interaction with other people, think about the possibility of becoming a volunteer. The need has never been greater in all communities. Economic trends and the movement of women into the paid work force have pared down many of the traditional sources of volunteers. Many worthy organizations—schools, hospitals, museums, social service agencies—are facing the reality of leaner budgets. To keep our communities friendly, productive, and nurturing places to live, we need more volunteers, not fewer. Fortunately, many retirees are answering the call, serving their communities, sharing their gifts, and helping others.

The rewards of volunteering are many. Is there a cause for which you want to work? A social agency you support? A community organization from which you have benefited? Ask if they need volunteers. Chances are they will say "Yes," and then

Background Checks: The New Reality of Volunteering

If you want to volunteer in a school or any organization that serves children, you will now most likely be required to submit to a background check. Other social service agencies are beginning to require checks as well. The extensiveness of background checks depends on the organization for which you want to work and the kind of work you will be doing. Simple checks require only your driver's license number and other identification. Deeper checks require fingerprinting.

You have to give your permission for a background check to be initiated. While it can be initially intimidating, most people come to understand that the existence of these checks effectively discourages many potential child predators and others who would abuse the trust relationship that is part of being a volunteer.

No one likes background checks, but they have come to be the rule when working with vulnerable populations. Safety is worth some discomfort and inconvenience for those of us who want to be volunteers!

"Thank you!" Almost every institution and organization has some work for volunteers that doesn't require special skills or training.

Do you have a special skill you can share? Can your work experience translate into volunteer activity? Do you have specialized knowledge or expertise? Volunteers don't just stuff envelopes and answer phones anymore! From retired businessmen's groups that provide volunteer assistance and mentoring for fledgling entrepreneurs, to the legion of museum docents and national park guides—if you have special knowledge or gifts to share, there's probably someone who would greatly appreciate your contribution. Volunteering in your area of expertise is a way to keep your skills sharp and your mind challenged.

Maybe you don't have a particular skill, but you do have time, energy, and a commitment to working with a certain population—for example, children, people with substance abuse problems, the developmentally disabled, women in crisis. Many organizations and programs offer training for volunteer positions. The training requires a serious time commitment, as does the volunteer commitment after training. Many people, however, find this level of involvement to be very satisfying, a worthwhile investment of their time and energy.

Would you like to volunteer but don't know where to start? Try the following:

- **Public schools** are always in need of volunteers. Check with your local school district office or just visit the school nearest you to find out how you can contribute your time and talents. Go straight to the office (the days are over when unidentified visitors can wander school halls). The school secretary or other office assistant can put you in touch with whomever is responsible for coordinating volunteers.

- **Hospitals** use volunteers for a number of jobs, from staffing hospital gift shops to providing hospitality and delivering mail to patients and families. Call your local hospital to see how you can help.

- **Community agencies** such as the United Way, Boys and Girls Clubs, the local senior center, and the public library are always in need of volunteers. Call the main number and ask to speak to someone about volunteer opportunities.

- **Parks and recreation departments** often use volunteers to maintain gardens and landscaping. If you want to put your gardening skills to work, call and find out if they need you.

- **Synagogues, churches, and other religious organizations** use volunteers in almost every facet of community life. If you are part of a religious community, let it be known that you have time, interest, and a willingness to serve. They will find a place for you.

- **Habitat for Humanity** is active in hundreds of communities around the country, creating low-cost housing with partner families. If your skills lie in the area of carpentry and home repair and remodeling, call your local Habitat chapter.

- **Small independent community service agencies** serving youth, families in transition, women in crisis, low-income persons, persons with disabilities, and other persons in need exist in every community. Pick up the phone or pay a visit. Let them know you are interested. Many small agencies only have the resources to provide volunteer orientation and training once or twice a year, so you may have a wait before they can put you to work.

- **Cultural organizations** such as museums, theaters, and sites of local interest often use large numbers of volunteers. If you love the theater but can't act, volunteer to paint scenery or take tickets, serve refreshments, or hand out programs. Museum volunteers provide everything from hospitality services to school tours. Most such community organizations also need help with fund raising.

Whatever your interest or ability, there is a volunteer job in your community that will meet a need, make your community a better place, and give you the satisfaction of knowing that you are still a person with gifts to give and talents to share. Most volunteers agree that they receive more from volunteering than they give. It remains one of the best ways to stay active and connected to others, working together towards the common good.

To Sum Up . . .

There are so many ways to stay connected to the world around you, to express yourself, expand your world view, make a significant difference in someone else's life. All of these activities add depth and meaning to life; they keep your mind agile and your body moving. They keep your emotions from growing rusty with disuse, and let you know that who you are in the world is of value. So, to borrow a line from the phone company, "Reach out and touch someone." You'll be glad you did. And so will they.

More Resources

- To find senior centers in your community, check the Yellow Pages. The **Eldercare Locator** (*www.eldercare.gov*) is also a good place to begin. Searchable by ZIP code, its directory will take you to your local senior resources; many states have full directories of senior centers.

> ## Quick Links
>
> >>> These web-based resources may be accessed through our website:
> www.aginginstride.org

- A good place to start looking for volunteer opportunities is the **U.S. SeniorCorps** website (*www.seniorcorps.org*), part of **AmeriCorps** (*www.americorps.org*), a network of national service programs that is part of the **Corporation for National and Community Service**. (*www.nationalservice.org*)

- The **FirstGov for Seniors** website has a section on work and volunteer opportunities. (*www.seniors.gov*)

- The **Mayo Clinic** website's "Senior Health Center" includes a section on nurturing relationships and the effect on health and well-being of having supportive connections with others. (*www.mayoclinic.com*)

ISSUE 4: NURTURING YOUR SPIRIT

Many cultures and most religious traditions look to the elders of the community as persons of wisdom and mature spirituality. There is something about the later years of life that leads one to spiritual contemplation. Much of life's work is done. Those past retirement age have already raised families, been productive in society, given much to their communities. Now the pace of life slows down, and there is time to reflect on life's experience.

As we age, the reality and inevitability of death grow more present. The older we are, the more people we know who have already passed from this life to whatever lies beyond. There is, for many, a growing curiosity about what lies on the other side of this life, a desire to complete life's work and be ready for what might be next.

Wisdom, life experience, the movement towards completing life and preparing for death—all these combine to bring a rich spiritual possibility to the last decades of life. For most people, aging successfully will involve some attention to spiritual questions and spiritual life.

What Does It Mean to Nurture Your Spirit?

Spiritual reality is defined in very different words, depending on the religious or philosophical tradition speaking. In all traditions, however, to pay attention to the realm of the spiritual is to pay attention to that which connects us. Spiritual reality connects us here in the world with other people, with creation, with the earth itself. Spiritual reality connects us to those who have gone before us, and those who will come after, and to the ground of being that holds together all reality. Spiritual questions are those that deal with the meaning of life, of death, of God, of evil, of what holds us together, and what pulls us apart. Nurturing our spirits means taking the time and effort to pay attention, to think, to begin articulating the meaning of what we have known.

Again, the later years of life are a uniquely powerful time for spiritual nurture, for making sense of our journey here on earth, developing perspective, readying the soul for the next step. There are a variety of ways to do this, both within conventional religious communities and, for those who are not drawn to organized religion, outside of traditional religious institutions and concepts.

Spirituality and Religious Communities

Religious communities provide structure, language, and companionship in the world of spiritual exploration. The language of Hindu spirituality is different from the language of Christianity; Judaism frames the spiritual differently than Buddhism. Even within individual traditions there are differences, such as the difference between Catholic and Protestant Christians, or Suni and Shi'ite Muslims. Each group offers its own path.

If you are currently part of a religious community, use the resources your community offers to engage the spiritual questions that are important to you. Many churches, synagogues, and other religious communities offer classes and groups focused specifically on the needs and questions of older adults. Sometimes it is helpful to be part of a group that is willing to discuss spiritual concerns. Listening to others articulate their life experience and how they find meaning in it may help you to do the same. Knowing that others share your concern provides support and companionship. Most groups devoted to exploring spirituality develop a rare closeness, a special relationship that comes from sharing everything from laughter to anger, confusion to rage, the questions that seem to have no answers, and the answers that seem completely clear.

Beyond classes and groups, most religious communities have people in the community who are looked upon as teachers, guides, or religious leaders. Priests, rabbis, ministers, imams, bishops—there are as many different titles as there are communities. If you find yourself needing a more individual approach to spirituality than groups afford, make an appointment to see your religious leader. He or she may know of reading material that will be helpful to you, or may prescribe a spiritual discipline. Sometimes just one-on-one conversation is what you need to point you where you want to go.

Many people find comfort and meaning in community worship and the religious rituals of their particular faith. If your worship tradition sustains you, then make a point of finding a way to attend worship regularly. If you have given up driving, most religious communities have volunteers who are pleased to give rides to other members. Many retirement communities provide transportation to places of worship; others provide worship opportunities within the facility. If religious observance is important to you, then make a point of going, even if it means calling a taxi. You owe it to yourself to take care of yourself spiritually. And as you have probably learned in the past, when life turns difficult, a strong faith or life philosophy can be a rock to which to cling.

Non-Traditional Spirituality

Many people consider themselves to be spiritual, but not religious. For one reason or another, traditional religious communities do not meet their needs. That doesn't mean they are without spiritual resources. Even those who are part of traditional religious communities might want to explore different approaches and understandings of spiritual truth. The resources below may be helpful to you as well.

If the spiritual task of later life is coming to see life as a whole, assessing the meaning and value of one's own life, then there are a number of ways to approach this task outside of religious communities. Spirituality is a popular topic these days, and your local bookstore or public library will carry a variety of titles that approach spiritual reality from many perspectives. Peruse the "Spirituality and Religion" section. Look at the titles that interest you, read a few pages, and select a few books to take home with you. Remember, though, that even though authors sometimes write as if their version of the truth is the only correct or reasonable one, there are many perspectives. Don't take what you read at face value. In the world of spirituality, as in all other aspects of life, there are those who provide valuable guidance and those who don't. Use your best instincts to separate the one from the other.

One increasingly popular way of approaching the spirituality of aging is through keeping a journal or writing an autobiography. There is something about writing things down that encourages the mind and heart to consider what is important and what is not, what has been meaningful and why. Many religious organizations, senior centers and community colleges now offer courses to help you write your life's history or keep track of your day-to-day search for meaning. Taking up an endeavor in a class framework both pushes you to stay focused and offers the possibility of making new friends, fellow seekers with whom you can connect more deeply than in many social situations.

Even without the support of a structured class, you can start to write out or make audiotapes or videos of your life history. As families have grown more dispersed, there is a growing interest in family history. Ask your children or grandchildren to interview you or ask you questions to which they want to know the answers. Doing a family history offers the opportunity for some positive interaction with family members and a chance for you to take a trip through your memories. Both can bring spiritual reward.

Electronic Spirituality

Many older people who are home-bound or who have not found a good fit in a religious community close to them find spiritual nurture through radio, television, and Internet religious organizations. Television evangelists, religious talk shows, and Internet chatrooms that focus on spirituality provide spiritual nurture and comfort for thousands of older adults.

Many of these organizations are, in fact, legitimate religious and spiritual communities. They provide a valuable service to those who watch, listen, and log on. However, a word of caution is in order. There are some so-called religious organizations that prey on vulnerable individuals, promising them spiritual benefit, but bombarding them with increasingly urgent pleas for money.

To Sum Up . . .

It is normal and healthy for older adults to be interested in issues of the spirit. Find a place where you can explore the questions and concerns that are most important to you. If you are part of an organized religious community, then use its resources and take advantage of the community support and spiritual guidance it offers you. If organized religion is not for you, then use the other resources available to help you articulate and answer the questions of meaning and value that are most crucial for you. People who take care of themselves spiritually approach life more positively and have a resilience that can help them through many of life's difficulties. Pay attention to your spiritual self and your particular spiritual needs. It's an important piece of living life the best you can.

More Resources

- The **American Society on Aging** website includes the "Forum on Religion, Spirituality and Aging." (*www.asaging.org*)

- The **U.S. Administration on Aging** has a collection of resources on "Faith-Based Services, Spirituality and Aging." (*www.aoa.gov*)

- The **Alzheimer's Association** offers a section on "Spirituality and Dementia Care" for people with Alzheimer's disease and other dementias. (*www.alz.org*)

- If you are unsure about the legitimacy of a charitable organization, check to see if it is listed on the website of the **American Institute of Philanthropy**. (*www.charitywatch.org*)

Quick Links

>>> These web-based resources may be accessed through our website:

www.aginginstride.org

Safe and Secure

INTRODUCTION

Have you ever had this experience? You decided to make a favorite recipe. Maybe it was a chocolate cake, or banana nut bread. Everything would have turned out perfectly, *except* that you forgot to add one small but essential ingredient, such as baking powder.

An experience like that—and we've all had them—teaches us that even small things can make an important difference in how the big picture unfolds. Safety is one of those things many of us take for granted. We sometimes forget that even a little carelessness can have big consequences.

As children, we had our parents watching out for us, reminding us when something was a risk to our safety. Later, as adults, we thought about safety and security for ourselves and our family. Many of the precautions we took were more a matter of habit than they were the result of consciously thinking about safety.

Now, as older adults, it's a good time to take a step back, to think actively about why and where we might be at risk, and what we can do to eliminate or reduce our safety risks. After all, it doesn't make much sense to do everything else right—stay physically active, maintain our connections with others, and all the rest—only to have all our fine work spoiled by one careless moment!

In Issue 5, we look at one of the big worries for many older people: how to keep from falling. In Issue 6, the subject is similar, but somewhat broader: how to make sure your home is safe and secure. In Issue 7, the focus is on a different but equally important safety concern: driving a car. Finally, in Issue 8, we look at going out and about, around your neighborhood or around the world, with confidence and security.

In the forms section, you'll find four forms to help you take up the personal challenge of identifying and dealing with the safety risk factors that apply to you:

- Form 5: *Checklist for Reducing Your Risk of Falling*
- Form 6-A: *Home Safety Inspection Checklist*
- Form 6-B: *Home Repairs and Home Modifications Checklist*
- Form 7: *Checklist for Older Drivers*

ISSUE 5: PREVENTING FALLS

The risk of falling increases as we age. The numbers tell the story. Every year, one in every three Americans over age 65 takes a fall. That's about 10 million falls every year. Many of these falls don't cause serious injury. That's the good news. The bad news is that many falls *are* serious and result in a hospital stay. In fact, every year nearly 10,000 Americans over 65 die from injuries caused by falling.

Hip fractures are an important part of the picture. Every year, more than a quarter million older Americans break a hip, most from falling. Breaking a hip means a lengthy hospital stay. For many, it also means that they won't be able to return to their own home when they're discharged from the hospital.

Along with the physical consequences, there are emotional and psychological costs associated with falling and the fear of falling. Those who experience a fall often feel embarrassed or discouraged about it. They worry, "Will I fall again?" and decide to limit their activity rather than risk another fall.

Not all falls can or will be prevented. No matter what our age, living an active life means taking some risks. But thousands of falls can and should be prevented. Preventing falls doesn't just happen. It takes some know-how and effort. There's work to be done! But this is a challenge worth accepting.

What Are the Risk Factors?

Our bodies change over time, and some of those changes increase the risk of falling. In addition, hidden dangers in our homes and out in the world may pose a threat. Some of these risk factors can be eliminated or reduced. Others are more difficult. Knowledge is power. The first step in cutting your risk is to have a clear understanding of the major risk factors.

The physical changes of aging make falling more likely. Most older persons, sooner or later, will experience problems with their eyesight, sense of balance, mobility, bone structure, and reflexes. Confusion, forgetfulness, and medical conditions such as stroke, Parkinson's, and Alzheimer's are also important risk factors.

These changes increase the chance that the person who falls will be injured. But physical changes are only one part of a bigger picture. In combination with physical changes, the following factors greatly increase an older person's risk of falling:

- **Environmental hazards**—Throw rugs, electrical cords, wet and slippery floors, rough floor surfaces, slick walkways and steps, and poor lighting are all examples of things or conditions that can trip you up.

- **Medications**—Most seniors take a variety of medications, both over-the-counter and prescription. Many medications cause dizziness, drowsiness, or other side effects that make it harder to maintain balance.

- **Things you don't expect**—Often, a contributing cause in a fall is a circumstance you do not expect and for which you have not prepared. You lean against a door, thinking it is latched. You walk down a poorly lighted walkway, not anticipating the small pile of weeds and clippings someone has left there.

- **Hurrying**—A former basketball coach used to tell his athletes, "Be quick, but don't hurry." Accidents are much more likely to occur when you are distracted by trying to accomplish a task quickly. Instead of focusing on what you are doing, you are worrying about having it done and not paying close attention.

Practical Steps for Reducing Your Risk of Falling

Although it is unrealistic to think all falls can be prevented, there are many proven ways of reducing the risk of falling. An excellent starting point is to give yourself a fall-prevention checkup. Now that you understand the major risk categories, ask yourself which ones apply—or could apply—to you. Use Form 5, *Checklist for Reducing Your Risk of Falling*, as your guide.

As you think about risks and possible prevention measures, consider the following suggestions:

- If you already have a fitness program or are in physical or occupational therapy, make fall prevention one of the issues you discuss. Lowering your risk of falling should be one of the explicit goals of your program or therapy. If you are not as physically active as you could be, ask your doctor about setting up an exercise program to build your muscle strength, joint flexibility, and coordination.

- If you have experienced episodes of dizziness, or if you think you may have a problem with balance, vision, or medications, talk with your doctor. Be persistent in seeking answers to your questions. Ask to have balance and dizziness problems tested, diagnosed, and treated.

- Eat right. A sensible diet—when, what, and how much you eat—helps improve a person's energy, stamina, and alertness, all factors for reducing the risk of falls. Alcohol can negatively affect balance and coordination and slow the reflexes, so be careful how much alcohol you consume.

- Be aware of your surroundings. Don't be tripped up by something you didn't anticipate. Get in the habit of thinking two steps ahead. That way you'll be giving yourself more time to react to your physical surroundings and the other people around you. Pay special attention whenever you are in new or unfamiliar surroundings: for example, your first hours or days in a strange hotel, or your first days and weeks in a new retirement living situation.

- Do a regular home safety inspection (see Issue 6 and Form 6-A). Look for obvious hazards, such as rough floor surfaces, throw rugs, poor lighting, extension cords, and clutter. While you are at it, consider some simple household safety modifications, such as grab bars in the bath or shower, a second hand rail on the stairs, better lighting in high traffic areas.

Using Physical Activity to Cut Your Risks

Physical inactivity is a major risk factor for falls among older persons. Lack of exercise leads to the following:

- Weakness and poor muscle tone.
- Decreased reaction time.
- Loss of bone mass.
- Poor circulation.

- Decreased sensation in hands and feet.
- Depression.

For most older adults, a program of regular exercise is one of the most effective ways to lower the risk of falling. (For more on exercise and the importance of staying physically active, see Issue 2, *Staying Physically Active*.)

Fear of Falling

Fear of falling exacts an enormous emotional and psychological toll. The experts tell us that fear of falling is almost as big a problem for seniors as falling itself. Of course, being concerned about a risk can be a good thing. You recognize a risk. You're afraid the worst might happen. You take smart steps to keep the risk as low as possible.

The problem comes when a person retreats, taking a "safe at any cost" approach. That's when fear of falling can trap a person in a vicious cycle that looks something like this:

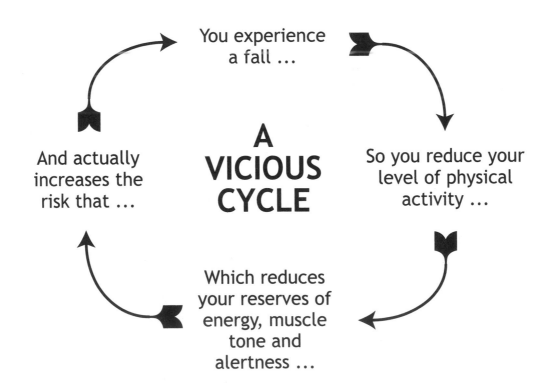

You experience a fall ...

A VICIOUS CYCLE

So you reduce your level of physical activity ...

Which reduces your reserves of energy, muscle tone and alertness ...

And actually increases the risk that ...

If fear of falling is something you experience, you're not alone. What matters is how you respond to your fear. Share your concerns with your doctor and others in your support network. If fear is holding you back, preventing you from doing some things your doctor is recommending, be proactive. Many hospitals, clinics, and senior centers now offer courses on fall prevention that can teach you to move around more safely and confidently. These courses train participants to identify environmental hazards, develop strategies for response, and evaluate assistive devices that might increase stability. Fight fear with information and planning, not inactivity.

Assistive Devices

For anyone with gait or balance problems, assistive devices—such as canes, walkers, or crutches—can provide added support and stability while walking. These devices should be prescribed by your health care provider, who will help you select the right type and size. It takes a little time to adjust to using one of these devices, but they can significantly reduce your risk of falling.

Preventing Serious Injury If You Do Fall

There are steps you can take to prevent or minimize the dangers of falling. The two most common precautions for older persons are subscribing to an emergency response program and wearing hip protectors.

Emergency Response Programs

When you subscribe to an emergency call service, you carry a personal call button like the one you would have next to your bed if you were in the hospital. The call button is built into a medallion you can wear around your neck like a necklace, or on your wrist like a watch, or you can put it in your pocket.

If you're alone and fall, and you can't reach the phone to call for help, you can press the button on your medallion. Pressing the button alerts the program's central call center that you have a problem. The call center will try to reach you by phone immediately. If you don't answer, they will call a designated responder for you, and make sure assistance arrives.

There's an enrollment fee for emergency response programs, but for many seniors and their families, the added peace of mind is well worth the cost. There's no doubt that being able to get help quickly can make the difference between slight or no injury and serious injury, or even death.

One last point about emergency response programs: if you enroll in one, be sure to wear your call button faithfully whenever you're alone, even if you're feeling fine and don't think you'll need it.

Hip Protectors

For an older person who knows he or she has a high risk of falling, wearing external hip protectors is another way to play it safe. Hip protectors won't prevent a fall, but studies show they can help prevent a hip fracture if you do fall.

Hip protectors are lightweight (but very strong) shields, usually made of plastic. They slip into pockets on the sides of specially designed briefs. They serve basically the same purpose as a bicyclist's helmet or a football player's shoulder pads: they protect you and your hip bones by absorbing and dispersing some of the impact from a fall.

Hip protectors are easy to wear, and the special briefs are easy to launder. Because you wear them as an undergarment, most people won't know you're wearing them.

Here again, there's a cost. You have to purchase the special briefs and the pads that slip in and out of them. From time to time they'll need to be replaced. But for anyone with a history of falling or with clear risk factors, the cost is probably worth it.

How Family and Friends Can Help

For most of us, preventing falls is easier to do with a little help from our support network. Here are some ways family and friends can help prevent falls:

- Gather information and understand the challenge.
- Provide encouragement and support.
- Conduct a home inspection and perform necessary safety modifications.
- Learn what can be done to safely assist a family member when walking, going up or down stairs, or getting into or out of a car.
- Offer transportation, so your loved one can stay active and connected.

- Play the role of advocate if your loved one's physician or other care provider doesn't seem to be paying enough attention to the problem.

To Sum Up . . .

Older adults will and should worry about falling. This worry will be well spent if it results in taking positive steps to reduce the risk of falls. Planning and action will make you safer. Retreating into fear and inactivity will make you less safe. Take charge; be smart; reduce your risks. Don't let fear of falling prevent you from living your life to the fullest!

More Resources

- "Check for Safety," a six-page safety checklist for older adults, is offered by the **National Center for Injury Prevention and Control** (part of the **Centers for Disease Control and Prevention**). (*www.cdc.gov*)

Quick Links

>>> These web-based resources may be accessed through our website:
www.aginginstride.org

- The **American Occupational Therapy Association** website offers "Home Safety Tips for People with Health Problems." (*www.aota.org*)

- The **AARP** website includes "Finding Universal Design Solutions That Meet Your Needs," helpful suggestions for modifying your home to make it safer and more senior-friendly. (*www.aarp.org*)

ISSUE 6: HOME SAFETY AND SECURITY

Every year more than three million Americans over 65 are involved in accidents, a large percentage of which take place at home. The risk of death by accident is three and a half times higher for people over 75 than for the population at large. In fact, accidents are the seventh leading cause of death among older adults.

Accidents at home are usually caused by simple things that most of us didn't think of as particularly dangerous when we were younger; for example, stairs that are dark or don't have handrails, showers or tubs without grab bars, worn carpeting, slippery or uneven floors. With a small investment of time and effort, accidents from these simple causes can be prevented.

Preventing Accidents in Your Home

There is no magic formula for preventing accidents in your home. Here, however, are some practical suggestions to help you get started:

- Make a conscious effort to understand the special risks and vulnerability of older adults. Take into consideration changes in physical agility, balance, strength, and eyesight, as well as use of medications that might cause dizziness or drowsiness.

- Make a home safety assessment. Use Form 6-A, *Home Safety Inspection Checklist*, as your guide. For best results, make this inspection a team effort, with the homeowner and a trusted friend or family member doing a careful walk-through of the home, making note of what needs to be repaired or modified.

- Follow up by dealing with the risks found during the inspection. This could be as simple as doing some home improvements or repairs yourself. It might involve arranging for some professional help. Put high-risk problems at the top of the list for immediate action.

Sometimes you will run up against a safety risk that just can't be removed. Discuss such risks with family and caregivers. Work out a strategy for coping, given the resources you have available.

- Don't take safety for granted. Even after a thorough assessment, you need to stay alert. Needs and situations change. A person's physical condition will likely change over time, raising the risk threshold for certain kinds of injury. Home safety efforts need to include both an initial assessment and regular follow-up checks. Plan to do an updated safety inspection at least once each year.

- Safety benefits from teamwork. If you can, work on safety as a family project. Everyone in the family, especially children who will be visiting or living in the same home with an older adult, should know what the risks and issues are. They need to be sensitive to potential problems. For example, spilling water on the floor or leaving small toys around can be safety issues anywhere. In the home of an older friend or relative, such carelessness can be especially dangerous.

- The most common household accidents involving the elderly are falls in bathrooms and on stairways. Start by identifying needs in those high risk areas, then move on to the rest of the home.

Fire Safety

Fires are often caused by forgetfulness. A pan of food is left cooking on the stove. A small appliance is turned on and forgotten. A cigarette or pipe is left somewhere where it can fall and ignite a rug, chair, or mattress. Because forgetfulness is one of the predictable problems older adults face, fire is a major risk to their health and safety. Be sure a home safety assessment includes fire prevention, warning, and escape.

Here are seven basic fire safety precautions:

- Your home should be equipped with an adequate number of well-placed smoke detectors/alarms. Smoke detectors are an inexpensive, sensible safety precaution. They are easy to install and check. Smoke detector batteries need to be checked often and changed every six months. Many people change their smoke detector batteries at the same time they change their clocks ahead an hour for daylight-saving time or back an hour for standard time.

- Hazardous materials, including combustible matter and flammable substances such as old paints and thinners, should be removed or stored safely. If you have questions about storing or disposing of hazardous materials, your local fire department can be helpful.

- Fire extinguishers should be placed in the kitchen and in hallways. Like smoke alarm batteries, fire extinguishers must be checked at regular intervals. Read the manufacturer's directions for recommended frequency, and tag each extinguisher with a label that tells when it was last inspected.

- Check for overloaded outlets or extension cords. See that electrical wiring, appliance cords, and connections are in good repair.

- Electrical appliances should be checked and in good working order. If safe use of appliances is a concern, look into the availability of appliances with automatic shut-off switches and other similar safety features.

- Heavily-used chimneys and flues should be cleaned from time to time.

- Escape routes from upper and lower floors of the home in case of fire should be planned and discussed. Do a walk-through rehearsal if you can.

Home Security

Unfortunately, older adults are easy targets for burglary and assault. Statistically, they are victimized more often than other age groups. Because of that reality, many older people living alone feel vulnerable. Here are several ways to make your home more secure:

- Doors and windows should be in good working order. All doors and windows should lock securely. If you have questions about what type of locks are best, talk with your local police community relations department or a local locksmith.

- Exterior lighting should be ample. Shrubbery should be cut back or removed to improve visibility from the street and neighboring homes.

- All exterior doors should have view holes. Never open the door to your home if you don't know who is on the other side.

- There should be at least one phone on every floor in the home and a phone by the bedside for emergencies.

- Emergency numbers should be clearly written out and taped on or next to the phone.

Making Repairs and Modifications

You can fix some things by yourself or with the help of handy friends, but doing it yourself is not always the best way to go. Poorly planned and built features can prove useless, or even dangerous. For example, a ramp that is too steep and lacks safety features is worse than no ramp at all. Grab bars that are not solidly anchored can cause rather than prevent falls. Form 6-B, *Home Repairs and Home Modifications Checklist,* can help you decide what home modifications might be necessary now, as well as down the road.

If you are hiring a handyman or contractor to do some of the work for you, be certain the person or company you select is reliable and trustworthy. Here are some helpful tips:

- Get recommendations from friends who have had similar work done.

- Be sure the contractor is licensed and bonded.

- Get references and check them.

- Check with the Better Business Bureau, your state's consumer affairs office, and your local licensing board, if applicable.

- Ask if you can see some of the contractor's completed projects.

- Get a written agreement, and don't pay the full agreed price until the work is completed to your satisfaction.

- Get bids from several contractors—but remember, the lowest bid isn't always the best choice.

Buyer Beware

Older adults are often targeted by unscrupulous contractors and service providers. Be wary of door-to-door repair sales. A common scam is for a salesperson to come to your door, claiming that his company is working on a job in your neighborhood and offering to do work on your house for a low rate. He might claim to have spotted dangerous conditions that should be taken care of "right away." But when the work is completed (if it ever is completed), the services and materials usually turn out to be shoddy and not to code. Never agree to any services until you have checked out the company.

Paying for Home Improvements

If you are concerned that paying for safety improvements is beyond your means, consider these options:

Assistance Programs—Most communities and all states have programs to assist older persons with home maintenance, seasonal weatherization, and needed repairs. Some programs are free of charge, except for the cost of materials, while others charge on a sliding scale, ability-to-pay basis.

Home Repair Loans—Government housing agencies and nonprofit organizations offer loans for home repairs and accessibility renovations, such as ramps, grab bars, and accessible kitchen and bathroom fixtures. Loans may be interest-free, or at below-market interest. Eligibility requirements apply, and the construction must not be merely cosmetic in nature. Home repair loan and grant sources include:

- Title III of the Older Americans Act, which includes home improvement grants.

- U.S. Department of Agriculture Section 504 Rural Development Home Repair Loans.

- Local Community Development Departments (block grants and city development monies).

- U.S. or local Department of Energy weatherization loans.

- Federal Emergency Management Agency (FEMA) for disaster assistance.

Contact your local Senior Information and Referral or Area Agency on Aging for a list of sources available in your area. Your local senior center may also be able to help you determine the programs for which you qualify, and help you apply for home loans and grants.

Reverse Mortgages—A reverse mortgage is a loan against your house that allows you to convert part of your equity into cash. The loan is paid back when the homeowner sells the house, dies, or moves out permanently. The loan can be in a lump sum, a line of credit, or monthly payments. Reverse mortgages are another area where you need to have your guard up. Be sure to work with a reputable lender, consult with your financial advisor if you have one, and do your homework before you make any commitments or sign any documents.

To Sum Up . . .

Whether home is a long-time family house, an apartment or condominium, or a shared residence with family members or friends, feeling safe, secure, and comfortable when at home is important for everyone! This is a gift you can give to yourself—or to a loved one—which will result in greatly increased peace of mind. Get some help. Get it done. Enjoy your home!

More Resources

- **The Consumer Product Safety Commission** offers up-to-date information about dangerous products and recalls, and a list of online publications concerning home safety and other safety issues. (*www.cpsc.gov*)

- The **National Fire Protection Association** website features fact sheets and information on a variety of fire safety topics. (*www.nfpa.org*)

Quick Links

>>> These web-based resources may be accessed through our website:
www.aginginstride.org

- The **U.S. Fire Administration**, a branch of FEMA, has online articles about special concerns for the dwelling places of older adults and those with mobility or sensory disabilities. (*www.usfa.fema.gov*)

- The **National Institute on Aging** website includes information and contact numbers to report crime against older adults, as well as suggestions for avoiding being victimized. (*www.nia.nih.gov*)

- **The Bureau of Consumer Protection of the Federal Trade Commission** offers numerous articles on fraud and scams that target older adults. (*www.ftc.gov*)

- **National Resource Center on Supportive Housing and Home Modification**. Online resources and publications to help make the home safer and more convenient for older adults. (*www.homemods.org*)

- **Universal Home Design**. AARP's introduction to the concept of "Universal Design," home design geared toward people of all ages and abilities. (*www.aarp.org/universalhome*)

- **National Reverse Mortgage Lenders Association**. Information and FAQs about reverse mortgages. (*www.reversemortgage.org*)

ISSUE 7: SAFETY BEHIND THE WHEEL

We Americans invest a lot of emotion in our cars. They have become a symbol of our culture at large. The ultimate sign of American independence, it often seems, is driving a car! Getting a driver's license is the first rite of passage to adulthood. For many, cars represent power, control, individualism, independence, mobility. It is no wonder that older adults sometimes want to continue driving longer than is smart or safe. In many people's minds, not having a car means being trapped, being dependent on others, losing a significant element of freedom and enjoyment in life.

In this issue, we will discuss staying safe behind the wheel as long as possible, and how to make a comfortable transition to being a non-driver.

Assessing and Improving Driving Skills

Older persons can take several steps to extend their capability as safe drivers. For example:

- Do an honest self-assessment. Use Form 7, *Checklist for Older Drivers*, as your guide.

- Take a class for drivers 55 and over. These classes focus on the impact of the aging process on the ability to drive safely. Specific strategies for safer driving are taught and discussed. Contact your local AARP office for more information. Automobile clubs, such as the American Automobile Association, and many senior centers also offer safe driving courses for seniors.

- Always keep your car in good repair. Many local affiliates of the American Automobile Association offer free safety checks. Watch for carpet and pedal wear that may cause an accelerator or brake to stick, or a foot to slip. Make sure windshield wiper blades are replaced regularly so visibility on rainy days is as good as it can be.

- Minor modifications to your car will enhance driving safety. You can install better side- and rear-view mirrors, a back-up warning buzzer, steering wheel grips, pedal adjustments. Your local auto parts store can show you a variety of available safety enhancements. If a particular feature improves visibility or your control of your automobile, it is probably a good investment.

- If your car is large and difficult to maneuver, think about trading down to a smaller car that's easier to handle and park.

- Make sure your driver's license and license plate tabs are current.

- Check that your auto insurance is adequate and current.

- If you are becoming nervous about driving, consider cutting back. Work out some practical compromises on when and where you drive. Route and time-of-day adjustments can make driving easier. Many people give up night driving, while continuing to drive during the day. Busy highways and rush hour traffic can often be avoided with some advance planning and allowance for additional travel time. Park-and-Ride lots let you combine driving your car and riding the bus.

- Don't let safe driving become a "taboo" subject in your family. Seniors have the right to make their own decisions as long as they're able, including the decision to keep driving. But family members have the right—and the responsibility—to be concerned about safety to their loved one and to strangers who might be hurt in an accident. There is obvious potential for conflict here, but you shouldn't let it reach that point. Be willing to talk candidly about the issue, and be open to some risk-reducing compromises. Work together on a plan that respects while it protects.

When a Person Should No Longer Drive

The normal physical changes of aging can make driving unwise beyond a certain point. Hearing loss, vision problems, decreased reaction time, memory loss, and lessened manual dexterity are all limitations that tend to worsen as a person ages. There comes a point when any one of these conditions or a combination of several make it difficult and risky to keep driving. A person who has lost depth perception, peripheral vision, and reaction time creates a hazard on today's crowded streets and highways. That person risks not only damaging his or her own car or another vehicle, but also injuring himself or herself or another person.

Older drivers know this. Most older drivers become increasingly nervous about their driving ability as they age. But they also can experience a powerful denial. Many seniors wait too long to give up their car keys. They keep driving until an incident occurs—a scare, a minor accident, or worse—and then quit driving without having made plans for what they will do without the car.

It doesn't have to be like that. When you first begin to have concerns about your driving, that is the time to begin planning your post-driving strategy. Think of this as just another challenge to be addressed, and then use your best problem-solving skills to keep yourself active and mobile.

The first thing to do when considering becoming a non-driver is to add up what owning and maintaining a car costs you. Car payments, insurance, repairs, gasoline, parking fees—all these should go into your calculation. For most people, the total is considerable. Think of those dollars as money available to you for alternative transportation.

Knowing you have this "transportation allowance" available to you, begin to calculate your alternatives:

- Do you live on or near a bus route? Where are the places you can conveniently travel using the bus? If you've never explored your local bus routes, take a field trip! Just hop on and take a ride some day, making sure you know how to return to the same spot. Look for grocery stores, dry cleaners, other shopping possibilities along the route.

- Do you have family or friends who might enjoy giving you a ride to church, to your doctor's office, to the barber or beauty shop, on a weekly shopping trip?

- Is there Dial-a-Bus service for seniors in your area? Where will they take you? How convenient is it? How much lead time is needed to use this service?

- How much do taxis cost in your community? Are there cab companies that take "standing assignments" on a daily, weekly, or monthly basis? Once you have figured out how the first three modes of transportation will work for you, use taxi cabs to fill in the blanks.

With this kind of planning, many seniors lose their anxiety over giving up driving. It still may not be easy, but having a workable plan for getting where you want to go is a major step forward.

When the time comes to put away the keys, be creative in your approach. You might try these suggestions:

- Leave your car in the garage for a while and see how you get along not using it.

- Take the opportunity of an illness or hospital stay to give up driving. Did you really miss it while you were recovering?

- Give your car as a gift to a favorite charity or to a grandchild.

- Sell the car and set the money aside to increase your transportation fund.

To Sum Up . . .

There are several ways an older person can promote safe driving: by doing a periodic self-assessment, by taking a refresher driving safety course, by considering changes in when and how to use the car. There are also ways to ease the transition to being a non-driver when that time comes. Be proactive; don't wait for circumstances to make decisions for you. If you're honest with yourself, you will know when you need to begin making plans. Giving yourself an extra margin of safety is the right thing to do for other drivers on the road, and it can, above all, be a gift to yourself and your family!

More Resources

- The **National Highway Traffic Safety Administration** website includes a section on "Older Road Users." (*www.nhtsa.dot.gov*)

- Information on **AARP's 55 Alive Driver Safety Program** can be found on its website. (*www.aarp.org*)

- The **American Automobile Association (AAA)** offers driving safety courses; some local chapters offer free automobile safety checks. (*www.aaa.com*)

Quick Links

>>> These web-based resources may be accessed through our website:
www.aginginstride.org

- The **Administration on Aging**'s Supportive Services Directory describes alternative transportation services in your community. (*www.aoa.gov*)

- For situations of memory loss or dementia, the **Alzheimer's Association** website includes helpful information on driving when a person has Alzheimer's, warning signs of unsafe driving, and suggestions for preventing a person with dementia from driving when it is no longer safe to do so. (*www.alz.org*)

ISSUE 8: OUT AND ABOUT

Staying physically active and connecting with other people are two important keys to successful aging, and mobility is one of the best ways to do both at once. You might think of this as an upward spiral: going out into the world leads to increased confidence and security, which encourages even more activity. "Getting out and about" doesn't just mean a trip around the globe or to an exotic locale. In your own country, in your own community, even in your own neighborhood, there are plenty of opportunities for active engagement with the world.

Some older adults hesitate to travel because they are afraid of illness or injury, or of getting lost, or encountering hazards along the way. Others are concerned about cost. But travel need not be unsafe or expensive. Packages designed for seniors, and discounts as well, are one of the "perks" of being an older traveler. You don't have to go to Europe or even cross-country to experience the benefits. A weekend church retreat, a visit to the state capitol with your local college's senior education program, a bike ride to a winery, a bus trip to a downtown museum—there are many possibilities, all offering intellectual stimulation, lasting memories, and new friendships.

Travel Safely

If you are going on a trip out of your area, here are some suggestions to ensure a safe and healthy trip:

- **Prepare for your trip in advance**. Know about any potential adverse conditions, such as extreme weather, civil unrest, or disease warnings. The U.S. State Department and the Centers for Disease Control and Prevention both offer announcements of unsafe conditions. (See "More Resources" for those web addresses.) You can check the weather right before you pack by going to *www.weather.com*.

- **Review your health insurance policy before you leave**. What are the conditions for receiving medical care out of your service area? If you are traveling abroad, will you be covered?

- **Make sure your immunizations are up to date**, and that you have received the specific immunizations recommended or required for the area you are visiting.

- **Bring along enough medication for your trip**, and pack it in your carry-on luggage. Especially if you are traveling abroad, leave medications in their original containers. If you are carrying any narcotic drugs, consider bringing a letter from your doctor verifying your medical need for the prescription.

Special Health Concerns for Airline Passengers

Gone are the days when traveling by plane was a pampering treat! Nowadays, long lines, delays, cramped seats, and jet lag can be the norm. You can minimize discomfort by following a few steps:

- Get plenty of sleep before you leave.

- Drink water and avoid alcohol and caffeinated beverages to avoid becoming dehydrated.

- Change sitting position frequently and walk down the aisle occasionally to avoid stiff joints or (in rare cases) dangerous blood clots.

- If you have a cold, take a decongestant and chew gum on takeoff and landing to avoid ear pain.

- Check with your doctor ahead of time if you have any questions about flying with your medical conditions.

Protect Your Money

You can make sure you're in control of your money by taking the following precautions when you travel:

- **Be careful when shopping for a vacation package**. Deal only with travel agencies and tour companies with a proven track record and strong reputation for value and honesty. Make sure you know what is included in a travel package so there will be no unpleasant surprises. Planning ahead helps ensure that you will have the relaxing, carefree vacation you want.

The "Ten Essentials"

Hikers and backpackers are careful to bring along their "ten essentials": compass, map, extra food and so on. When you travel, pack smart; take the things you're sure you'll need, but leave the rest. Here's a different set of "ten essentials" for those of us over 55, to help us be prepared as we travel.

1. If you will be bringing a suitcase or luggage set, invest in a sturdy but lightweight style with wheels.

2. Bring an appropriate supply of your medications with you. If you're going to be checking luggage, keep your medications in your carry-on items.

3. Select comfortable, supportive shoes and socks. Nothing ruins an outing faster than sore feet. Bring along some moleskin, blister pads or adhesive bandages, just in case.

4. Bring a spare pair of glasses or contact lenses, and if you use reading glasses, don't forget to bring a pair or two.

5. Dress appropriately for warmth and comfort. Check the weather before you leave—but be prepared for a change. Dressing in layers helps you be ready for whatever weather you encounter.

6. Carry personal identification, including emergency contact information. If necessary, wear a medical alert bracelet, necklace, or medallion.

7. Carry currency, identification, passport and other important papers in a secure pocket or carrier.

8. Bring along an organized itinerary, complete with addresses, phone numbers, and other notes. Be sure to leave a copy with a friend also, in case someone needs to reach you in an emergency.

9. Invest in a guidebook to your destination, or borrow one from your local public library. Be sure the book you choose is up-to-date. Even if you are only exploring your own area, you might be surprised to find a variety of interesting attractions and sites.

10. Bring your address book or printed address labels so you can send postcards. If you're traveling domestically, bring stamps with you so you don't have to find a post office.

- **Carry most of your money in traveler's checks or use an ATM card**. Don't bring more cash than you think you will need for a few days, and carry only the credit cards you will use on the trip. Be aware that, in many countries, money changers factor a "commission" into their exhange rates. If you prefer, bringing an ATM card will allow you to withdraw cash at the current exchange rate—and avoid these additional charges. Also, some countries still operate on a "cash only" basis. Check with your travel agent before you leave, and consult your bank to see if your card will be operable in the places you're visiting.

- **Guard your valuables**. Don't pack anything irreplaceable (such as family photos or heirloom jewelry). Help prevent theft by carrying money and valuables securely, in a front pocket or money belt. Carry handbags tucked under your arm, not by a strap.

- **Check your auto insurance policy**. If you will be driving outside the country, your auto insurance will probably not be valid. Check ahead about buying adequate short-term insurance for your trip.

Special Assistance If You Have a Disability

Some older persons are reluctant to travel because they feel insecure negotiating the crowded service desks and corridors of busy airports and other transportation terminals. A person with hearing difficulty often has the hardest time hearing when there is significant background noise. Someone suffering from dizziness, limited vision, or mobility problems may fear falling or being jostled by crowds. If you are basically able to travel, but just need a little extra assistance, take advantage of these services available to travelers:

- **Boarding assistance**—Most airlines and rail lines have wheelchairs available for those unable to walk long distances, and some also offer formal "meet and assist" programs. These programs assure that a traveler in need of assistance will be met at the check-in counter and given help getting to the point of departure, onto the plane or train, and off safely at the other end. It is best to confirm when booking tickets that you will need either wheelchair transportation or "meet and assist" service. And don't hesitate to take advantage of pre-boarding if you need the extra time or feel unsafe in the crowding of general boarding.

- **Oxygen**—Persons with medical conditions requiring the use of an oxygen tank can travel safely on most kinds of public transport. Airlines have strict requirements about oxygen use. These usually include a letter from a physician explaining the person's oxygen requirement and a statement certifying that the oxygen provided by the airline is acceptable. If you are a supplemental oxygen user, make sure that you understand the regulations regarding oxygen use on whatever mode of transport you choose. You will also need to make arrangements ahead of time for a supply when you reach your destination.

- **Disabled accessibility**— Most aircraft are wheelchair accessible, though some small commuter planes are not. Trains and ships generally have a limited number of disabled-accessible cabins or compartments. Many resorts offer specially designed rooms and suites for use by people in wheelchairs. When planning your trip, these options can be researched and reservations for special facilities confirmed in writing before the trip begins.

Even if your physical condition makes travel more of a challenge for you, many obstacles and potential problems can easily be overcome with a little advance planning.

Safe, Healthy Walking

When we think of potential travel hazards, we might forget that even walking requires some care. Older adults can be at greater risk of injury or accident due to slower reflexes, decreased vision and hearing, and joint stiffness. But this shouldn't stop you from participating in one of the best and easiest forms of exercise, one that can improve your life in so many ways. Here are some of the keys to safe, healthy walking:

Wear comfortable, lightweight, loose-fitting clothes. Dress for the weather. Wearing several thin layers lets you adjust to the day's variations in temperature. A hat and gloves are especially important in cold or rain.

Well-fitting shoes are a must! Casual shoes with rubber or crepe soles are recommended, with a laced shoe offering the best support for your feet. A good walking shoe should include:

- Proper fit.

- Flexibility.

- Arch support.

- Elevated heel of ½ inch as a cushion.

- Leather or nylon mesh upper to allow for "breathing."

Before lacing up those walking shoes, check your feet:

- Keep toenails properly trimmed.

- Avoid tight-fitting socks.

- Use protective material for corns and calluses.

- See a podiatrist if your feet hurt.

Proceed at your own level of fitness. Start with a minimum five-minute warm-up and end with a 5–10 minute cool-down. Do some stretching exercises before and after. Remember: your body responds to changes in physical activity. Always listen to your body's messages.

Obey pedestrian safety rules. Most pedestrian injuries involve cars. Cross at crosswalks, obey "walk/don't walk" signals, and don't cross against the light. Be alert at intersections, checking carefully in both directions before crossing the street. Choose routes with sidewalks and paths when possible.

Make yourself visible. When walking, you want to see and be seen. Watch carefully for cars—check right, left, and right again. Wear bright colors in the daytime. At night, carry a flashlight. Wearing reflective materials can also make you more visible to drivers, so look for shoes, jackets, vests and backpacks with reflective strips.

To Sum Up . . .

Mobility is an important aspect of aging successfully. Getting out and about—whether it be a trek in Nepal or a trip around the block—supports independence and a sense of well being, and helps maintain connection with the world. Social contact combined with physical benefits make outings doubly beneficial. Special travel packages are available for older adults, so do your homework as you choose a vacation. Taking reasonable precautions can help ensure a successful and safe trip, so travel safe and smart!

More Resources

- The U.S. government's **FirstGov for Seniors** website includes information about travel and leisure. (*www.seniors.gov*)

- The **U.S. State Department's Bureau for Consular Affairs** includes a section of special tips for older travelers. (*http://travel.state.gov*)

- **Elderhostel** specializes in educational travel for older adults, offering tours and local events geared toward seniors. (*www.elderhostel.org*)

- The Centers for Disease Control's **National Center for Infectious Diseases** website includes information about health conditions and other concerns relating to world travel. Also within the CDC site is the **National Center for Injury Prevention and Control**, which includes information on safe travel, as well as pedestrian injury prevention. (*www.cdc.gov*)

Staying in Your Own Home

INTRODUCTION

Where is home for you? Is it the house in which you raised your children, or a smaller house, apartment, or condominium where you moved when you retired? Is home a place you live alone, or with your spouse, another family member, or longtime friend? The place called home looks different to each person, but for most, the place you identify as home is the place you want to stay.

As you age, there are good reasons for choosing to continue to live in the place you now call home. Staying in your own home means staying where your roots are. Especially if you have lived in the same community for a long time, there is comfort in knowing the grocer and the letter carrier, where you like to shop and have your hair done. Friends, neighbors, and family nearby provide companionship and support. A neighbor who always brings the morning paper upstairs, a friend who stops in for coffee twice a week, the young family next door who enjoys having surrogate grandparents for their young son and daughter—all these intertwine to create a fabric of community that is difficult to recreate if you move.

As you grow older, living on your own can present a series of challenges. Taking care of the garden, managing home maintenance and repair, keeping up with basic housework, the cooking, and the laundry—as energy and physical ability decrease, these ordinary jobs grow more difficult. The good news is that as the senior population has increased, so has the variety of senior services available in most communities. Many of these services are designed specifically to help seniors remain safely and comfortably in their own homes.

The next several issues focus on identifying and meeting the needs of older adults living independently. In Issue 9, we provide an overview of the senior services network that exists to support those living on their own. We also guide you through a realistic needs assessment that will both help you decide whether living independently is right for you, and give you direction in putting the service network to work for you or a loved one.

Issues 10 and 11 deal with arranging for in-home personal care and health care services. Finally, Issue 12 will introduce you to adult day programs, a relatively new approach to meeting both the social and health care needs of seniors living at home.

In the forms section, you will find three worksheets to help you as you work through these issues and opportunities:

- Form 9: *Needs Assessment for Living on Your Own*
- Form 10: *Worksheet for Hiring a Home Helper*
- Form 11: *Checklist for Choosing a Home Health Care Agency*

If staying where you are is one of your goals, roll up your sleeves! Use the resources in this section to help you develop a plan that allows you to remain safely and comfortably in your home.

ISSUE 9: SUPPORT SERVICES FOR SENIORS LIVING AT HOME

A story is told about a sailing ship off the coast of South America on which the crew had run out of fresh water. The situation was becoming desperate when the captain signaled a passing ship to ask for help. The other ship sent back a message: "Lower your buckets." That made no sense to the thirsty sailors, but they did as they were told and were surprised when they brought up not saltwater, but fresh water. The ship, it turns out, was passing the mouth of the great Amazon River.

The moral of this story is, know what's around you! It applies to the network of senior services, in that many older people don't use the services available to them simply because they don't know what's there, or don't understand the process of gaining access to what is available.

In this section, we'll introduce you to the range of support available to seniors living on their own. Program specifics vary from one community to the next, but you probably will be pleasantly surprised at the variety of services available to you. Having services available is only one part of the equation. In order to make the best use of the range of possible services, you must be willing to do two things: one, you need to honestly and carefully understand your needs; and two, you need to be willing to accept help. For many people, both sides of the equation are difficult. Many older adults are reluctant to admit that they have needs or to ask for or accept help. It takes both time and perspective to understand that the way to preserve independence is to know what help you need and to go after it!

The Senior Services Network

The array of programs for seniors and caregivers has grown to the point that it is now an impressive community service network. Some senior services have grown up as governmental mandates, others exist in the realm of free enterprise. Some are free to all or free to those at certain income levels. Others require payment. Understanding the diversity of programs will help you find and use services that best fit your situation.

When you take advantage of governmental agencies and programs, you shouldn't feel that you are asking for a "handout." These agencies and programs are supported by your tax dollars. Specific eligibility requirements sometimes apply, but many of these agencies are there to serve all seniors. In helping seniors live healthier and more productive lives, the services are benefiting the community as a whole. Don't hesitate to take advantage of what they have to offer.

Here are some of the senior services available in most communities:

Senior Information and Referral

Senior Information and Referral, often called "Senior Information and Assistance," is a publicly funded program available in all communities across the country. Phoning your local Senior Information and Referral office is a great place to start if you want to research the services available in your particular community. If you are assisting an older adult from a distance, get in touch with that person's local Senior Information and Referral program. The trained advocates who answer the phone will connect you with appropriate services, explain eligibility requirements, and follow up to ensure that needs are being met.

Care Management

Care management services help you locate, use, and coordinate services. Care managers may be acting in an independent, fee-for-service capacity, or as an extension of some other agency or program. A care manager's role typically includes:

- Assessing a client's needs.
- Arranging services.
- Explaining issues.
- Monitoring how things are going.

For more on care managers, please turn to Issue 42, *Working with a Geriatric Care Manager*.

Assistance for Living at Home

Many agencies and programs direct their energies toward assisting seniors who choose to live independently in their own homes.

Home care programs include:

- **Home health care**—Supportive care and supplies in the home.

- **Chore and personal care service**—Assistance with household tasks, shopping, and other personal activities of daily living.

- **Emergency response systems**—Devices that connect individuals at home with emergency services.

- **Reassurance programs**—Regular telephone contacts to persons who are unable to leave their homes.

- **Respite care**—Temporary assistance to give caregivers time away from their responsibilities.

- **Household services**—Assistance with home safety inspections, home repairs, and modifications for safety and energy efficiency.

Nutrition Programs

There are two kinds of nutrition programs for seniors: congregate nutrition sites that offer meals served at designated locations and times, and "Meals On Wheels" delivered to an individual's home. Many Meals On Wheels programs deliver a hot noontime meal five days a week; others deliver frozen meals, typically one week's supply at a time.

Transportation

Transportation resources often include van services such as Dial-A-Bus and senior discounts on taxis and public transit.

Alternative Housing Options

Many older adults decide it's time to move. For them, the work or expense of keeping up a house or living alone in an apartment is too much. Alternative retirement housing options include:

- Home sharing programs.
- Low-income senior apartments.
- Retirement communities.
- Assisted living facilities.
- Adult family homes.

Health Care and Mental Health Services

Many community-based health care resources are available to assist older adults. They include physician referral services, medical and dental care, health screening programs, home health care providers, hospice care providers, and mental health counseling and therapy.

Information and Support for Specific Diseases and Conditions

Information and support services for seniors with certain diseases and medical conditions (and for their family members) are especially important. These programs offer an opportunity to learn more about a particular illness and to share experiences with others facing similar problems. Many disease-specific groups offer education workshops, health fairs, health screening opportunities, help lines, and support.

Legal and Financial Assistance

Services are also available to assist seniors and caregivers in sorting through legal and financial issues such as Medicaid eligibility, Medicare and supplemental insurance benefits, preparing advance directives, and keeping track of and paying bills.

Informal Sources of Assistance

Formal, high-profile senior service agencies and programs are only part of the total network of senior support. Family members, friends, neighbors, and community organizations such as churches, youth groups, and service clubs provide an important set of less-formal senior resources. These personal, one-to-one resources are especially good for meeting the occasional challenges of living at home. The personal connections made also provide seniors with opportunities for companionship and recreation.

Doing a Needs Assessment

Knowing the types of services available is only helpful if you understand your own needs. Are there ways in which you could use some help? If so, with what tasks or activities? Questions like these seem straightforward enough. However, it is difficult sometimes for an older person to step back and ask, "What aspects of independent living are going smoothly?" and "Where could I use some outside assistance?"

A "needs assessment" is a professional term for something that is usually very quick and easy to do. It's just sitting down and listing the ordinary tasks and responsibilities that go into living on your own, such as buying the groceries, making sure the lawn gets mowed in the summer and the sidewalk gets cleared of snow and ice in the winter, doing laundry, and getting to doctors' appointments. You don't have to make your own list, however.

In the forms section, we've included Form 9, *Needs Assessment for Living on Your Own*. Use it to help you see the big picture and set some priorities. Then, when you call Senior Information and Referral or look in the phone book for help, you will be clear on what will be most helpful to you.

Obstacles That Sometimes Prevent Getting Help

For many of us, being willing to ask for and accept help is difficult. We have spent our lives proud of our ability to take care of our own needs, as well as the needs of others. It's not easy to admit that the time has come when help is both welcome and necessary. However, one of the keys to successful aging, to maintaining the greatest amount of independence for the longest time, is being wise enough and honest enough to ask for and arrange for what you need.

So, be alert to the possibility that an attitude of "going it alone" may negatively influence decision making, perhaps without you even realizing it. Remember to keep these realities in mind:

- Senior services are not a form of charity. Rather, they are part of the social commitment we make as families, communities, and as a society-at-large. You wouldn't think of school for your children as charity, so why should support services for seniors be any different?

- Being on the receiving end of services is not something that should make you feel embarrassed or guilty. All emotionally healthy adults need to learn to both give *and* receive.

- We all value our independence. But the truth is that seeking out and accepting available senior services will often increase, rather than reduce, your independence. For example, accepting help from the local Kiwanis Club in tacking down throw rugs and fixing loose floorboards may keep you from breaking a hip. Signing up for Meals On Wheels may help maintain your health and energy through good nutrition when the alternative would be eating poorly planned, nutritionally deficient meals that could lead to physical decline.

Tips for Working with Busy Agencies

Working with busy social service agencies and programs can sometimes be frustrating. Workers want to be prompt, pleasant, and helpful, but they often have large caseloads and multiple responsibilities. Here are some tips for working positively with senior service providers:

- Before you call, gather all the information you may need, such as Social Security and Medicare numbers, and names of current service providers.

- In your first contact, be brief and to the point. Be specific in explaining your situation and the kind of help you need.

- Be patient and persistent. Sometimes it takes several referrals to line up the help you need.

- Ask the agency for the best time to call or visit.

- Keep track of the date and time of each call you make, the name of the person with whom you speak, and what is said. If necessary, check back to see that your request is being handled as promised.

- If someone unresponsive or rude to you, get back to Senior Information and Referral, or contact the program supervisor.

To Sum Up . . .

Most communities today go to great lengths to provide support for their older citizens living at home. To take full advantage of these programs and services, three things are needed: you must know what services are available; you must have a reasonably accurate picture of your own needs; and you must be willing to ask for and accept help where you need it.

The purpose of senior services is not to infringe on independence, but to promote it. Don't ask for help where you don't need it. It's good to continue doing for yourself those activities you can do safely and comfortably. But if there are things you are beginning to wonder about—issues or concerns that could be affecting your independence, safety, or quality of life—the smart thing is to let the support network do what it does well.

More Resources

- **The Eldercare Locator** is the nationwide toll-free service to help seniors and their caregivers find local services. Information specialists can take your call on Monday–Friday, 9:00 a.m.–8:00 p.m. (Eastern time) at 1-800-677-1116. Information is also available at the Eldercare Locator website. (*www.eldercare.gov*)

- **The Resource Directory for Older People** is a government publication listing federal agencies, national organizations, professional societies, volunteer and non-profit groups that specialize in helping older adults. The directory may be available at your public library, or you can use the directory online. (*www.aoa.dhhs.gov/directory/default.htm*)

- The **U.S. Administration on Aging** website has information and resources for older adults and their caregivers, including fact sheets and state contact numbers. (*www.aoa.dhhs.gov*)

Quick Links

>>> These web-based resources may be accessed through our website:
www.aginginstride.org

ISSUE 10: HIRING A HOME HELPER

Is it becoming more difficult for you to take proper care of your yard or bend over to take the laundry out of the dryer? Does it seem like too much effort some days to cook or take care of basic housework? Do you find yourself bathing less often because you are worried about slipping and falling in the shower when you are alone? Then you are probably a good candidate for a home helper!

A home helper is someone who comes into your home to help with:

- Personal care needs, such as cooking, bathing, or transportation.
- Household chores, such as laundry, housekeeping, or yard work.

Home helpers may come every day of the week or only occasionally. They can be hired to do just one chore or several. You can find them through an agency or independently. However large or small your personal and household needs, finding the right home helper can be an essential element in your plan to stay safely and comfortably in your own home.

What Are Your Needs?

The best place to begin is with an overall needs assessment. Remember, Form 9, *Needs Assessment for Living on Your Own*, is available to use as a guide. In listing your needs, be as realistic as possible. This is one of those times it pays to be honest with yourself. It is important to keep doing the jobs you can do with some effort; however, you should not be doing jobs that exhaust you, jobs that you no longer have the strength or dexterity to do, or jobs that make you feel unsafe. Remember that your goal is to design a plan that will allow you to remain safely in your own home. If you are not honest in setting up the plan, it's not going to work.

How Do I Find Someone?

There are many places to begin your search for a home helper. Senior Information and Referral can be helpful here. They keep a listing of agencies that specialize in providing services for seniors. Your local Yellow Pages is another good place to begin. Depending on the services you need, try looking under the listings for home health care, home care services, eldercare services, cleaning services, housekeeping, or yard maintenance.

Especially in smaller communities, the informal network can also be a good source of referrals. Go to your local senior center, and ask if they have someone they will recommend. Check through your church or ask a neighbor whose home always looks well-kept if someone takes care of it for her.

Depending on the mix of services you are seeking, you may be looking for one helper or several. As you investigate the options, remember to write down the name of each person with whom you have spoken, the scope of services that person or agency will provide, and any other important information.

How Much Will It Cost?

The cost of home help can range from free volunteer services to basic help at minimum wage to higher-skill services at $8 or more per hour. You should count on paying more for help provided through a cleaning company or home care agency, although hiring through an agency has its advantages. Call around to find out who provides the kinds of services you need and how much they usually charge. Don't forget to include volunteer and government-supported programs. Then work out a plan based on how much you can afford to pay.

Choosing Carefully

Once you know your needs and understand your resources and your budget, the next step is to make a careful selection. Use Form 10, *Worksheet for Hiring a Home Helper*, to organize your information.

In making your selection, be sure to:

- **Ask questions**—Get a clear picture of the person's/agency's experience, training, standards, and pay expectations.

- **Check references**—Ask for the names of other persons the person or agency has served. Then call the references and listen carefully to what they tell you.

Should You Hire a Home Helper Directly or Go Through an Agency?

Both options have plusses and minuses. Here are some points to consider:

Going Through an Agency—Advantages:

- The agency is responsible for screening, training, and supervision. If something goes wrong, you can look to the agency to fix it.

- An agency may offer greater flexibility by assigning different persons to different needs.

- You don't have to worry about tax withholding and other responsibilities of being an employer.

Going Through an Agency—Disadvantages:

- You will have to pay more, since the agency needs to cover its overhead.

- More turnover in helpers is likely; expect different helpers for different tasks/needs. If it is important to you to have the same helper all the time, you should let the agency know, and expect to be flexible on hours and days available.

Hiring Someone Directly—Advantages:

- Your cost will probably be less.

- If you get a good helper, you may develop a supportive one-on-one relationship.

Hiring Someone Directly—Disadvantages:

- You are responsible for screening the person and checking references.

- If there are problems, you're on your own in working things out as an employer.

- If the person you hire is your employee (not an independent contractor), you must meet the legal obligations of an employer, such as withholding and reporting income taxes and paying Social Security taxes. To learn more about your legal requirements as an employer, contact the Internal Revenue Service, or you can find the information on their website (*www.irs.gov*).

- **Be clear about what you expect**—Get off to a good start by being specific about your needs, how much you are willing to pay, and things like smoking/non-smoking, being on time, and wanting a consistent helper.

Managing the Relationship

If you start out being clear about your needs and the scope and quality of work you expect, your relationship with any service provider will go more smoothly. The first few times a person works in your home, it is important to give clear, constructive feedback on how you think they are performing their work. Deal with any problems that arise promptly and candidly. Any serious issues should be reported immediately to the agency, or to the person if you've hired directly. Remember, never tolerate any form of physical or verbal abuse or intimidation. Promptly report such behavior to the authorities (Adult Protective Services or similar agency, or to the police). Positive feedback and expressions of appreciation, given promptly when earned, are also important. Two other tips for building a strong relationship:

- Give the helper the name, address, and phone number of another family member to contact if the helper has questions or concerns.

- Give the helper's full name and work schedule to other family members, so when they call and the helper answers, they will be aware of the household support being provided.

To Sum Up . . .

Hiring qualified, reputable home helpers can help you meet your needs and greatly extend your ability to continue living safely and comfortably at home.

When hiring in-home help, you have two options: go through an agency or hire someone directly. Each approach has its own advantages and disadvantages. Either way, it is critical that you start with a clear sense of the tasks with which you want help, that you do your homework gathering and checking references for individuals and agencies, and that you understand how services are charged and how much you will be paying. For successful relationships, give honest feedback early and often, letting your helpers know in clear terms what you need and how they are doing.

It takes significant work to begin a positive relationship with a home helper. Consider that work an investment in yourself and your independence! If you follow the necessary steps at the beginning, the rest of the relationship will go more easily, and it will help you meet what is for you an important goal: maintaining a good quality of life while remaining in your home.

More Resources

- **The Eldercare Locator** is a nationwide toll-free telephone number and online service from the U.S. Administration on Aging. The Eldercare Locator service operates Monday–Friday, 9:00 a.m.–8:00 p.m., Eastern Time, and can be reached at 1-800-677-1116, or online. (*www.eldercare.gov*)

- **The Family Caregiver Alliance** website includes information on hiring in-home help and related services. (*www.caregiver.org*)

- Your local **Area Agency on Aging** may have a list of home helper/ chore services workers and agencies. A directory of state agencies can be found on the **U.S. Administration on Aging** website. (*www.aoa.dhhs.gov*)

- The **Internal Revenue Service**'s website includes information about employment taxes for household employees. (*www.irs.gov*)

Quick Links

>>> These web-based resources may be accessed through our website: www.aginginstride.org

ISSUE 11: HOME HEALTH CARE

Chronic health problems and/or occasional acute health crises will eventually challenge most older adults. You know how it goes. Your friend was very healthy for a man in his 70s until he fell and broke his hip and needed to go through rehabilitation. Your sister has chronic lung problems causing her to need supplemental oxygen. It used to be that almost all major health issues required care in a hospital or nursing home. However, with the growth of home health care, many health concerns that formerly required institutional care can be treated in the comfortable and familiar surroundings of your own home.

Many people do prefer to receive health care at home, and in many cases home care is less expensive than going to a nursing home or transitional care facility. It's worth doing a bit of research to see what the options are, and to determine if you are a good candidate to receive home-based health care services. In this section, we will look at the options and considerations.

Is Home Care the Right Choice?

Most people, if given the choice, prefer to receive health care services at home rather than at a hospital or nursing home. However, personal preference isn't the only thing to consider. *Before making a choice for home health care, you should make sure you understand what services will and will not be covered by Medicare, Medicaid, or private insurance (see pages 76-77).* You should also ask yourself the following important questions:

- What are my medical and personal care needs?

- Is the medical technology I need available and safe for home use?

- Is the physical layout of my home practical for living with my condition? Is the bathroom too far from the bedroom? Can simple modifications make my home more suitable?

- Are medical facilities located nearby, in case of emergencies or procedures that can't be handled by home health workers?

- Who else lives in my home, and what degree of support can they provide? Will I have enough privacy to allow me to rest comfortably?

- What will the cost be, compared to a hospital or nursing home?

What Services are Available?

The home health care field is growing every year, and many specialized services can be provided in the home. To help you begin your research, here are some categories of professionals who can help:

- **Home health aides** are trained to provide custodial care, such as helping with activities of daily living, such as dressing, bathing, getting in and out of bed, and using the toilet. They may also prepare meals for the patient and do light housekeeping tasks related to care.

- **Certified nursing aides (CNAs or NACs)** are health aides who have received special training. The training requirement varies from state to state. In addition to personal care, CNAs can perform simple medical procedures such as taking temperatures, changing dressings, and administering medications.

- **Registered nurses (RNs) and licensed practical nurses (LPNs)** provide skilled medical services beyond those that home health aides offer. Nurses can conduct an assessment to determine the care needed and monitor the patient's condition. They perform hands-on procedures such as changing wound dressings, inserting catheters and IV lines, and giving injections.

- **Rehabilitation services** provide care to help maximize the patient's quality of life, independence, and safety, and to restore the patient to the highest possible level of function.

  - **Physical therapists** work with patients who have lost muscular strength, coordination, and range of motion. They provide treatments designed to help the patient regain body strength and function.

  - **Occupational therapists** provide treatment and training for patients who need help relearning the activities of daily living, such as eating, dressing, grooming, and safely transferring from bed to chair or wheelchair.

- ° **Speech/language therapists** work with patients who have impaired speaking ability. They provide treatment to maximize the ability to speak, or to help the patient communicate even if he or she cannot speak. They also work with swallowing disorders.

- ° **Respiratory therapists** care for patients who have trouble breathing on their own. They provide therapy to help the patient breathe, and instruction on using mechanical help, such as supplemental oxygen or ventilators.

- **Registered dietitians** visit the home to develop and monitor an appropriate nutritional plan for the patient, including special diets, such as low-fat, low-sodium, or high-calorie.

- **Social workers** often coordinate other helpers to create a safe, effective home care plan. They help patients locate needed services and navigate the paperwork maze. Social workers are also concerned with how to best meet the patient's social and emotional needs.

- **Technical services** involving a product or piece of complex equipment are also available in the home. **Infusion therapy** companies provide equipment and services for intravenous (IV) medications, such as antibiotics, pain relief drugs, nutritional therapy, or chemotherapy. Home **enteral therapy** means feeding through a tube when the patient can't receive adequate nutrients by eating.

- **Durable medical equipment companies** provide home care equipment that will be used over an extended period of time, such as oxygen delivery systems, wheelchairs, walkers, and hospital beds. They can also furnish wound care dressings, incontinence aids, and other products and supplies.

Locating Home Health Care Providers in Your Area

Once you have completed an evaluation of your situation, have decided that home health care is a good choice, and have determined which services you will need, the next step is to locate suitable providers. Here are some places to start:

- Your physician or hospital discharge planner may make recommendations.

- A geriatric care manager can help assess your needs, then locate and set up a care network. Care managers may work alone or as part of an agency or organization.

- Senior community referral services, such as your local Area Agency on Aging or Senior Information and Referral, are often able to give referrals.

- Look in the Yellow Pages under "Nurses," "Nursing Services," "Home Health Services," "Home Care," or "Social Service Organizations."

- Home health care agencies provide a range of services, from initial evaluation and care planning, to placing home health care workers, to supervising the care you receive. Many home care agencies are affiliated with hospitals. Agencies are licensed, and they recruit and screen personnel.

- Nurse registries are employment agencies for home care nurses and aides. They will provide a list of candidates from which the client selects. Depending on the law in your area, nurse registries may or may not be licensed or subject to state regulation, so be a cautious consumer and check references. Nurses or nurse aides located through a registry typically act as independent contractors, so they are not supervised as they would be if they were employees of a home health care agency.

Who Pays for Home Health Services?

Home health services are paid for in a variety of ways:

- **Private health insurance**, Medicare supplement ("Medigap") policies, and long-term care insurance may cover home care. Coverage is usually limited to services that are "medically necessary," "reasonable," and less expensive than in another setting.

- **Medicare** is the largest source of payment for intermittent skilled services, but numerous administrative restrictions apply. Medicare covers home health services for persons who are essentially confined to their homes, who need part-time or intermittent care (such as skilled nursing, home health aide services, or therapy), but who do not need to be in an institutional setting. This includes people who have been recently discharged from a hospital and those with chronic health problems that require ongoing treatment. Other specific coverage limitations apply, so be sure to check before assuming Medicare will cover the care you need. Before care begins, your home health care provider must tell you how much of your bill Medicare will cover, and what items or services you will be responsible for.

- **Medicaid** programs from state to state cover many home health services as an alternative to more expensive institutional care. Contact your state medical assistance office to find out what your state's program covers. Payment under Medicaid depends on meeting the eligibility requirements in your state. See Issue 32, *Medicare and Medicaid,* for more information.

- **Charitable organizations**, such as United Way, also contribute significantly to the costs of home health care provided by nonprofit agencies.

Choosing and Working with a Home Health Agency

Use Form 11, *Checklist for Choosing a Home Health Care Agency*, as a guide to the questions you should ask before choosing a home health agency. Form 11 also includes questions to ask when checking a reference you've been given, as well as factors to include in evaluating how well your home health agency is doing and where improvements are needed.

To Sum Up . . .

It's nice to stay at home if you can. Home health services are becoming more sophisticated all the time, and they provide an increasingly important alternative to hospital or nursing home care.

When selecting a home health agency, it is important to be clear about what your needs will be, ask questions before making your selection, and follow up with the references you've been given.

More Resources

- The **National Association for Home Care and Hospice** is the trade association for home care and hospice providers. The "Consumers" area of their website includes information about home care, including the online brochure "How to Choose a Home Care Provider." (*www.nahc.org*)

> **Quick Links**
>
> >>> These web-based resources may be accessed through our website:
> www.aginginstride.org

- The U.S. government's **Medicare** website includes a booklet entitled "Medicare and Home Health Care." Also on the Medicare site, you can find **Home Health Compare**, which gives information about Medicare-certified home health agencies, searchable by state, county, ZIP code, or name. (*www.medicare.gov*)

- **State Medicaid Toll-Free Lines**. List of phone numbers for state Medicaid programs. (*http://cms.hhs.gov*)

- **The Eldercare Locator** is a nationwide toll-free telephone number and online service from the U.S. Administration on Aging. The Eldercare Locator service operates Monday–Friday, 9:00 a.m.–8:00 p.m., Eastern Time, and can be reached at 1-800-677-1116, or online. (*www.eldercare.gov*)

ISSUE 12: ADULT DAY PROGRAMS

It would be great if all of us could maintain our independence throughout our lives. However, millions of seniors in our country live with significant physical or cognitive impairment. Many of these older adults continue to live at home alone, even though their isolation poses some level of risk. Others continue to live with a spouse, or move in with a relative or friend. Quite often, it is a positive arrangement for all parties. The older adult needing care is able to receive it from those closest to him or her, and the person doing the caregiving is able to translate love and concern into concrete acts of care and support. Even in the best of situations, though, it can be difficult for both caregiver and care receiver to be together 24 hours a day. Both can benefit from some "away" time, a change of scenery and routine that provides particular services to the older adult and allows the caregiver time for other activities.

To meet the needs of at-risk seniors, both those living alone and those living with a caregiver, a new kind of senior service has been developed: the adult day center. Almost unheard of 20 years ago, such centers are now becoming an integral part of the senior service network, both in metropolitan areas and, increasingly, in smaller towns.

What is an Adult Day Center?

Sometimes listed as *adult day services*, *adult day care centers*, or *adult day health centers*, these are places where older adults and other physically or mentally challenged individuals can go during the day for socializing, for recreation and activities, for help with personal care, and for safety. Adult day *health* centers also provide health and rehabilitation-related services.

The majority of participants in such programs are over 65, but adult day centers are open to any adult with a physical or cognitive disability. Participants in adult day centers most often live with family members, but many still live alone in their own homes, in assisted living communities, or in adult family homes.

Adult day centers exist to help their clients maintain the greatest possible independence and level of function. Centers provide activity-based care and learning in a secure environment. They provide a base for social interaction and help for participants and families as they work out issues in daily life and caregiving. The following are services most commonly provided:

Social Activities and Intellectual Stimulation

- Group and individual activities.

- Community outings and field trips.

- Therapeutic recreation, designed to be fun, but also for rehabilitation benefits.

- Dementia-appropriate activities, such as music, pet therapy, or sensory programs.

- Ability-appropriate and adaptive activities for participants with physical disabilities.

Health Care and Rehabilitation Services

- Care for health problems, such as diabetes or congestive heart failure.

- Minor medical services, such as medication management, blood pressure checks, diabetic monitoring, and wound care.

- Rehabilitation therapies, such as physical, occupational, or speech therapy.

- Rehabilitation services such as gait training, ambulation, exercise and strengthening classes, fall prevention, and help performing activities of daily living (ADLs).

Many adult day centers also provide mental health services, such as counseling, education and support groups, psychiatric evaluation, and support for Alzheimer's patients and their families. Some centers also offer assistance with personal care, such as haircuts and shampoos, shaving, foot and nail care, and bathing. Most programs include at least one full meal and nutritious snacks. Adult day centers are accustomed to accommodating special diets, and easily meet a variety of needs. Finally, some programs provide their own transportation, or are willing to arrange special transportation with the community's public transit or taxi services.

Adult day programs vary greatly in the range of services they provide. You will need to check your local options to see what specific services are offered in your community. However, adult day programs provide a cheerful, positive environment for socialization, education, and activity for adults with limitations and special needs. They can be one important element in a plan to allow an older person to remain safely and securely in his/her own home.

Locating an Adult Day Program in Your Area

For a recommendation or list of adult day centers in your area, consult:

- Your family physician, social worker, care manager, or hospital discharge planner.

- The Yellow Pages, under "Adult Supervisory Care" or "Day Care-Adult."

- Your local Area Agency on Aging or Senior Information and Referral phone number.

- The National Adult Day Services Association website (*www.nadsa.org*), which has an online searchable directory.

- The National Eldercare Locator (1-800-677-1116), a service of the U.S. Administration on Aging.

When looking for an adult day center, think about the specific needs of the participant. Here is a checklist to use as you begin your search:

Will the participant need:

- Social activities, companionship?
- Mental stimulation?
- Exercise?
- A secured environment?
- Nutritious meals and snacks/special diet?
- Health monitoring?
- Assistance with personal care?
- Medication monitoring?

- Personal care, such as bathing, hair and nail care, shaving?
- Health care procedures?
- Rehabilitation, such as physical, occupational, speech/swallowing therapy?
- Transportation?

Questions to Ask About Adult Day Centers

Once you have located the centers in your community, you will want to call and find out the particulars of each program. Questions to ask include:

- What criteria must a client meet to be accepted to the program?

- Are there any conditions that would make the client ineligible for this particular center, such as memory loss, not being able to eat unassisted, combative behavior, or not being able to transfer to a chair?

- What are the center's hours? Are they open weekends? Holidays?

- What are the professional credentials of its personnel? Are staff members licensed to provide the necessary medical care?

- Does the program meet the social and regular health needs of the potential client?

- What meals are provided? Can special diets be accommodated?

- Are there facilities for bathing, hair washing, grooming?

- Does the center provide transportation?

- Is the environment safe and secure?

- What are the charges, and what services are included?

- Does the center accept Medicare/Medicaid?

Pay a visit to the center during regular hours. Talk with the person in charge, and observe the participants. Ask to see the monthly activity calendar and menu. Observe the facility, staff, and clients, and pay attention to your impressions.

Ask if the participant can visit the center for a trial period, so that both participant and family can get a feel for the center. If possible, this trial period should last several days so that the participant has time to adjust to the new faces, location, and routine before making a decision about the program.

The Transition Period

Adjusting to new surroundings and a new schedule can take time, especially for those suffering from memory problems and confusion. Family or other caregivers can be helpful in the process. Ask staff at the center for suggestions about how to help your loved one make a smooth transition. In the beginning, a family member or friend may want to spend time at the center with the participant. Remember, however, that one of the goals of adult day centers is time away for all of you! Don't be concerned if your loved one is unable to remember everything he or she did during the day. The staff can give you the information you need. Also, don't be surprised if the participant is unusually tired or out of sorts during the transition period. Change is difficult for all of us. Once a good transition has been achieved, it is important that the caregiver remember to use these hours in the week as a time to relax and take care of the rest of life. Adult day centers exist as much to benefit caregivers as participants. Enjoy your time off, knowing that your loved one is safe and well cared for.

Paying for an Adult Day Center

The typical charges for adult day centers range from $25 to $75 per day. In certain cases, part of these charges can be paid by Medicaid, the Veteran's Administration, or the participant's private health insurance or long-term care insurance. Caregivers may also qualify for a tax credit for qualified programs.

Some centers charge for services on a sliding scale, depending on a person's income. Other funding may be available, and the intake coordinator of the center will often work with participants and families to explore the available payment options.

When weighing the expense of an adult day center, remember that the cost of a day program must be weighed against the alternatives of assisted living, in-home care, or nursing home care. In many cases, adult day centers provide a cost-effective alternative to such programs.

Setting the PACE

In the field of senior services, PACE stands for Programs of All-Inclusive Care for the Elderly.

PACE programs provide adult day services to eligible seniors. They are funded in part by Medicare and in part by Medicaid. Currently there are 29 PACE sites in cities around the country, with more expected to open in the future. For a list of PACE sites and more information on the services they offer, visit the website of the National PACE Association, *www.natlpaceassn.org.*

To Sum Up . . .

Adult day programs are an innovative approach to providing care for older people and their families. With the services and support these programs offer, many seniors can continue to live at home and still have regular access to many of the benefits provided in more structured—and more expensive—residential care settings. Adult day programs are not for everyone, but they can make a significant difference in quality of life, both for participants and those who care for them at home.

More Resources

- The **National Adult Day Services Association** offers information about adult day programs. (*www.nadsa.org*)

Quick Links

>>> These web-based resources may be accessed through our website: www.aginginstride.org

- The **Easter Seals Foundation** website includes a checklist entitled "How Do I Choose an Adult Day Services Provider?" (*www.easter-seals.org*)

- **The Eldercare Locator**, a nationwide toll-free telephone number and online service from the U.S. Administration on Aging, operates Monday–Friday, 9:00 a.m.–8:00 p.m., Eastern Time, and can be reached at 1-800-677-1116, or online. (*www.eldercare.gov*)

Other Senior Living Options

INTRODUCTION

The experience of moving evokes a range of emotions. If your family moved frequently when you were growing up, or if you have moved often over the years, the thought of moving one more time may not be intimidating for you. If the last time you moved was 20, 30, or 40 years ago, the thought of moving now may seem overwhelming.

In the previous section of this book, we discussed strategies and resources for staying in your own home. Now we look at other senior living options, including moving into a residential community that caters specifically to older owners or renters.

Issue 13 focuses on understanding the types of retirement living options available. Today's retirement communities come in many shapes and sizes. What do they all have in common? How do they differ from one another? What does "assisted living" mean? What is a "continuing care retirement community"? Are there retirement housing opportunities especially for seniors on a limited budget?

Issue 14 covers shopping for a particular facility or community, comparing possibilities, and selecting the one that will best meet your needs. What should you look for when you visit or take a tour? What questions should you ask before you sign on the dotted line?

Issue 15 will be of interest if you have already decided to move. We want to help you complete your move to a new home as smoothly and successfully as possible.

In the forms section, you will find three worksheets to help you understand and pursue your retirement housing options:

- Form 13: *"Is It Time to Move?" Retirement Housing Planning Sheet*
- Form 14: *Worksheet for Evaluating a Senior Living Community*
- Form 15: *Retirement Living Move-in Guide*

ISSUE 13: YOUR RETIREMENT HOUSING OPTIONS

"Is it time for me to move?" Most older adults ask themselves this question many times before they make a final decision. Staying right where you live now may have many advantages, especially if you currently live in a smaller house, condominium, or apartment where you feel comfortable, and if housekeeping and maintenance are not a problem. But before you decide to stay, you should at least take a look at the variety of housing options that have been developed specifically for seniors over the past two decades. The growing number of older adults in our society has made seniors a sought-after market in the area of housing. Most communities contain a wide range of senior housing alternatives, and more are being developed all the time.

Understanding Your Options

Looking into senior housing options is an important aspect of planning for the future. Your housing choice will have a major influence on your activity level and quality of life. We've tried to simplify the decision-making process for you with the "decision tree" below. Each "branch" of the tree represents a new decision point.

Retirement Housing Decision Tree

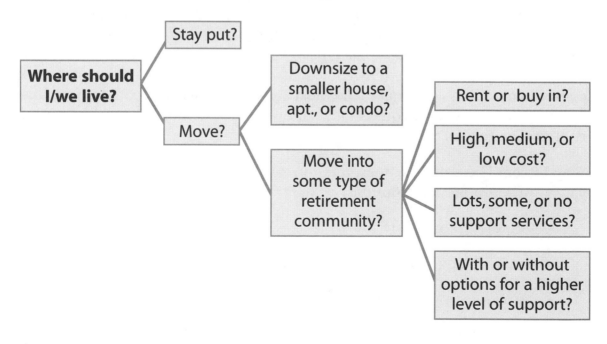

Step One: As the diagram suggests, the first questions to ask are: *Should I move? Or am I better off staying where I am?* These may seem like simple questions, but don't be fooled. To come to a thoughtful answer, you need to ask yourself some more tough questions. For example:

- What are my needs now, and how are they likely to change as I grow older?

- How long will I be able to meet changing needs where I live now?

- How do the costs and inconveniences of a move balance against the benefits of living in a retirement community?

- If I expect to move at some point, would it be smarter to move now, while I am healthy and active? Is it better to wait as long as I can before moving?

To come to a good decision about whether or not to move, you need to take an honest look at your current situation, decide if it is still working for you, and estimate how long you think it will continue to work. Of course, none of us has a crystal ball. We can't tell what the future will bring. So you need to ask yourself whether you want to make housing decisions planning ahead for an uncertain future or whether you want to deal now with your present needs and desires and make future decisions as your circumstances change. If the time is right to consider a move, then go on to step two of the decision tree.

Step Two: The second branch on the retirement housing decision tree asks this: *If I'm thinking about moving, should I be looking at a smaller independent living space? Or, should I consider some type of residential facility or community that specifically serves seniors like myself?* Just as with the first question, the hard work comes in deciding what makes the most sense for you, given both current and possible future needs. If you want to explore specific senior residential options, continue on to step three.

Step Three: These are the questions you need to ask yourself as you look at the variety of senior housing options:

- Should I rent or buy-in?

- Am I looking for an expensive, moderately priced, or inexpensive option?

- Am I looking for a high, medium, or low level of support services?

- Am I comfortable with the possibility that I may have to move again as my needs change? Or do I prefer an independent living or assisted living community that offers the option of receiving a higher level of care, if I later need it, right in the same building or complex?

As you think about where to live and whether or not to consider a move, there's no better way to start than by stepping back and looking seriously at what you really need and want. Form 13, *"Is It Time to Move?" Retirement Housing Planning Sheet*, in the forms section, serves as a practical worksheet to guide you through this process.

As you add up all the pros and cons of various services and support, be sure to think about not only where you are now, but also where you are likely to be two, five, or 10 years from now. Take into account the amount of money you have available each month or year to spend on housing. Consider your family members and friends. Who would you like to live near? What elements are most important to you in a housing situation? Is it location, ambiance, convenience, proximity to family and friends, or level of care provided? There is no "one size fits all" answer. Your particular mix of answers to these important questions will guide you in choosing a living situation that suits your needs and desires.

Overview of Retirement Housing Options

Type	Description
Homesharing	As the name implies, this is an arrangement where two or more people share the same home. Each person has his or her own room, possibly even a whole floor. The kitchen, dining room, and other common spaces are shared.
	Your local Senior Information and Referral program may keep a list of people interested in sharing their home, or who are looking for a home to share. Private matching services that charge a small fee are also available in some communities.

Type	*Description*
Senior Housing	Senior housing refers to any type of housing—mobile homes, single-family houses, or apartments— limited under the Fair Housing Act to people over a certain age. The emphasis is on independent living with few, if any, services offered.
Low-Income Senior Housing	Low-income senior housing units are developed using public funds or mortgage guarantees under a federally sponsored housing program. Often, large senior housing projects or planned retirement communities include a certain number of units that have been set aside for seniors who qualify under low-income programs. To be eligible, you must meet a minimum age requirement and have income or net worth within the specified limit.
Retirement Living Communities (also called Congregate Care Communities)	Retirement communities offer independent senior living in apartments, townhouses, or detached homes or cottages. They serve seniors who are generally in good health and able to live without personal care or health assistance from the staff. These independent living units may be part of a larger campus that also includes assisted living and skilled nursing. Retirement communities offer services such as housekeeping, dining, transportation, and an activities program.

Type	*Description*
Continuing Care Retirement Communities (also called CCRCs, Integrated Care Communities, and Life Care Communities)	These are essentially retirement communities with an important added element. They are intentionally structured to provide a full range of care—from independent living to assisted living to skilled nursing care—all in one complex or on one campus. In a CCRC you are able to stay in an independent apartment for as long as possible, knowing that personal care and even skilled nursing care will be available, if and when you need them. Most people who move to a CCRC or similar multi-level community expect it will be the last move they will make. Some CCRCs charge a straight monthly rental. Others require an up-front "buy-in." The buy-in, if there is one, may or may not be refundable if you later decide to move elsewhere.
Assisted Living Facilities and Communities	Assisted living combines some features offered by an independent living retirement community—privacy, independence, a home-like setting—with some of what a nursing facility can offer, such as help with personal care needs and some health care services. Assisted living facilities and communities are licensed at the state level, with definitions and requirements varying from state to state. A typical assisted living unit is a studio, one-bedroom, or two-bedroom apartment with a kitchenette and private bathroom. Services include help with personal care needs, some health care services and help with medications, housekeeping, dining, laundry service, and an activity and recreation program.

Type	*Description*
Adult Family Homes (also called Adult Foster Care Homes)	These are single-family homes that have been licensed by the state to provide room, board, and support services, usually to four to six older adults. Regulations and oversight vary from state to state. For someone who is being released from a hospital and does not need 24-hour supervision or skilled nursing care, an adult family home may provide a convenient interim housing solution. It can also be an affordable, home-like option for a frail or chronically ill senior who needs long-term care.
Residential Health Care Facilities	Some states—for example, New Jersey—license residential health care facilities, or "RHCFs." They are similar to assisted living facilities, but may offer less in the way of health care services and support.
	RHCFs serve residents who are self-mobile, do not need 24-hour skilled nursing care, and need only a limited amount of help with activities of daily living, such as bathing, dressing, and grooming. They provide room and board, housekeeping and laundry service, medication supervision and assistance, and transportation and recreation activities. Health care support and monitoring services are provided under the direction of a registered nurse. They offer semi-private and private rooms with or without private bathrooms, and common areas for dining and recreation. Most facilities are required to have staff (but not nursing staff) on site 24 hours a day.
Nursing Facilities	Nursing care facilities today play two important roles. They provide rehabilitation or "sub-acute" care for persons who have just been discharged from a hospital but are not yet able to return home, and they provide extended (or "long-term") care to frail or chronically ill persons who require a higher level of skilled nursing and medical supervision than is available elsewhere.

More About . . .

Retirement Living Communities

Retirement living communities are much like other planned residential communities, except that they only accept older adults. That means the amenities, such as pool, exercise facility, and dining room, will be shared by people who are generally the same age with generally the same interests. Recreational and social activities are also planned specifically with seniors in mind.

Retirement living communities typically offer residential services, such as housekeeping, transportation, and a meal plan. If you are in a retirement living community and need in-home care for a short period, you can usually make such arrangements with a local home health agency. However, if you need help on an ongoing basis, an independent retirement living community is probably not your best option.

Assisted Living Communities

There are approximately one million older Americans living in assisted living facilities and communities these days. That's between 2 and 3 percent of the over-65 population. Residents choose assisted living because it offers the combination of a private, home-like residence—often a studio or one-bedroom apartment—and support services to meet personal care and some health care needs. These personal care and health care services are in addition to the basic services that typically go with retirement housing options, such as housekeeping, laundry, transportation, and meal service.

As the diagram below suggests, assisted living is an important middle option for seniors who are concerned about their present or future ability to live independently, but who are also a long way from needing the skilled nursing care of a nursing home. On what we call the "senior living continuum," assisted living gives many seniors a best-of-all-worlds option.

Senior Living Continuum

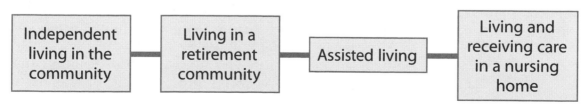

If you are interested in the assisted living option, you will want to investigate the services offered and how much they cost. Remember that services vary widely. Some facilities only provide limited help with personal care, health care needs, and medication management. Others include a broad range of health care services. Some now offer specialized care for persons with Alzheimer's disease or other dementias.

Make sure you understand the *maximum* level of care available in each facility. Assisted living is often advertised as "aging in place," meaning that as a person ages and needs progressively more support, the assisted living facility will be able to respond. In reality, a person's needs may exceed the level of care for which the facility is licensed and staffed. When that happens, the person is required to move. Make sure you understand the limitations of each facility and what procedures would be followed if the time were to come when your needs could no longer be met there. Issue 14 will help you in this selection process and includes a checklist you may wish to use in comparing two or more choices.

Continuing Care Retirement Communities

Continuing Care Retirement Communities, or CCRCs, are an attractive option for many seniors. What makes CCRCs special is their multi-level approach to care. A typical CCRC offers independent living units, personal care or assisted living units, and skilled nursing beds, all within the same building, campus, or complex. Residents move to a CCRC while they are still active and in good health, knowing that a higher level of care—up to and including 24-hour skilled nursing care—will be available to them if they need it in the future.

Financial arrangements for CCRCs vary, but there is often a buy-in payment that may or may not be refundable if you die or decide to move out soon after moving in. Moving to a CCRC is usually more expensive than moving to an independent living or assisted living community, and there may be net worth requirements in order to qualify for admission.

Many CCRCs have long waiting lists, so if you are interested, it's probably a good idea to fill out the paperwork and give your first choice a deposit well before you actually plan to move. In most cases, coming to the top of the wait list does not mean you have to move right away; you can ask to have your application carried forward—at or near the top of the list—until you are ready to move.

A final thought about CCRCs: because these communities emphasize true multi-level continuing care, you must be relatively healthy and independent when you move in. Some people wait too long before deciding to make their move. If you like the idea of living in a CCRC, you need to act while you are still healthy and active, rather than waiting until your health and activity level have declined to a level that disqualifies you for admission.

Retirement Housing on a Tight Budget

Much of the retirement housing available these days tends to be for middle- or upper-income individuals, but not all of it. In most communities there are government-subsidized housing units set aside for low-income seniors. The easiest way to explore the possibilities in your area is to call Senior Information and Referral and ask for help in finding a housing match on your particular budget.

To Sum Up . . .

Everyone is different. The right retirement housing option for you depends on your particular combination of needs and preferences. Sometimes the options may seem as overwhelming as the thought of moving itself. In truth, if you have been honest in your self-assessment, are clear about your preferences, and understand the major categories of housing options, your choices will quickly narrow to a handful. In Issue 14, we will guide you through the process of evaluating the potential new homes that make their way onto your short list. When you choose the right facility, you will be ready to make your move. It is important not to let yourself get discouraged! For most older adults, once the decision-making process is done, completing the move to a senior living facility opens a door to new friendships and opportunities.

More Resources

Quick Links

>>> These web-based resources may be accessed through our website:

www.aginginstride.org

- The **National Center for Assisted Living** website (*www.ncal.org*) offers information on choosing an assisted living facility.

- The **Assisted Living Federation of America** website includes consumer information about locating an assisted living community. (*www.alfa.org*)

- The **U.S. Administration on Aging's** website includes fact sheets on making the decision about where to live. (*www.aoa.dhhs.gov*)

- The **Continuing Care Accreditation Commission** website includes a list of accredited communities and general information to use as you make your decision. (*www.ccaconline.org*)

- **AARP**'s website features articles and information about comparing housing options. (*www.aarp.org*)

ISSUE 14: CHOOSING A SENIOR LIVING COMMUNITY

You've thought through your situation and needs, and the signs point in the direction of a move to some type of senior living community. Now what? How do you go about choosing the facility or community—and even the particular housing unit at that facility or community—that will be the best match for you? It's time to begin the evaluation process.

Four Rules of Thumb for the Savvy Shopper

You've probably moved before. In this mobile society, most people move several times over the course of a lifetime. In many ways, making a move to a senior living facility is no different from making any other move. Yes, it is a major decision, but it is just one more in a long series of important decisions you have made throughout your life. There are no guarantees of success. However, your chance of finding a new home that is a good match for you is greatly increased if you're willing to take the time to do some research and pay attention to your decision making. Here are four simple but important guidelines:

- **Begin early and take your time.** Don't feel rushed. Don't feel you have to jump at the first opportunity that presents itself.

- **Get the facts you'll need to make an informed choice.** Visit before you decide. Don't accept advertising at face value. Think of housing as a product, like a car or a brand of soap. You'll get your best buy if you are a thoughtful consumer who puts your own interests and needs first.

- **Be realistic in assessing your needs.** Consider not only your needs today, but also how those needs may change as time goes by.

- **Don't make this decision alone.** Talk about your options and plans with close family or friends. Don't forget, a move will most likely involve a financial outlay and affect your overall well being, so don't be afraid to discuss your move with your doctor, lawyer, financial advisor, or other trusted professional.

Consider what you're trying to accomplish in terms of a three-step process:

Step 1: Create a Short List of Your Best Options

You've made the decision about what type of facility interests you. Now you want to first list, then sort your options. Coming up with a preliminary list of choices is easy and need not take much time. Depending on the size of the town or city in which you've decided to live, the list might be long or relatively short. Make a list of all suitable facilities, each with a few attributes that seem to set it apart. For example:

Horizon Terrace, assisted living, Medford, built about five years ago, Beverly's sister lives there, close to Medford General

There are several sources you can use to develop this preliminary list, including:

- The Yellow Pages of your local phone book.

- Ads in your newspaper or in local magazines that cater to a senior audience.

- Senior Information and Referral.

- Your doctor or other senior care or health care professional for a referral.

- Friends and family.

- The Internet.

Once you have listed all the possibilities, you can begin your sorting process. If your list has more than 10 facilities on it, start with location. Pull from that longer list the eight to 10 facilities that are closest to the neighborhood where you would like to live. Now it's time to do some phone calling. You're going to call the facilities on your shorter list and ask some basic questions. Make sure you have pencil and paper on hand when you start calling. While you might think at the time that you can remember the information about each option, after you've called two or three places, it's easy to get confused. When you call each facility, tell them you are a prospective resident, or that you are calling on behalf of a prospective resident, and ask for the following information:

- Does the facility have a website you can visit or a brochure or information packet they can send you?

- Are there any upfront costs, and what is the range of their monthly fees for the size of unit that interests you?

- What services does the facility provide?

- Is there a waiting list, and how long is it?

- Are there particular days of the week or times of day when you may tour the facility and talk with a staff member? Is it helpful to make an appointment in advance?

With this new information, are there facilities on your list that don't fit your price range or don't offer the services you desire? Cross them off. What is your preferred time frame for moving? If facilities have waiting lists that don't work with your time frame, cross them off your list. You can always come back to them later. Once you receive the information the facilities have mailed to you, are there places that just don't appeal to you? Again, cross them off, knowing that you can always reconsider.

You should have enough information to have narrowed down your choices to a short list of no more than four facilities. Now it's time for a closer look!

Step 2: Visit. Ask Questions. Compare.

There is no good substitute for a personal visit. Occasionally a situation arises when a personal visit is simply not possible, and then you have to do your best with phone calls and letters. However, in most cases, an investment of time and money in visiting your top housing options pays for itself many times over.

You should plan to spend an hour or two for each visit. Talk with as many staff members as possible. Try to speak with current residents. If you call in advance and plan your visit close to a mealtime, most facilities will give you a complimentary meal, and you will have a chance both to mingle with the residents and to gather important information about the food service. There are many things you want to see, and questions you want to remember to ask. Form 14, *Worksheet for Evaluating a Senior Living Community,* is a checklist that will help you know what to look for, what questions to ask, and what factors to consider. Take a copy of this form with you on each visit so you won't forget to ask an important question.

You will want to compare your potential new homes on the basis of:

- Location.

- Availability of the type of unit you're seeking.

- Availability of services you need or think you may need.

- Prospects for not having to move again, either because this community provides a full range of care, or because the facility has an affiliation or transfer arrangement with another more intensive care provider nearby.

- Cost and affordability.

- Reputation, including the comments of current residents.

Along with the information you receive, pay attention to your personal impressions about such things as:

- Who the residents are and how healthy, happy, and comfortable they appear.

- Whether the facility seems to foster an active, interesting lifestyle.

- Whether the staff seem friendly, capable, and service-minded.

- Whether the building and grounds are attractive and well maintained.

The combination of hard information and your intangible impressions will lead you to make the best possible choice for yourself. This place is going to be your home. Choose carefully, and don't be afraid to follow your best instincts.

Step 3: Know What You Are Buying

It is important to know exactly what you are buying. Be assertive in getting answers to the following questions:

- **What documents will you be asked to sign at move-in?** Most senior living providers have their own rental agreement, move-in information packet, and Resident Guide or Handbook. Ask for copies of these to peruse at your leisure before you make your final decision.

- **How much will you have to pay?** If there is a base or standard monthly rate, what does it include? More importantly, what *doesn't* it include? Is there an initial buy-in cost? Can that be refunded under any circumstances? Most rates are understandably subject to upward adjustment. Like everything else, the community's or facility's costs are probably rising, so at some point you may have to pay more. Ask what the history of past rate increases has been. Is there an increase under consideration at the moment?

- **What are the rules?** A senior living community is like any other communal living situation. There are rules that apply to everyone. Whether you are a smoker or a non-smoker, you will probably want to know what the smoking policy is. Pets, noise levels, and guests are other issues that are likely to be covered in a policy statement or rule somewhere. Make sure you read the Resident Guide or Handbook carefully. If you still have unanswered questions, don't be shy about asking.

- **What would happen if you or your spouse were to experience a decline in health status?** Would you be free to arrange for an independent home health or personal care provider to come in and care for you? At what point might you have to move out because needed services could no longer be provided? What help will the facility give you in arranging for a transfer?

To Sum Up . . .

Selecting one senior living community over other possibilities is a major decision. But it should also be an enjoyable—even an exciting—experience. After all, you are turning an important new page in your life. Now that the decision is made, it's time to focus your attention on making this move as smooth and positive as possible. It's time to get settled into your new home.

More Resources

- The **National Center for Assisted Living** website includes a directory of state Centers for Assisted Living, as well as consumer information for comparing and selecting assisted living facilities. (*www.ncal.org*)

- The **Assisted Living Federation of America** offers information on finding and selecting a senior residence. (*www.alfa.org*)

- The **American Association of Homes and Services for the Aging** website features a section for consumers and caregivers with articles and information about selecting a senior living community. (*www.aahsa.org*)

Quick Links

>>> These web-based resources may be accessed through our website:

www.aginginstride.org

ISSUE 15: MAKING A SMOOTH TRANSITION TO A NEW HOME

Moving to a home in a senior living community is a new beginning in your life, not unlike starting off in a new job. There's no way to avoid some anxiety, uncertainty, and surprise. But, like that new job, your new home can also open some exciting opportunities for you. So, if you are about to make a move, it's time to do more planning! There are concrete steps you can take to make your move as easy and comfortable as possible.

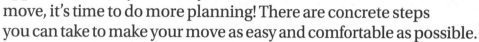

Some Practical Considerations

Are you one of those people who has moved often in your life? If you are, then you probably have a system for deciding, packing, and hauling. You may not need the following suggestions. However, if you haven't moved much in your life, or if it's been a long time since your last move, the following practical suggestions may prove helpful:

Plan Your Move

What are the space limitations of your new home? What furniture and personal belongings will fit? What can you do without? It is always a good idea to decide *before* you move what furniture and other large items you will want and need to take with you. Most facilities have scale drawings available of their residential units. You can get one of these, make several photocopies, and then try out various plans for arranging your furniture and other household items. Remember to measure your furniture to avoid unpleasant surprises on moving day. How much storage does your new home contain? Again, it's best to plan the organization of your closets before you move to make sure everything has a place. If you have a well-organized plan, you can pack your belongings according to their location in your new space, making the unpacking process much faster and easier.

Less is More

Trimming back the size of your household can be a negative or positive experience, depending on how you look at it. Deciding what to keep and what to leave always takes time and energy. However, many in this situation come to

What Do I Do With Great-Uncle Harold's Portrait?

It's difficult to know what to do about those special things in your life and the life of your family—photographs, home movies, heirlooms and antiques, little things that have sentimental value.

- If you are too hasty—you throw things out or take them to Goodwill without enough thought—you can cause real pain and regret in your family.

- If you cling too much to the "treasures" you've accumulated over the years, you may simply not have room for all of them and you will be making more work for yourself and possibly for others.

Look for a middle ground. Here are some suggestions:

- If you have furniture, mementos, or other household items you won't be keeping but that might be of interest to your children, grandchildren, great-nieces or nephews, invite them to come over and make some selections. Be clear about your timeline. This visit may be a wonderful opportunity for sharing old memories and family stories, and forging a stronger connection to the younger generation.

- Home movies can now be converted safely and inexpensively to VHS or DVD format. Your 35mm slides, photographs, and photo albums can also be copied to digital format. You may or may not feel competent to tackle these projects yourself, but you probably have a nephew or granddaughter who understands newer technology and would love to take on such a project for you. Ask for a volunteer.

- With the keepsakes you decide to either keep for yourself or give away to family, and with all of your photographic memories, it is a real gift to your family to label pictures, furniture, other mementos so that others can appreciate their significance. The portrait of the stern-looking man in the celluloid collar may be of limited interest to your grandson until he learns that picture is of famous Great-Uncle Harold who made his fortune during Gold Rush days.

welcome the chance to scale back. They call it "living leaner and cleaner," and it can have its own rewards.

For example, it can be fun and satisfying to give unneeded possessions to family members—for instance, to a grandchild who is just starting out in his or her very first apartment. You may wish to give some household items to Goodwill, the Salvation Army, a local organization that works with the disadvantaged, or to a friend or family member you know could use them. You might decide to hold a garage sale. If you don't have enough for a sale on your own, see if friends and family members want to join you in your new commitment to "lean and clean," and share a sale with you.

Ask for Help

If you are worried about the work involved in your move, or the decisions and arrangements you will need to make, ask for help. Family and friends are usually eager to get involved, and they can help the process happen quickly and smoothly. If you don't have family or friends nearby, call Senior Information and Referral or your local senior center. Often they know of local volunteer or for-hire resources that can lighten your load considerably. Call your local moving companies. Find out the difference in price for the moving companies to do your packing for you. The additional cost may be worth it.

Before the Move . . .

- Understand your new space limitations.
- Decide what you can and cannot take.
- Dispose of surplus furniture, clothing, etc.
- Discontinue old services such as phone, cable TV, and newspaper; sign up for services if needed
- Give change of address notice to Post Office, family, friends, bank, etc.
- Arrange for moving company or helpers.
- Pack whatever the movers won't be packing.
- Label each item or box with contents and its location in the unit.

Make Your Move a Team Effort

Whether you use professional or volunteer help for moving, there will be a lot of work to be done on moving day. Ask at least one or two friends or family members to be part of your moving team. Not all members of the team have to be able to carry furniture and lift heavy boxes. Volunteers can help with cleaning, packing, and unpacking at the other end. Having a friend with a strong sense of humor can be as important as another pair of strong arms. Most family and friends are pleased to be of help, especially when there are donuts, cookies, or pizza on hand for your crew.

Work Through the Details

There are always auxiliary tasks associated with moving that you need to remember. These may not need to be accomplished immediately, but make a list and check off each task as soon as it's done. As Form 15, *Retirement Living Move-in Guide,* suggests, your list might include these tasks:

- Notify people of your change of address. This includes both friends and those with which you have business: the phone company, other utility providers, creditors, insurance carriers, financial institutions, Social Security.

- If you are moving to a new area, you will want to choose and get acquainted with a new primary care physician.

- Again, if you are moving to a new area, you may want to find a faith community where you are comfortable.

On Moving Day . . .

- Supervise arrangement of furniture and other larger items.
- Unpack kitchen and arrange new drawers and cupboards.
- Unpack clothing and set up new closets.
- Hang pictures and arrange personal items.
- Set up books and bookcases.
- Present a friendly first impression to new neighbors.
- If you have helpers, don't forget treats!

- Change your voter registration.

- Search out the best places to shop and take care of errands.

Take Advantage of the "New Resident" Resources Available

Most senior living communities are welcoming places. Staff and residents are accustomed to helping people get settled. If staff, volunteers, or other residents offer help and support, just say yes. Congratulations! You've made your first efforts to know the members of your new community.

Let Your Sense of Curiosity Run Free

It's too easy for all of us to get set in our ways. The old and familiar seem more worthwhile than the new and the unfamiliar. Now is a good time to exercise your curiosity and your sense of adventure, even if they are a bit rusty! Ask all the questions your want. For example: *Who are my new neighbors? Is there an exercise class? When does it meet? If I'm interested in volunteer opportunities, whom should I contact? What's next on the social calendar?* If mobility and safety are not a problem, get out and walk. Explore your new neighborhood. Take up a new

After the Move . . .

- Introduce yourself to new neighbors, and take advantage of "new resident" resources.

- Sign up for upcoming social and recreation opportunities.

- Learn about and join groups, clubs, or classes that interest you.

- Learn about and begin using exercise facilities, programs, or classes.

- Introduce yourself to the administrator, resident services director, and workers you meet.

- Check out your new surrounding community for shops, parks and places of interest.

- Select a new primary care physician, if necessary.

- Select a new faith community, if appropriate.

- Switch your voter registration.

hobby or learn to play bridge. Try every day to think of positive things to tell yourself about this new transition. As in so much of life, the attitude you bring to your move will determine how well you adjust and how quickly you begin to thrive in your new environment.

When Things Aren't Going Smoothly

What should you do if you've tried to do everything right, and still, after a week or a month in your new home, it's not turning out quite as you had hoped and expected? If you find yourself unhappy in your new home, the first thing to do is to determine the reason for your unhappiness.

If the Problem Concerns the Facility

Are there expectations you had for services or quality of care that are not being met? Have you had a problem with staff or other residents? Is there some other problem that management should address?

Most of us don't like to complain. However, when you live in a residential community of any kind, it is important that those in charge know when you are dissatisfied or upset. Most people who work in senior housing are professionals who genuinely care whether or not things are going well. All residential facilities have an accepted process by which a resident can make formal complaints. Before things get to the formal complaint stage, though, you might want to talk with the facility's director about whatever is making you unhappy. Often, small misunderstandings and problems can be cleared up with little fuss.

In talking with the facility director or other staff, remember to be both courteous and assertive. Your concern deserves to be heard, but we all react best when we believe that those talking with us respect our humanity and basic integrity.

If you have tried to resolve a complaint or dispute and don't seem to be making headway, you may need to consider your options:

- Is there an outside advocacy agency with jurisdiction over issues like yours? In many states, the long-term care ombudsman has oversight in assisted living and other residential care settings, as well as nursing homes. See Issue 27, *Your Rights as a Resident* for more on ombudsman programs.

- Is your issue one that affects other residents? If so, is it time to talk together about how you might get the issue resolved to your satisfaction? Is there a Resident Council or similar group you can address?

- Is the problem so serious that it might mean you selected the wrong living situation and should consider another move? If so, what does your move-in contract say about notices of intent to move, refunds, and other contractual obligations?

If the Problem is About You

With any major change, there is predictably a low point, a time of disappointment, a let-down after the first rush of activity is over. If this is happening to you, don't be too surprised—and don't let it concern you too much. Instead, be patient and gently persistent. Making friends and becoming well connected takes effort and time. Consider the following strategies:

- If your facility or community has a social worker and/or an activities coordinator, talk with them about your situation and concerns. They can't make your friends for you, but they can suggest some additional opportunities you might not have considered. Don't be shy or embarrassed about asking for help. The professional staff is there to ease your transition.

- Get involved. We know we repeat this a lot, but getting involved in social activities, joining a faith community or a hobby club, is good for both your mental and physical health. It will add to your sense of well-being.

- Ask specifically about volunteer opportunities available in your new situation. People who volunteer together share a common bond and often become friends. If you have time, volunteering is one of the most rewarding things you can do with it!

- Listen to yourself talk. Often, people fall into an unintentional habit of complaining. Their attitude comes across as more negative than it really is, and people are put off by their supposed negativity. Are you balanced in expressing the positive and negative feelings that you have? Are you as quick with a compliment as with a complaint? It's something to keep in mind. Remember that others are drawn to those who face life with humor and graciousness.

- Ask around. Talk with other residents who have moved in fairly recently. Is what you are feeling unusual or fairly typical? You may be surprised to find that you are far from alone. Right there, you have found something important that you have in common with at least a few of your new neighbors.

It's difficult when things don't go as smoothly as we would wish. If your feelings that something is wrong persist more than a few weeks, it is important that you work to understand what is bothering you, then set about solving the problem. Whether the difficulty lies with the facility or with your adjustment to life in this new place, it's good to have the problem out in the open and begin working toward a solution. Remember: this is your new home. It is important for you to feel comfortable. Take steps to get the problem solved, so that you can enjoy this new adventure.

To Sum Up . . .

Change can always bring with it a level of uncertainty. However, experience teaches us skills for planning and taking care of ourselves, and gives us the patience to understand that change takes time. The vast majority of people who move into some variety of senior housing report that the move becomes a positive change in their life. You can do this, with planning, a renewed sense of adventure, and the help of family and friends. Moreover, the chances are that your life will be better for it!

More Resources

- The **Assisted Living Federation of America** website contains a "Consumer Information Center" that includes articles about moving—and helping someone move—to a retirement community or assisted living facility. (*www.alfa.org*)

Quick Links

>>> These web-based resources may be accessed through our website:
www.aginginstride.org

Health Concerns of Older Adults

INTRODUCTION

If you ask most people what is important to them, good health usually makes it onto the list. Especially as we age, we come to appreciate our health and not take it for granted. We wish and hope that we will be among the "lucky" ones who stay healthy and active well into their 80s and beyond.

But how much does luck really have to do with it? Asked more positively, what can we do, if not to ensure our good health, at least to increase the odds in our favor? Some aspects of feeling good and being healthy are tied to our genes or other factors beyond our control. However, there is much that each of us can do to minimize our chances of disease and disability, to maintain our present level of health, even to improve how we feel and how our bodies function. Almost without exception, no matter where you begin, you can make a significant difference in how you feel every day.

This group of issues covers a variety of topics about how to maintain and improve your physical health and sense of well-being. Issue 16 contains a general overview of how to stay healthy, while Issue 17 addresses your relationship with your primary partner in health care: your doctor. Issues 18–22 focus on five of the crucial elements in managing health: the use of medications, memory changes and dementia, dealing with stress and depression, good nutrition, and urinary incontinence. In Issue 23, we help you create a framework within which to manage serious or chronic health concerns. Finally, Issue 24 deals with questions of consent, medical decision-making, and your ability to control the course of your health care even when you are unable to act for yourself.

The forms connected with these issues include:

- Form 17: *Checklist for Communicating Clearly with Your Doctor*
- Form 18-A: *List of Current Medications*
- Form 18-B: *Medications Check-off List*
- Form 24: *Personal Values Statement*

Your body is important! The better you understand how it works, and what you can do to maintain and enhance its function, the more you will be able to live your life as you choose. So get moving, do your part, and enjoy the benefits.

ISSUE 16: STAYING HEALTHY

Nothing affects quality of life more directly than the state of our health. As we grow older, there is a common feeling that our bodies are "betraying" us. We often feel as if we are losing control of our ability to do the things that are important to us. Unfortunately, physical problems can erode our sense of who we are, and a downward spiral begins.

This issue is your guide to common health challenges, issues, and conditions, and, yes, opportunities to take control over your physical and mental well being instead of letting them take control over you. The more you know, the more effectively you can meet challenges and live your life the way you want to live it.

Taking Control

For older adults, taking control of health involves a different way of thinking than when we were younger and didn't think much about health at all. We are generally unprepared for new health problems and we find them scary and often depressing. One aid to successful aging is learning as much as possible about the particular health issues you encounter and how to manage them well.

There is no one way to age, and certainly there are many physical problems that each of us might encounter during our lifetime. In this book, we cannot cover all of them. However, we will provide an overview of the most common health problems in aging and give you tools and strategies for making good choices so that you can live a full and active life, regardless of the physical problems that challenge you.

When you become discouraged, remember that making a positive change to take control over one problem virtually always impacts all the rest. You need to develop your own personalized "health improvement strategy." You should develop this strategy in partnership with your doctor, who can add support and refinements. But following through on the plan will be up to you; it is yours alone to control. You *can* do it!

Health Improvement Strategies

Begin by thinking about your goals for your life. What is most important to you and what is keeping you from getting there health-wise? What are the current health concerns that you are dealing with (or not dealing with)? Make a list if that would be helpful to you. Then focus on the following three questions:

- What problems can you fix?

- What problems can you control?

- What will be required to fix what can be fixed and control what can be controlled?

Schedule for Preventive Care

Preventive care visits should include:

- An overall physical exam with blood pressure screening, weight, and pulse every one to two years.

- Screening for common cancers:
  ○ Mammograms every one to two years.
  ○ Prostate screens with digital exams and PSA every one to two years.
  ○ Colon cancer screens with hemoccult tests every two years.
  ○ Sigmoidoscopy/colonoscopy every five to 10 years.

- Updates on immunizations:
  ○ Tetanus every 10 years.
  ○ Flu shot every year.
  ○ Pneumonia shot once.

- Screening for health conditions associated with aging every one to two years.

- Follow-up on all chronic conditions every year, or as your health care provider suggests.

As you think about and organize the answers to these questions, be both realistic and optimistic. You want to develop a plan that is workable for you, and yet challenges you to improve those areas of your health that can be improved.

Now it's time to turn your attention to preventive care. Good preventive care is just as important as monitoring your current health concerns. Early detection can often make the difference between a minor health concern and a major problem. Work with your doctor to develop a health management plan that includes appropriate cancer screening, blood pressure monitoring, immunizations, and overall prevention strategies.

Once you have developed this plan, make sure you follow it! The best personalized plan is useless unless you follow through.

The past 20 years have seen great strides in the field of geriatric medicine. We now understand that good geriatric medicine can improve your chances of living a long, healthy life by paying attention to the most common problems that contribute to functional decline, the downward slope on the healthy aging curve. Being screened and treated for seven common conditions may improve both your quality of life *and* your ability to control chronic diseases you might face, such as diabetes, heart or lung disease, or arthritis.

These conditions are:

- Physical inactivity.
- Falls.
- Medication-related complications.
- Dementia.
- Depression.
- Poor nutrition.
- Urinary incontinence.

Each of these seven conditions contributes to what in medicine is called your "physiologic reserve." This reserve governs your ability to bounce back to good health after acute illnesses, or better yet, to avoid acute illnesses entirely. Because your understanding and monitoring of these conditions is so important, we have devoted an entire issue to each one of them. Please read these issues carefully and pay attention to how they apply to your current health condition. Then, in partnership with your doctor where needed, you can begin to make your plan. Pick one or two areas to begin. Encourage yourself by remembering that progress in one area will lead to improvements in others. Also remember that the single most important thing you can do to improve your overall health and increase your physiologic reserve is increasing regular physical activity. With a clear plan and a little concentrated work, you truly can become the best you can be!

To Sum Up . . .

As our bodies age, it is easy to become discouraged and feel like our health is out of our control. That is a mistake. No matter what your health problems, there are steps you can take to fix or manage them, to maintain and improve your quality of life and physical function. In partnership with your doctor, you can get the information you need to monitor your concerns, to prevent small problems from becoming larger, and to make good decisions. You can develop your own personal health improvement strategy, see it through, and enjoy the benefits of being the healthiest possible you!

More Resources

There are many reputable online websites having to do with senior health issues. Here are just a few of them:

Quick Links

>>> These web-based resources may be accessed through our website:
www.aginginstride.org

- **Mayo Clinic Senior Health Center** (*www.mayoclinic.com*)

- **Healthscout** (www.healthscout.com)

- **Health and Age** (National Institute on Aging/ National Institute of Health) (*www.healthandage.com*)

- **Medem Senior Health Library** (*www.medem.com*)

ISSUE 17: TALKING WITH YOUR DOCTOR

How well do you and your doctor communicate? It's an important question because a positive relationship with your doctor is essential in getting good health care. Many people, both doctors and patients, feel that the fast pace of health care visits today leaves little time for asking questions or really getting to know each other. It used to be customary that doctors took the lead during an office visit and patients followed. Now it's important for every visit to be a two-way partnership with the patient clearly stating problems, worries, or desires; the doctor offering his or her expertise and experience; then patient and doctor together making decisions about treatment or next steps.

You and your doctor, or other health care provider, need to work as a team to keep you healthy and solve your medical problems. If something is worrying you, be sure to tell your doctor first thing during a visit. If you don't understand what the doctor is saying, speak up. If you don't agree with a recommendation or treatment your doctor suggests, ask questions right away. The responsibility for good communication rests with both you and your doctor. The following tips can help you build a great partnership, whether you are working with a new doctor or one you've known for years.

Your Doctor's Team is Your Team

Remember, you aren't just working with your physician; there is an entire primary care "team" there to serve you. Get to know the nurses, physician assistants, pharmacists, and social workers or counselors who work with your doctor. They are each experts in their fields and can be a valuable source of specific information. They work closely with your doctor and often have more time to review and explain information about your care and answer questions you may have.

Prepare for the Visit

Write down all the issues you want to discuss. For example, do you have a symptom that is concerning you? Do you need a flu shot? If you have more than one concern, make a list and be sure to talk about the most important concern first. If your list is long or time runs out, you may need to have a return visit to adequately address all your issues; however, if you have a list and prioritize it, on this first visit you will have discussed your most urgent problems. If you have listed the other problems, the doctor may well be able to save you time by ordering tests immediately, so you both will be prepared for your next visit. You may want to use Form 17, *Checklist for Communicating Clearly With Your Doctor*, to organize your questions.

Many people are reluctant to talk about problems that are embarrassing or uncomfortable, such as depression, sexual issues, or incontinence. But it pays to be brave! Don't leave these issues for the end of the visit. You'll be worried the whole time, and might not hear what the doctor is saying about other issues. Talk about the hardest things first, and then you can relax and get the most out of your visit.

Make an *accurate* list of *all* medications you take, both over-the-counter and prescription, for the doctor to review at each visit. Include herbal supplements and vitamins. Misunderstandings about the medications you are taking can lead to other health problems. Some doctors even recommend you bring all your medicine in a bag at each visit. For more on managing your medications, see Issue 18, *Using Medications Safely*, and Forms 18-A and 18-B.

Focus as Clearly as Possible During the Visit

If you have only 15 minutes with the doctor, you will want to use them well. Being organized means that you will take only the amount of time necessary to state your concerns and desires. Be clear, listen well, and take notes. It is often helpful to have a friend or family member along on the visit, especially if you are worried or if you have difficulty hearing. Be sure to tell your companion ahead of time what major concerns you want to address, so he or she can help you focus on those concerns. Sometimes it's helpful just to have another person hear the doctor's explanations and recommendations. If your friend can write down what the doctor says, then you have a written record to help you remember exactly what was said so you have the best possible information for making decisions.

Be Sure You Can See and Hear as Well as Possible

If you use hearing aids or glasses, take them to the visit so that you can interact with your health care team as well as possible. If you have problems getting around—for example, if you use a cane, walker, or wheelchair—or have other special needs, be sure to get to the visit a bit early so that your needs can be accommodated and you won't feel rushed.

Be Assertive and Ask Questions

Update your doctor on what has happened for you since your last visit, including new symptoms, new worries, the results of any new treatments, how you've been feeling in general. Answer the doctor's questions as honestly as you can. Not telling the truth because you're embarrassed, or feel you ought to be doing better, is not helpful. If you don't understand what your doctor is recommending, ask questions until you are clear. It's fine to ask why a particular medicine is being prescribed, whether there are cheaper or safer alternatives, whether a certain procedure or medicine is really necessary. You have a right to know exactly what your choices are and why you might choose one course of action over another. There are no dumb questions! If you don't ask, your provider will just assume you understand.

Be honest about your feelings and desires. If time runs out and other patients are waiting, be willing to talk with the doctor later for further discussion and clarification, either in person or on the phone.

Be Prepared to Set Goals—and Meet Them!

Once you understand your options and your doctor's recommendations, you'll want to make a plan, set goals for yourself, and discuss with your doctor how to meet them. The more you know about your choices and options, the easier it will be to make informed choices, really understand what it will take to comply with chosen treatments, and *do it* successfully!

To Sum Up ...

Having a good relationship with your doctor is an important element in staying as healthy as possible. Doing your part to make that happen is a worthwhile investment of your time and energy. Be prepared. Be organized. Be focused. Ask questions. Make the best possible choices for yourself. And follow through. Your doctor will appreciate your effort, and you will get the most out of the doctor-patient relationship!

More Resources

- "Talking with Your Doctor: a Guide for Older People" can be found on the National Institute on Aging/National Institutes of Health website's **Age Pages**. (*www.healthandage.net*)

Quick Links

>>> These web-based resources may be accessed through our website:

www.aginginstride.org

- The **AARP** website includes a section called "How to Talk to Your Doctor," as well as an online article for caregivers entitled "Caregiving: Communicating with Health Professionals." (*www.aarp.org*)

- The **American Academy of Family Physicians** website features articles about communicating and working with your physician. (*www.familydoctor.org*)

ISSUE 18: USING MEDICATIONS SAFELY

Medications play a big role in managing health problems. Remember, however, that all medications, whether prescribed by a doctor or bought over the counter, have potentially toxic side effects that can cause you significant problems, either immediately or after long-term use. Knowing how to use medications safely is essential for everyone.

What are Medications?

Medications fall under one of two major categories:

- **Prescription medications** are drugs that can be used only under a doctor's supervision by written prescription.

- **Over-the-counter medications** are drugs available without a prescription, and include aspirin, Tylenol®, cold preparations, antacids, and all herbal or "natural" supplements and vitamins.

Both prescription and over-the-counter medications can have serious side effects for some people and need to be used properly, both when used alone, and especially when used in combination with other medicines.

Risks and Benefits of Medications

When taking medications, remember this simple rule: *take only what you need to control the health problems you have, or are at risk of developing.* Medications can play a major role in improving health and prolonging life, in treating and preventing diseases. For example, an aspirin a day can help prevent heart disease and stroke; appropriate medications for existing heart disease can help prevent heart attacks and congestive heart failure. Medications for arthritis and other painful disorders can allow you to participate in the kinds of exercise that can actually improve your condition and prevent joint replacements in the future.

Even a single medical disorder may require the use of more than one drug. A combination of conditions or diseases, such as diabetes, emphysema, arthritis, and high blood pressure, requires the use of multiple medications. The more conditions and drugs involved, the more caution is required.

Always remember that *increasing regular physical activity can decrease or possibly even eliminate the need for many medications.* For example, in diabetes, regular exercise has been shown to improve blood sugars better than *metformin*, a commonly used medication. (For many patients, the best approach will include both medication and exercise.) In arthritis, joints become healthier and less painful with regular exercise, requiring less pain medicine. Aerobic exercise strengthens the heart and blood vessels and increases lung capacity, often decreasing the need for medications to treat heart and lung disease. We tend to look immediately to drugs to "fix" medical problems, but getting regular exercise is often the best medicine. Given the high cost of medicines these days, this is doubly good news! If you can safely reduce or discontinue any medication, in consultation with your doctor, it will benefit both your body and your finances.

Overmedication and Drug Interactions

Appropriate use of medications focuses on two areas: avoiding overmedication and staying away from drugs that tend to cause serious side effects for people as they age.

Overmedication can occur if a person:

- Fails to stop using a drug when recommended by a doctor.

- Uses another person's medication.

- Takes a medication in excess of recommended dosage.

- Uses a number of different medications that have a similar effect.

Some drugs are known to cause potentially serious problems for older people. Talk with your doctor about avoiding side effects and using the best, safest medications for your age and medical condition.

Some drugs can have serious interactions with certain other drugs. If you are seeing two or more doctors at the same time, this can present a special challenge. Every provider needs to know *all* medications you are taking. Keep a complete, updated list of the medications you take, both prescription and over the counter, and carry it with you to every visit with a health care provider. Form 18-A will help you make your list. Keep a copy of your medication list in your purse or wallet at all times. It's a good idea to give the list to your health care representative, in case you are admitted to the hospital for an emergency and your list is not with you.

For all medications, you should carefully follow the doctor's or pharmacist's instructions as to frequency of dosage, length of treatment, proper storage, consumption with or without food, and other special instructions. Following instructions will help ensure the best results and minimize adverse effects.

Questions for Your Doctor or Pharmacist

It is very important for you to have information about the medications you are taking and know how to take them correctly. When your doctor prescribes a medication, be sure to ask:

- What is the name of the medication?

- What is it for?

- How often should I take it?

- How long must it be taken?

- Are there foods I should not eat or other medications I should not take while I am on this medicine? Can I safely drink alcohol while I am on it?

- What side effects should I know about?

- What side effects or problems should I report to the doctor?

- What should I do if I miss a dose?

- Do I need any instructions on how to take it properly?

It is often helpful to write down your doctor's instructions so that you will remember them accurately when you get home. If you have questions, ask your pharmacist or call back to your doctor's office.

Simple Rules for Taking Medications

Below are some important guidelines for taking medications safely.

- Review all of your medications at each doctor visit, and focus on eliminating any that are unnecessary.

- Be sure to take all the medication prescribed for you.

- Develop a system for keeping track of all medications you take. You might use a chart to record when you take them. (See, for example, Form 18-B.) Or use a container with compartments, which can be found in any pharmacy, to organize a day or even a week's medication. Keep your complete updated medication list with your medication container, along with the instructions for taking each drug.

- Drink a full glass of water when taking tablets or capsules. What a great reminder to drink enough water each day!

- Always take medications standing or sitting, not lying down.

- Chew chewable tablets thoroughly and then drink a glass of water.

- Vigorously shake bottles of liquid medications before use.

- Request regular bottle caps if you have difficulty using the childproof ones.

- Always store medications out of the reach of children.

- If you use antacids or laxatives, take them either two hours before or two hours after taking other medications.

- Report symptoms to your doctor, who will help you decide if the symptoms are caused by the medication and if you should stop taking it.

- Increase your daily exercise program to minimize your need for medications.

- Do not take more or less than the prescribed amount of medication, unless directed to do so by your doctor.

- Do not stop taking a medication suddenly without checking with your doctor, even if you feel better. Abruptly stopping some medications can cause serious problems.

- Do not mix alcohol and medicines, unless approved by your doctor. Many drugs react in a negative way when combined with alcohol.

- Do not take medication prescribed for someone else or give your medicines to another person.

- Do not transfer medication from its original bottle to another, since you may become confused about the contents.

- Do not keep medications that are old or expired in your medicine cabinet.

- Do not ignore side effects—call your physician!

Become an Educated Consumer

There are many medication guides on the market, some of them directed specifically toward older adults. Read about the medications you are taking. Ask questions of your doctor or pharmacist if you don't understand why you are taking a particular medication or how you should take it. The more you know and understand, the more likely you are to get the best effect from your medication.

To Sum Up . . .

Taking the right medications correctly is an important part of controlling or preventing health problems. Make sure that both you and all your health care providers know *all* the medications you are taking. Learn all you can about what you are taking and why. Ask questions. It's your body! Being responsible about the medications you put into it will minimize problems and help you feel your best.

More Resources

Quick Links

>>> These web-based resources may be accessed through our website:

www.aginginstride.org

- The "Consumer Information" sections of the **U.S. Food and Drug Administration (FDA)** website features information about medications and how to use them correctly. (*www.fda.gov*)

- The **U.S. National Library of Medicine**, along with the **National Institutes of Health**, provides a website, **MedlinePlus**, which includes a Drug Information section. (*www.medlineplus.gov*)

- The U.S. **Agency for Healthcare Research and Quality** website has a section entitled "Your Medicine: Play It Safe" and other information for consumers about the use of medications. (*www.ahcpr.gov*)

ISSUE 19: MEMORY CHANGES AND DEMENTIA

For most people there is no more feared consequence of aging than "losing our minds," and in the process, losing our "selves." Most important to our ability to live our lives well is the combination of mental processes we call "cognition" or "knowing." This combination includes the ability to learn new things, intuition, judgment, language, and remembering. Having a clear, active mind at any age is important, but as we get older it can mean the difference between dependence and independent living.

Memory changes are a natural part of aging; they occur throughout our lives. The brain changes with age. The process by which it can receive and process information slows, but most often we don't even notice. Many centenarians complete their lives fully cognitively intact.

Think of the brain as a set of billions of telephone wires trying to make connections. The older we get, the more "phone numbers" or memories we have stored and must sort through in order to call up the memory we want. Over time, some of the connecting links will break down; it will take a little longer to access information. When we are under stress, the system becomes really challenged. In such times, we usually are thinking of lots of things at once, and as with the old phone "party lines," there can be a lot of interference and static in making the connection we want. Sometimes we can't make the connection at all, leaving us frustrated and worried about our memory, adding more stress and clogging the system even more. Memory lapses are simply traffic jams in the brain.

The good news is that in recent years researchers have learned more about how the brain functions and what causes breakdowns in the cognitive system. We know better how to prevent cognitive decline, and even how to improve memory. One of the most exciting new discoveries is that while some brain cells (or "neurons") die over time, we now know that it is possible to grow new ones, no matter how old we are! Just as we discussed earlier with muscle cells, it *is* possible to positively affect how our minds and our bodies age, but it takes work. You have been working all your life; now is a good time to focus that work energy on keeping your mind sharp.

The Dementias

The problem many people worry most about is the risk of developing dementia. Dementia is defined as a decline in both memory and at least one other cognitive function, including:

- **Language**—The ability to name things when asked.

- **Executive functions**—For example, keeping a checkbook in order.

- **Visual spatial skills**—For example, being able to draw a clock accurately.

Dementia affects only about 5 percent of people over 65. Alzheimer's disease is the most common cause, representing about 70 percent of the dementias. Other progressive disorders, such as vascular or blood vessel disease, Parkinson's disease, or Lewy Body disease account for another 25 percent. Unfortunately, completely reversible dementias make up less than 5 percent and are due to factors such as drug toxicity, thyroid disease, and metabolic mishaps in the body.

A Special Note on Alzheimer's Disease

Because Alzheimer's disease is such a devastating problem, it's important to understand some of the realities of the disease. It usually strikes older adults, but may also occur in middle age. At present, an estimated four million Americans have Alzheimer's, most of them over the age of 80. There are many excellent books written about the disease. If you or a loved one has received this diagnosis, we encourage you to read some of them. The Alzheimer's Association has branches in nearly every community and offers a wealth of support and education, not only about the disease but also about memory changes in general.

The average length of time from diagnosis of Alzheimer's to death is 10 years. The onset of the disease is slow and insidious. No one knows the cause. The disease is characterized by the development of "neurofibrillary tangles" and plaques, caused by something called "amyloid protein deposits," which cause brain cells to stick together and become dysfunctional. Symptoms include a gradual deterioration in memory and function. Alzheimer's disease appears to be irreversible, and we have yet to find an effective treatment. Significant research continues, and there are hopeful steps forward in the area of medications that can slow the disease process and improve quality of life. There is some hope that we will one day have a vaccine or understand the cause of this disease well enough to prevent it altogether.

As the disease progresses, patients have trouble understanding concepts and processing new information. They experience increasing difficulty in carrying out tasks in the home or at work. Co-workers and family report having to "cover" for them. Restlessness, changes in personality, and disorientation also occur, becoming more pronounced over time. The most common comment from families about living with Alzheimer's patients is that their family member "just isn't the same person they were two years ago." The patients themselves generally have less and less insight into what is happening to them, often denying any problem at all. However, they become more and more fearful, knowing something isn't right and not being able to comprehend what it is.

In later stages, Alzheimer's disease is characterized by a lack of concern for appearance or bodily function, significant sleep disturbance, and irritability. Eventually, Alzheimer's patients are no longer able to care for themselves; they are unable to manage without assistance in basic daily functions such as eating, grooming, dressing, and using the toilet.

The outcome does not have to be as devastating as we often think. There are many wonderful stories about people who, even in the later stages of the disease, are able to laugh, be joyful, sing, and certainly, love. Medications and behavioral techniques can help control some of the most problematic symptoms. Therapeutic activities, physical exercise, and careful attention to nutrition and hygiene are also important. The goals of caring for a person with Alzheimer's disease are to keep the person safe and to make the most of his or her remaining abilities in a supportive environment in which comfort, dignity, and self-respect are maintained.

It is just as important to take good and loving care of the family and friends who are caregivers! The caregiver role can often feel like a long, lonely, and devastating road to travel as one watches one's loved one slip away. The biggest difference between the caregiver and the patient in this disease is that the caregiver knows what is happening. It is extremely hard. Take extra loving care of yourself if you find yourself in this situation. Read the section in this book on caregiving (Issue 43, *Sharing Your Home*) and be sure you have a good support system to help you, whether it is family and friends, or people you've met through the Alzheimer's Association. Never feel guilty about asking for help or taking time for yourself. No one can do this job alone. Nor *should* they. Be kind to yourself. Remember you will do a better job taking care of your loved one if you are not exhausted and worn out.

Take Control—You *Can* Make a Difference!

The good news is that we *do* know how to improve memory and all cognitive functioning, as well as how to prevent or slow decline, *no matter* what age we are. You can even have fun in the process! Don't worry about your memory. Follow these simple rules to keep yourself as sharp as you can be.

- Exercise your body every day. Physical exercise of all kinds not only increases the blood flow to your brain, bringing it needed food and oxygen, but also releases the brain chemicals that make you feel alert, energetic, and happy. Exercise will improve your "problem-solving" ability virtually immediately. It also stimulates the growth of new neurons. The effects last for about 24 hours. We've all had the experience of feeling better able to deal with the challenges life presents us after we've exercised. Even people with Alzheimer's do much better on days they physically exert. Do it daily.

- Your mind needs to be exercised as often as your body. We used to think that doing crossword puzzles or playing Scrabble or card games were the best exercises. They are good, but we now know that those activities simply keep the brain connections you already have intact. It's important to learn *new* things and make *new* connections all the time. Memorize a new poem, learn a new language, take up bridge if you've never played, or sign up for a continuing education class at your local college. Challenge yourself to learn something new every day.

- Be socially active. Interact with people every day, do volunteer work, join clubs or organizations that interest you. Being with people stimulates the mind's connections in ways we can never do alone. And it feels good.

- Eat a healthy diet full of antioxidant-rich fruits and vegetables. Keep calorie intake at a moderate level. Too much food dulls the brain because it takes all your blood supply to digest it!

- Take a multivitamin. But don't overdue vitamin replacement. Too much of anything can cause harm.

- Check with your doctor to see whether he or she recommends taking one ibuprofen tablet each day if you have a family history of Alzheimer's disease.

- Control cholesterol, high blood pressure, diabetes, and other chronic medical conditions.

- If you smoke, quit!

- Don't take any medications you don't need.

- Control your stress through meditation or other relaxation techniques.

- If you suffer from depression, loss, or grief, seek help.

If you continue to worry about your mental functioning, let your health care provider refer you for cognitive testing. You will learn what particular areas of cognition you can improve, and individualized strategies for improvement.

To Sum Up ...

For most of us, our greatest fear about aging has to do with cognitive function. But in reality, many people live to a very old age with their cognitive functions unimpaired. The fear of Alzheimer's disease and other forms of dementia is far more prevalent than the diseases themselves. Though memory does change over time, you can effectively exercise your body and brain to maintain and even improve your cognitive function. So what are you waiting for? Turn your fears into action. Your reward will go beyond mere peace of mind. You'll have fun with the new things you are learning!

More Resources

- The **American Geriatrics Society** website's Patient Education Forum has a section on memory and memory loss. (*www.americangeriatrics.org*)

- The **Alzheimer's Association** website contains a wealth of information, news and updates for people with Alzheimer's and their families. (*www.alz.org*)

Quick Links

>>> These web-based resources may be accessed through our website: www.aginginstride.org

The Association also offers a 24-Hour Contact Center, staffed by professionals who understand dementia and its impact. Call (800) 272-3900 with questions or concerns about memory problems, dementia, or Alzheimer's disease.

- The **Alzheimer's Disease Education and Referral Center (ADEAR)** is a service of the National Institute on Aging. Their website (*www.alzheimers.org*) has information, practical suggestions, and other resources. They also have a toll-free number (1-800-438-4380).

- The **Mayo Clinic** website has a section on memory, memory loss, and staying mentally sharp. (*www.mayoclinic.com*)

- The **Family Caregiver Alliance** website offers information for family members who are caring for someone who has Alzheimer's, related dementia, or head injury. (*www.caregiver.org*)

ISSUE 20: DEALING WITH DEPRESSION, LONELINESS, AND STRESS

Life is stressful; none of us can escape that fact. Every day of our lives, we face both new and familiar types of stress. As we get older, we experience losses of all kinds: not being physically able to do some of the things we used to do, sometimes feeling our bodies are betraying us, memory changes, the loss of beloved family and friends, needing to stop driving, changing homes. The list can go on and on. All too often, one particular stress or a combination of stresses can become overwhelming and lead to clinical depression.

What is Depression?

Depression is an illness. It can have a number of symptoms, both physical and mental. It affects the whole person: body, mind, and spirit. Depression can begin suddenly, as a result of a specific event, or come on slowly over time without apparent cause. Symptoms include:

- Feeling sad, helpless, hopeless, irritable, or blue.
- Lack of energy.
- Changes in normal eating, sleeping, or sexual patterns.
- Memory changes and the inability to concentrate.
- No longer feeling pleasure in activities that would normally bring you joy.
- Trouble keeping up with normal activities at home or at work.

The Causes of Depression

Clinical, or chemical, depression is the result of a chemical imbalance in the brain that significantly affects how you think, feel, and act. There is a small area in the brain that researchers call the "well-being center." When the body or mind is stressed, this center releases chemicals into the blood stream that counteract the bad effects of stress and allow us to soon feel "normal" or "fine" again. Stresses can be social, psychological, or physical in origin. Some stresses are easy to recognize, but many are not. Examples include:

- Specific events in a person's life, such as the death of a spouse, child, or friend; change in life circumstances, such as needing to change homes or no longer being able to drive; feeling lonely; health problems; or financial worries. Even happy events like marriage or having a baby can be stressful.

- Chronic pain.

- Nutritional deficiencies, such as lack of vitamin B-12 or folic acid, or poor nutrition in general.

- Medical conditions, especially low thyroid or other hormone changes, surgeries, an acute illness, heart disease, stroke, Parkinson's disease, or other neurological conditions.

- Side effects of specific medications, overmedication, or the effects of a combination of drugs.

Every human being, under enough stress for a long enough period of time, will become chemically depressed. This simply means that the effects of the accumulated stresses over time have become too much for the well-being center to counteract. Feeling good or fine or joyful is totally dependent on that center making the right chemicals in our brain and releasing those chemicals into our bodies. When we can't make enough of them, we feel sad or apathetic, sometimes anxious, and often feel more pain, both physiological and emotional. We can't feel normal "good" feelings without them.

How much stress it takes to make a person chemically depressed is very much determined by our genetics. Some people naturally have a lot of these chemicals and it takes a lot of stress to depress their system. Others make less, and a little stress can cause them to be chemically depressed. This trait runs in families.

Most people will experience sadness or other symptoms of depression at some time in their lives. Depression can range from a minor problem to a life-threatening illness. If you experience the symptoms listed above for two weeks or more, it's time to do something about them. The good news is that depression is a very treatable illness.

Diagnosing Depression

The first step in reversing a depression is recognizing or diagnosing it. Depression can become disabling if not properly treated. All too often, people are resistant to the idea that they might have a true depression, feeling that somehow they should just be able to handle whatever is troubling them and get a better attitude. But depression *is* an illness that results from a chemical imbalance in the brain and it can respond successfully to treatment.

Think of depression like you think about diabetes. The diabetic's pancreas doesn't make enough insulin for release into the body to help use sugar well. Over time, the body becomes sick as a result of too much blood sugar. The same is true for depression, where the brain is no longer making enough of its normal chemicals to help us feel good. Just as the diabetic cannot make more insulin by simply trying, the depressed person cannot simply try to make more neurochemicals. We have to do something to get them produced again!

A thorough exam by a physician or other qualified professional is the first step. The goals of such an evaluation typically include:

- Ruling out the possibility of other medical disorders.
- Reviewing all medications for possible side effects.
- Identifying the cause of the depression.
- Determining appropriate treatment options.

Just as depression can be brought on by other physical or medical conditions, it may also resemble other illnesses. For example, many symptoms of depression, such as memory lapses, problems with concentration, lack of energy, or loss of interest in formerly pleasurable activities, are sometimes mistaken for Alzheimer's disease or other dementias. It's very important to consult a professional to identify and treat the clinical signs of depression.

What Treatments Exist for Depression?

Depression is very treatable. Although clinical depression affects many older adults, it should not be accepted as just another part of the aging process. It is not! Sometimes people are hesitant to talk about depression or to have it diagnosed and treated. But treating depression can make a significant difference in a person's health in general and overall quality of life.

Treatments can include one or more of the following:

- Good self-care.
- Counseling.
- Medications.

Good Self-Care

Depression often causes people to have low self-esteem, to feel powerless to change things, and just not to like themselves very much. When people feel this way, they tend to withdraw from family and friends and quit doing the things they like to do. Staying away from family, friends, and pleasurable activities actually makes them feel even worse, and they begin a downward spiral that is difficult to break.

If you are experiencing signs of depression, it is most important to take good care of yourself. Here are some simple first steps:

- Make special times with family and friends. Talk with them about what you are feeling if you can, or simply enjoy just being around them. Everyone needs support from people who care about them.

- Make time for activities you enjoy. Think about the activities you have enjoyed in the past: hobbies, reading, music. Plan to do those things even if you don't feel good. It will be worth it!

- Confront negative thoughts. Depression leads people to think negatively about themselves. Depression also brings guilt, making people feel bad about events in the past. Remember that these thoughts are the depression speaking, and *not* reality. Work to change negative thoughts into positive ones. For example, instead of feeling guilty about past problems, try to concentrate on things you did *well*, and congratulate yourself.

- Increase physical activity! Exercise itself increases the brain's neurochemicals and will make you feel better quickly. It also increases the body's natural pain killers (endorphins) and so will help alleviate pain. *And*, exercise makes people feel good about themselves. (See Issue 2, *Staying Physically Active*, for suggestions on how to begin.)

- Set goals for yourself and take one step at a time. It's not easy to care for yourself while depressed. Get organized. Make a list of the things you are going to do to take care of yourself and begin actually *doing* them, one at a time. The activities will make you feel better, as will the satisfaction of checking them off your list!

Counseling

Talking with a mental health professional may help identify the stressors that have led to depression, aid in developing strategies to get rid of those stresses, and provide you with support as you learn to take care of yourself. Counseling may also enable you to begin changing negative thought patterns and develop better coping skills.

When choosing a counselor, it is important to find someone who is a good "fit" for you. There are counselors who specialize in working with older adults, as well as counselors who specialize in treating depression. Ask your doctor for recommendations. If you know a friend who has had a good counseling experience, ask him or her to share the counselor's name. Check your health insurance to see if mental health benefits are included. Often, insurance carriers require that you use someone from their approved list in order to be covered.

The most important thing, however, is that you choose a counselor with whom you feel comfortable. When you call to make an initial appointment, talk with the counselor over the phone for a few minutes. Tell him or her what your problem is and ask what their approach might be to working with depression. Counselors expect this. Like you, they want a good match between their personality and approach and your comfort.

Many older adults avoid counseling. There is a generational attitude of keeping one's problems to oneself, not asking for help. Self-sufficiency is a good thing, but when it keeps you from getting the help you need to feel better, it is a misplaced virtue. You want to make the best of your life, and be able to enjoy these years. Get the help that will allow you to dispel your depression as quickly as possible.

Medications

Anti-depressant medications work by helping your brain makes its normal neurochemicals again. These medications can help with sleep, improve energy, and reduce anxiety and negative thoughts, allowing you to feel like yourself.

Sometimes it takes a few tries to find exactly the right medicine for a given person; everyone is different. But almost everyone can find a medication that will help restore his or her own natural chemical balance.

The goal is to find the medication that works best for the individual. These medications do not change one's personality and are not addictive. They do take a while to work. Think of the well-being center as a neurochemical factory. The factory has closed down during a depression, and in order for the medications to work, the machines have to be restarted, the workers called back in, and enough chemical made for the person to feel the difference. This process takes an average of three weeks.

Once the medicine is working, research tells us that a person should continue taking it for at least six to eight months. If the time is shorter, the potential for recurrent depression is high, probably because the person has not had enough time to get the stress that caused the depression under control. And remember the caution on stopping medications: abruptly stopping an anti-depressant may actually cause a recurrence of the depression. Carefully follow your doctor's instructions.

Depression and Suicide

The most serious consequence of untreated depression is suicide. About one fifth of all successful suicides are committed by people over 65, particularly men.

What are some of the warning signs of possible suicide? They include depression and anxiety, often accompanied by heavy alcohol consumption, especially after a significant loss such as the death of a spouse, a divorce, or major health problems.

Effective treatment to reduce the risk for suicide exists. Watching for warning signs and seeking help early are important; the earlier the intervention, the greater chance of success.

If you or someone you know needs help, call the **National Hopeline Network** at 1-800-784-2433 to be connected to a trained counselor at a suicide crisis center near you. A list of state and local suicide and crisis hotlines can be found at *http://suicidehotlines.com*.

To Sum Up . . .

Remember, depression is a very treatable illness!

The first steps in treatment are recognizing the symptoms and looking for the cause. Don't delay in discussing these things with a health care professional if any of the symptoms rings a bell for you or your family member. Living with depression is no fun and no one has to "just live with it." Practice good self-care every day, and if symptoms of depression persist, see a counselor and/or talk with your doctor about medication.

More Resources

- The **National Institute of Mental Health** offers a number of fact sheets on their website. (*www.nimh.nih.gov*)

- The **U.S. National Library of Medicine** website is a good place to start to find a wide range of articles dealing with depression. (*www.medlineplus.gov*)

> > > These web-based resources may be accessed through our website:
> www.aginginstride.org

- The **Medem Medical Library** has information about depression from the *Journal of the American Medical Association*, the American Psychiatric Association, and other medical societies. (*www.medem.com*)

- The **Mayo Clinic** website contains information about depression, as well as other information in their Senior Health Center section. (*www.mayoclinic.com*)

ISSUE 21: THE ROLE OF GOOD NUTRITION

Good nutrition is always important, but over time it plays an increasingly important role in our health and how we feel. Eating either too little or too much can have significant effects on overall health. For most people, older age is a very different stage of life from earlier years when you could eat anything and not seem to suffer any more significant consequences than occasional heartburn!

It's time for you to take a little more care with diet. The benefits will be significant; you will feel better every day, and it will help you manage most chronic medical problems, from diabetes to hypertension and heart disease, cancers, and even susceptibility to the common cold.

Life-Threatening Undernutrition

The most under-recognized threat to health is what we *don't* eat that we should, whether it is calories or vitamins and minerals that are essential to keeping us healthy. People who are underweight, or normal weight but without adequate muscle, are at high risk for becoming debilitated after any significant illness or injury.

If you were to suffer an illness or injury, you would need calories to sustain you during the acute event and in healing. Generally, sick people can't eat as they usually do, and so need to get calories from the body, usually from muscle cells. The amount of "food reserve" in the body is part of that important "physiologic reserve" we mentioned earlier. If that reserve is inadequate, many people will never regain their former strength and ability to function after a serious illness or injury. In other words, they will be unable to "bounce back."

Examples of undernutrition that may threaten health include:

- **Being underweight**—Lack of physiologic reserve leads to fatigue, poor recovery after illness, and higher risk of death in the event of a life-threatening disease.

- **Losing more than 10 pounds over six weeks without trying**—Unaccounted-for weight loss is sometimes caused by depression, stomach or colon problems, or cancer.

- **Lack of appropriate caloric or vitamin intake**—Low calorie count or vitamin deficiencies often lead to fatigue, a weakened immune system (and therefore more illness), mental confusion, and depression. A low calorie count can also cause side effects with some medications and lead to hypoglycemic episodes for diabetics.

Undernutrition can be life threatening. See your health care provider right away. He or she can prescribe a diet to promote weight gain, possibly with nutritional supplements, and potentially save your life.

In treating this condition, the most important thing to understand is *why* an individual suffers from undernutrition, and to correct the underlying problem or problems. Here are some common causes:

- **Loss of appetite** may result from chronic illness, from the body's decreased ability to tell us we are hungry, or from a lessened sense of taste.

- If **physical limitations**, such as stroke, arthritis, or Parkinson's disease make eating difficult or discouraging, an occupational therapist can help to make eating easier. Look for helpful adaptive devices, such as large-handled spoons and non-skid plates.

- **Chewing and swallowing** can also be problems. Missing teeth, poorly fitting dentures, stroke, or other conditions that affect swallowing can all cause difficulty. Good dental care is essential. Therapy is available for swallowing difficulties. Meals can be prepared with food processed to make eating easier.

- **Depression and loneliness** may cause loss of appetite. Eating is often a social activity, and people who live alone are less likely to prepare nutritious meals. (See Issue 20, *Dealing with Depression, Loneliness and Stress*.)

- People on a **limited income** may skimp on nutritious foods. Help is available through a variety of senior nutritional programs, such as Meals On Wheels. Simple, inexpensive recipes for nourishing meals are also available.

- Some **medications** change how our bodies process food. Some block absorption of certain vitamins and minerals. Others decrease appetite.

- Some **digestive disorders** make it harder for the body to use nutrients.

The Healthy Diet

Everyone benefits from a healthy diet, one that assures that you avoid the unhealthy extremes of undernutrition on the one hand, and obesity on the other. Even if you've never given much thought to nutrition—or if, like many of us, you've thought "someday I'll watch my diet"—now is the time to start choosing foods to improve your health and well being. Here are several practical points to use as a guide in reorienting how you eat and how you look at the role good nutrition plays:

- **Make sure your diet is well-balanced.**

   A nutritious diet provides sufficient vitamins, minerals, protein, carbohydrates, and fat—but not too much fat! Include a good balance of foods from all the food groups. If you eat a variety of foods every day, especially good portions of fruits and vegetables, you will get the nutrients you need.

- **Maintain a healthy weight.**

   Being overweight can cause health problems, or make them worse; for example:

   - High blood pressure, diabetes, heart disease, and certain forms of cancer are linked to obesity.

   - Excess weight puts extra strain on the bones and joints, aggravating arthritis and osteoporosis.

   - As people gain weight, they tend to become more sedentary and get even less exercise, accelerating the downward spiral of unhealthy aging.

- **Limit fat and cholesterol.**

   Our bodies need a certain amount of fat—and even cholesterol—to stay healthy. The average American diet, however, provides too much fat. Watch your consumption of meat, dairy products, fast foods, desserts, and other high-fat and high-cholesterol choices. High-fat/high-cholesterol diets are linked to an increased risk of heart disease, stroke, colon cancer, and other disorders.

- **Watch your sodium.**

  We need some sodium (salt) in our diets. But salt occurs naturally in food, and usually provides adequate sodium. Most Americans consume too much salt, leading to an increase in blood pressure, kidney disease, and heart conditions.

- **Make sure you get enough calcium and vitamin D.**

  Getting enough calcium can be a challenge, but it's necessary for good nerve function and for preventing osteoporosis (a condition in which a person's bones become fragile and fracture easily). You need 1,500 mg of calcium and 800 mg of vitamin D every day. Dairy products are a good source of calcium, but older adults less easily digest milk and milk products. Add other foods, such as broccoli and spinach, which also contain calcium. Vitamin D is just as important as calcium; it acts as a "bridge" to allow calcium into your bones to make them strong. Add up what you are getting in your diet and take supplements if needed, to ensure you are getting the recommended dosage of both every day. Here's another place where exercise is good for you! It stimulates your bones to take up the calcium and become stronger.

- **Don't forget fiber.**

  Dietary fiber helps prevent chronic intestinal diseases and constipation. It also makes you feel full faster, so you tend to take in fewer calories. Fiber is found in many plant products, so choose whole grain breads and cereals and plenty of vegetables and fruits.

- **Take vitamin and mineral supplements when appropriate.**

  These may be recommended, but don't overdo it! You can actually take a harmful overdose of some vitamins, and older adults process toxic substances less efficiently. Your health care provider can recommend appropriate supplements.

- **Some diseases or conditions require special diets, such as:**

  - Low-sodium diets.
  - Individualized meal planning for persons with diabetes.
  - High-fiber diets.

- ○ Low-protein or low-potassium diets.

- ○ Meals specially prepared for people with chewing or swallowing difficulties.

Always follow closely the special diet recommendations of your health care provider; an appropriate diet will help manage any chronic diseases you might have and can make the difference between illness and wellness.

To Sum Up . . .

Over time, changes occur in the way our bodies use food and other nutrients. Activity level often decreases (though it shouldn't!), so we need fewer calories to maintain a healthy weight. The need for nutrients remains the same, so we need to "eat smart" and avoid any foods that have many calories but few nutrients. Eat well and be healthy!

More Resources

- The **U.S. Department of Agriculture** website contains information about the dietary guidelines, including the familiar "food pyramid." (*www.usda.gov*)

Quick Links

>>> These web-based resources may be accessed through our website: www.aginginstride.org

- The "Information for People Over 65 Years Old" section of the **U.S. Food and Drug Administration** website has information about a variety of nutrition-related topics. (*www.fda.gov*)

- The **American Medical Association** offers an online fact sheet entitled "Nutritional Basics: How Does My Diet Affect My Health?" in their collection of literature. (*www.medem.com*)

- The **American Dietetic Association** offers fact sheets and consumer information on their website. (*www.eatright.org*)

ISSUE 22: URINARY INCONTINENCE

No one likes to talk about urinary incontinence. However embarrassing it might be, leaking or losing control over urine is very common, and can significantly interfere with everyday life. Incontinence affects nearly 20 percent of women as they get older, and a substantial number of men. One patient recently quipped, "I know the location of every bathroom in town!" in an attempt to find some humor in a not very funny situation. The problem can escalate to the point where people don't want to go out in public for fear of an "accident." Incontinence can even be a significant cause of falls if a person has to hurry to get to a bathroom in time.

People often fail to talk with their doctors about incontinence problems, believing it is just "something I have to live with." You don't. There are many excellent treatments that can help. The place to start is by understanding how the bladder works, and what is causing the specific problems you are experiencing.

How the Bladder Works

The kidneys make urine all day long to get rid of extra fluid and other waste products. Urine travels through tubes, called *ureters*, to the bladder, which is like an expandable balloon. The urine is stored in the bladder and contained by a set of muscles in your pelvis called the *sphincter muscles*. They keep the bladder closed tight and hold it in place. When you are ready to go to the toilet, your brain signals the nerves that control your sphincter muscles to relax and causes the nerves surrounding your bladder muscles to contract, expelling the urine through a tube called the *urethra*.

Causes of Incontinence

There are three major kinds of incontinence:

Stress Incontinence

Stress incontinence occurs when the pelvic muscles that keep the bladder sphincter closed are too weak to do a good job. Stress incontinence occurs most often for women, especially women who have had children, or those for whom a hysterectomy has weakened support for the bladder. Stress incontinence is most bothersome when there is added pressure in your abdomen, caused by activities such as coughing, sneezing, or laughing. Kegel exercises (see the box "Exercise for Control" later in this issue) can often solve the problem. Occasionally, surgery to "tack up" the bladder to the abdominal wall is helpful; however, *always* begin with three months of Kegels, 50 times a day, adding them to your regular exercise routine. Even if surgery is eventually recommended by your doctor, strong pelvic floor muscles will be important in determining its long-term success.

Urgency Incontinence

Urgency incontinence happens when the nerves controlling the bladder muscles are "hyperactive," causing the bladder to contract against your will. The nerves can become overactive as a result of a bladder or vaginal infection or irritation, some medications, caffeine, alcohol, or nerve damage. With this form of incontinence, you don't receive a signal in time to reach the bathroom before the bladder begins to contract and empty itself. In solving this problem, first see your doctor to check for infection and review medications that may be making the problem worse. You should also stop all caffeine and alcohol intake, and be sure to drink eight glasses of water a day. Concentrated urine irritates the bladder and makes the problem worse. The best treatments, if the problem persists, are Kegel exercises and bladder training to develop control over both the sphincter muscles and the muscles of the bladder itself.

Overflow Incontinence

Overflow incontinence is the result of an obstruction to the flow of urine through the urethra. The urine backs up in the bladder, and, as the bladder becomes full, urine can begin to leak out. In addition, an obstruction can often keep the bladder from emptying completely when you do void, creating a high risk of bladder infections. In men, this condition is most often caused by an enlarged prostate; in women, it is usually a result of a narrowing of the urethra, or *stricture*. Symptoms are usually an irritating "dribbling" that you may not even know about until after the fact, and a feeling that you never completely empty your bladder. Overflow incontinence should be treated by your physician, who can test to see if your bladder empties completely after urination.

Taking Control

As you work to control your incontinence problem, you first need specific and accurate information. Begin with a "bladder diary" where you record all of the following:

- How many times you go to the bathroom.

- How much urine you void (small amount = 2 tablespoons; medium = $1/2$ cup; large = 1 cup or more).

- How much and what you drink.

- When you "leak" urine; for example, when laughing, coughing, exercising, hear running water, or for no particular reason.

This record will give good clues as to your type of incontinence and what you can do about it. Your diary will also demonstrate your progress as your bladder and pelvic floor muscles get stronger.

Bring the diary to your doctor, who can help you determine what kind of incontinence you have and help you make a plan to correct it. The treatments really work! Have patience, and be persistent. Building the muscles of the bladder and pelvic floor requires the same dedicated work as building any other muscle group in the body. The good news is you can do the exercises anywhere, any time, and no one will even know!

Keep Drinking Enough Water

Drinking enough water is very important, even if you are dealing with incontinence. If you don't take in enough water, your urine becomes more concentrated—something you can see just in its color. The more water you drink, the less concentrated your urine is, which reduces irritation to your bladder and skin.

Exercise for Control!

Kegel Exercises

First, you'll need to find the right muscles to exercise. Try to stop the flow of urine while you are sitting on the toilet. To do this, you use the muscles of your pelvic floor. These are the muscles you want to isolate and work in this exercise! Now, move on to the exercise itself.

Do the exercise at various times lying, sitting, and standing. You want to gain strength in all positions.

- Isolate the pelvic muscles, being sure to relax the muscles of your buttocks, legs, and stomach.

- Be sure to breathe while exercising.

- Pretend your muscles are pulling up an elevator; pull in a little and stop at the first floor to let people off and on, then up a bit more to the second floor, again letting people off and on.

- You want to develop a pattern of very slow contraction of the muscles. When you are at the top floor, hold there as long as you can (those folks in the penthouse take a long time to move off and on!), then slowly begin your way back down, again stopping at every floor to let folks on and off.

Try starting with three floors and as your control improves, increase to 10 floors. You'll be surprised at how quickly you'll make progress, even if at first you can hardly feel any contraction at all!

Do 50 Kegels a day to make the best progress. At less than 20 seconds each, that's only 15 minutes total. That's much less time than you would spend searching out bathrooms or worrying about a possible accident! Try to pick out some usual activities that can trigger you to do Kegels no matter where you are; for example, riding in a car, standing in the grocery line, watching TV or reading, and just before you fall off to sleep. It's well worth it, and after a while, they become an unconscious part of your day.

Bladder Training

The bladder wall is a muscle and, like all muscles, it can be trained with regular exercise to do what you want. If you find that you are going to the bathroom more often than every two to three hours, try this exercise to make your bladder muscle stronger.

- If it has been less than two hours since your last trip to the bathroom, wait for five minutes after you feel the urge to go.

- Do Kegel exercises to prevent leaking while you wait and relax with deep breaths. The urge will pass as you let the bladder muscle relax.

- Add another five to 15 minutes to your waiting time every week until you can wait two to three hours between voidings.

Training your bladder muscle to relax will reduce your urge to go and decrease leakage over time. *Don't* run to the bathroom when you get the urge or go more frequently than every two hours. Doing so makes the bladder weaker and able to hold less urine, resulting in worsening urge incontinence, the old "downward spiral." All people able to do regular Kegel exercises should be successful in strengthening their bladder control muscles.

A Note on Incontinence Aids

Until you become confident in your ability to control your urine, you may well benefit from the new disposable undergarments that are quite effective in controlling odor as well as leakage. These undergarments are as inconspicuous as regular underwear and allow people to stop worrying about embarrassing accidents. Do not use menstrual products—it is very important to protect your skin from irritating urine. Use over-the-counter products daily, such as Desitin®, vitamin A and D ointment, or Bag Balm® if you are often wet or irritated. Change pads often and rinse residual urine away. And remember to check with your doctor about any signs of chronic irritation.

To Sum Up . . .

Urinary incontinence is both embarrassing and inconvenient. However, rather than suffering in silence, you will be better off recording your symptoms, talking with your doctor, and taking the necessary steps to diminish or even cure the problem. Life is too short and too precious to let this problem get in your way. So take charge and feel better!

More Resources

Quick Links

>>> These web-based resources may be accessed through our website: www.aginginstride.org

- The **American Academy of Family Physicians** offer an informative online brochure on their website. (*www.familydoctor.org*)

- The **U.S. Food and Drug Administration** website has information on causes and treatment of urinary incontinence. (*www.fda.gov*)

- The website for **The Mayo Clinic** includes a thorough examination of urinary incontinence in their "Senior Health Center" section. (*www.mayoclinic.com*)

- **The Cleveland Clinic Health Information Center** site includes a searchable list of articles on health-related topics. (*www.clevelandclinic.org/health*)

ISSUE 23: CHRONIC DISEASES AND CONDITIONS

Managing chronic health conditions is one of the primary challenges of aging well. Unfortunately, there are many of these conditions. To list all the possibilities is beyond the scope of this book. Instead, in this issue we will give you a framework to help you come to terms with chronic health problems so that they impact your quality of life as little as possible.

Diagnosis

Your doctor has just informed you that you have a chronic health problem. What are you going to do? It is easy to feel discouraged or depressed when the doctor tells you that you have a condition that is not easily "fixed." That discouragement can begin a downward spiral into decreasing health and wellness. Don't let it! There is virtually no chronic medical condition that cannot be improved by your intentional attempts at improvement.

This is where your long-acquired life skills come into play. You've received tough news before, and dealt with it well. It might not be what you would choose, but you know you have no choice but to play the hand life deals you. It's time to take control. Give yourself an hour to complain to your best friend, but then go to work. Your first task is to find out everything you can about your newly diagnosed condition. There are many good medical reference texts that are written for a non-professional audience and are available at local libraries or bookstores. Your doctor probably has information to get you started. Or go online and check your favorite search engine, but remember to be careful in evaluating information you find on the Internet. Do you know of a friend or acquaintance who is living life with the health problem you have? Ask that person for references. Better yet, make an appointment to sit down and talk face to face. Just remember, it *is* possible to learn everything you need to know to take control of any disease or chronic medical problem.

Management

There are several principles for managing any chronic condition, whether it be diabetes, heart disease, lung disease, chronic pain, neurological diseases such as Parkinson's, arthritis, or...the list is long.

These principles include:

- **Become an active partner with your health care provider**. Develop a plan together for managing your condition. Set goals for self-care and medical care and stick to them!

- **Learn everything you can about your specific conditions** so that you can know what to expect and how to manage problems that may arise.

- **Remember that virtually ALL chronic conditions are helped by regular physical activity**. Make a specific plan for how to increase activity in your life and follow it.

- **Use community organizations for help and support**. Most chronic illnesses and conditions have organized community support groups whose purpose is to help people understand and live with their condition. These groups, such as the American Diabetes Association, the American Lung Association, and the American Arthritis Association, also offer support and help from others with similar problems. Work with your health care team to learn about the community groups that may be most useful for you.

Control

The goal in managing all chronic conditions is for *you* to control them instead of the other way around. That does not mean your health problems are insignificant in the living of your life. It does mean that you use your ability to gather information, to plan, and to manage your condition so that health issues have the smallest possible negative impact on pursuing your life goals and dreams. It will take discipline on your part. You will have to make choices and weigh priorities. Many people have actually taken the occasion of learning of a chronic health problem to improve overall health and well-being instead of letting things fall apart. You can be one of them! You still have things to do and a life to live. So take control and move on.

Chronic Pain

One of the most significant causes of disability as we age is chronic pain. Managing pain effectively is essential to being able to live life to the fullest. There is much confusion in society about the appropriate treatment of chronic pain;

many people worry about becoming addicted to pain medications and choose to live with the pain, becoming more and more disabled as a result.

Many doctors also have biases which lead to undertreating pain. The first step should always be to search for the cause of the pain, and to deal with it if possible. Unfortunately, finding and eliminating the cause of pain isn't always possible; that's when effective measures to manage persistent pain become the goal. In an effort to develop a reasonable medical approach, the American Geriatrics Society convened an expert panel to review the research on pain management and to develop guidelines for physicians. Here's a summary of their recommendations, in plain language:

American Geriatrics Society Guidelines for the Management of Persistent Pain in Older People

- Persistent pain that has an impact on physical function, psychological function, or quality of life should be considered a significant problem and treated appropriately.

- Acetaminophen should be the first drug to consider in the treatment of mild to moderate muscle or joint pain.

- Traditional nonsteroidal anti-inflammatory medications (e.g., ibuprophen, aspirin, or naproxen) should be avoided in those requiring long-term daily treatment, because they can cause serious stomach irritation over time. The newer COX-2 inhibitors, e.g., Vioxx or Celebrex, are preferable if acetaminophen is not enough.

- Opiod analgesic drugs like oxycodone are effective in helping control severe pain and have a low potential for addiction. As with all medication, they need to be closely monitored by physicians for possible adverse side effects.

- ALL people with persistent pain should have an individually designed program of physical activity to improve strength, flexibility, and endurance. This program should be continued indefinitely.

Remember, relieving chronic pain is essential to remaining active, and a physically active lifestyle is the very best treatment for chronic pain!

To Sum Up . . .

For many of us, chronic health conditions are a part of growing older. That doesn't mean you should feel discouraged or depressed, nor use that discouragement to spiral downward into poorer health. Use your ability to gather information, to plan, and to manage your condition so that health issues don't unnecessarily curb your dreams, but rather encourage you to take control and live the life you want to live.

More Resources

For information about a wide range of diseases and conditions, here are some good general health websites:

Quick Links

>>> These web-based resources may be accessed through our website: www.aginginstride.org

- The **American Medical Association**'s Patient Education Resources can be found on their website (*www.ama-assn.org)*. They can also be accessed through the **Medem Medical Library**. (*www.medem.com*)

- **The Mayo Clinic**'s extensive website has information on a wide variety of conditions. (*www.mayoclinic.com*)

- The **Cleveland Clinic Health Information Center** website includes a searchable list of articles on health-related topics. (*www.clevelandclinic.org/health*)

- Healthfinder is a service of the **U.S. Department of Health and Human Services**. (*www.healthfinder.gov*)

- MedlinePlus Health Information is a service of the **U.S. National Library of Medicine** and the **National Institutes of Health**. (*www.medlineplus.gov*)

ISSUE 24: INFORMED CONSENT AND ADVANCE DIRECTIVES

Health care today can be a bewildering business. The days when a person could sit down in the doctor's office for a leisurely chat are pretty much over. Because of the general consciousness about lowering health care costs and trying to provide efficient medical care, doctors, and all who work in doctors' offices, are busier than ever. Less time is scheduled for ordinary patient visits. Nurses, nurse practitioners, and physician assistants do much of the work that physicians used to do themselves. Many positive things can be said about modern medicine, but often for patients, it feels like they are being swept along in a system where an ever-changing team of people, many of them strangers, are doing things patients may not even understand.

If you have ever felt that way, this issue is for you! In the next several pages, we will be discussing patients' rights in health care—the legal and practical steps you can take so that you are in charge of what happens to you medically in your doctor's office, in the hospital, at home, or in any institutional care setting.

Informed Consent: The Most Basic Patients' Right

Informed consent is the legal term for your right to be in charge of your own health care and to make your own decisions. It means your right to accept—or refuse—medical treatment.

Both the words "informed" and "consent" are important. In fact, you should think of your right to decide as two separate rights that are closely related to one another.

First, your doctor or other health care provider must explain your medical situation to you before treatment begins, in language you can understand. This gives you the facts you need to make an informed decision for yourself, instead of relying on guesswork or someone else's opinion. Second, once you have been informed, you have the right to give or refuse consent. It's up to you to say "yes" or "no" to whatever your doctor is recommending.

Together, informed consent gives you the right to decide what is best for you, based on your values and priorities.

Getting the Necessary Information

Before treatment begins, or before it is changed in any important way, your doctor must tell you:

- What your medical condition is.

- What kind of treatment he or she is recommending.

- What this course of treatment is expected to do for you.

- What the risks and benefits of treatment are.

- What other options you have, including the option of doing nothing.

Most doctors want to do a good job of communicating with their patients. However, not all of us take in information at the same rate or in the same way. Making sure you have the information you need requires a conscious partnership between you and your doctor. It is the doctor's job to share information with you. It is your job to let the doctor know if he or she is doing a good job. You have the responsibility to let the doctor know if you understand what is being said, if you need more information, or if you need things to be explained in a different way.

The following suggestions may be helpful in making sure you get the information you need to make good decisions for yourself.

- **Repeat back to the doctor in your own words what you think he or she is saying to you.** Ask the doctor to clarify points that you don't understand. Don't worry that you might not be saying it correctly, or that you are taking up too much time. Answering questions and making sure you understand information is just as much a part of the doctor's job as ordering tests and writing prescriptions.

- **Have a family member or friend with you when you see the doctor.** Though this person doesn't have to be present during the physical exam if that makes you uncomfortable, have him or her come into the room when you are discussing things with your doctor. Often, two pairs of ears hear better than one. It can also be helpful for the person with you to write down what the doctor says. Then, when you get home, you can look at those notes to help you remember the important parts of the conversation. Especially if you are hard of hearing, or tend to be forgetful, or if you are discussing a potentially serious medical condition, having a person with you to help you understand the information and get your questions answered is a good idea.

- **If you think of questions after you leave the doctor's office or as you are discussing what the doctor said with someone else, write those questions down.** When you're pretty sure you know all the questions you want to ask, then call the doctor. Again, answering your questions is part of a physician's job. However, a doctor's time is limited. If you gather your questions to ask all at once, you will make the best use of both your time and the doctor's time.

Making Your Decision

Once you have all the necessary information, you will decide what course of treatment is best for you. Often, the decision is simple. Sometimes, however, there are difficult choices to be made, either because you disagree with your doctor's proposed course of action, or because all of the treatment options have significant risks as well as benefits. When you are having a difficult time making a decision, you might want to try the following:

- **Find out when the decision has to be made.** Do you have to make this decision right now, or some time today, or this week, or within the next month? What are the consequences of putting off the decision? Once you understand when the decision has to be made, then within that framework, you can take the time you need to make a good decision.

- **Talk over your decision with a person or several people whom you trust and who share your values:** family members, friends, or your spiritual advisor. Get clarity about what is most important to you, and make your decision from that perspective.

- **Call your primary care physician and talk with him or her** if you have been consulting with a specialist physician—for example, a cardiologist or oncologist.

- **If the decision you are being asked to make is a major one, you might want to consider a second medical opinion.** In serious matters, many insurance carriers will pay for a second opinion. Even when insurance won't cover the cost, you might want to pay for a second opinion yourself for your own peace of mind.

- **When you make your decision, communicate it clearly to your doctor and then make sure that the doctor has understood you.** Especially if you are choosing something other than the doctor's proposed course of treatment, you need to make sure that the doctor is completely clear about what you do or do not want.

If you take the time to make sure you understand the information you are given and what choices you have before you, you can make good health care decisions for yourself. Even when you feel tentative about a decision you have reached, remember: no one else can make a better decision for you. No one else knows you or your values and priorities, better than you do.

Some decisions are difficult by their very nature, because the medical situation itself is scary or overwhelming. Make the very best decision you can, and then let yourself come to peace with it.

Most of the time, it doesn't help when we second-guess ourselves. None of us can make perfect decisions all of the time. If you have done your homework, heard and understood the pertinent information, and based your decision on what you believe to be right, then you've made the best possible decision for yourself in any given situation.

Advance Directives: When You Are Unable to Make Your Own Decisions

We like to think that we will always be capable of making our own health care decisions. Sometimes, however, it doesn't work like that. A stroke, an automobile accident, being too frail or confused to understand medical treatment information—any number of circumstances could occur that might limit or take away a person's immediate ability to make health care decisions. Fortunately, you have the power to think and act ahead of time for such situations. The legal documents that allow you to do this are called *advance directives*, and they come in two varieties:

- A *Health Care Appointment*, also called a *Durable Power of Attorney for Health Care* or a *Health Care Proxy*, is a document that lets you give someone else—usually a close friend or relative—the power to make decisions for you if a time comes when you can't speak for yourself.

- A *Health Care Directive* or *Living Will* is a document that lets you say what kinds of care you would or would not want if you were nearing the end of your life. A health care directive usually refers to "life-sustaining measures." These are advanced medical treatments that can keep a person alive past the time when death would very likely occur. Examples include:

  - **CPR**—emergency restarting of a person's heart or breathing.

  - **Ventilation**—using a machine to breathe for a person.

  - **Dialysis**—mechanically cleaning and filtering the blood, usually the work of the kidneys.

  - **Tube or needle feeding**—giving basic nutrition to a person who has lost the ability to swallow.

  - **Antibiotics**—fighting an infection that could hasten death.

Health Care Appointments

If you were unable to make health care decisions for yourself, who would be the person you would most trust to make those decisions for you? That is the person you should appoint as your health care representative. If for some reason your first choice person were not available to act for you, who would be your second choice? Most forms designating a health care representative allow you to name a back-up.

Although no one is under any obligation to fill out a Health Care Appointment, it is the most flexible sort of advance directive. Your health care representative can make decisions for you in a wide variety of unforeseen situations. Your representative has a legal obligation to make decisions for you based on what you would have chosen for yourself. Therefore, the appointment of a health care representative significantly extends your ability to control your health care decisions.

If you wish to name an individual as your health care representative, it is a good idea to ask the person if he or she is willing to take on that responsibility. If the person agrees, then you should sit down with him or her and have a frank, detailed conversation about your feelings and values concerning health care and the kinds of treatment you would or would not want. Along with this conversation, be sure to give your health care representative copies of your advance directives.

Note: If you've been asked to serve as someone's health care representative, be sure to see Issue 45, *Serving as a Person's Health Care Representative*, and Form 45, *Health Care Representative's Discussion Checklist*.

Health Care Directives

If death were near, would you want your life to be extended by use of a ventilator? What about a feeding tube? What about antibiotics? Some people would respond "yes" to some or all of these questions; others would answer "no." If you fill out a health care directive, that document will ask you a number of questions about specific treatments to which you would say "yes" or "no" if you were at the end of your life. It is a common misperception that you should fill out a living will only if you don't want any life-sustaining treatment at all. In fact, your living will allows you to specify precisely what treatments you would like and which ones you would refuse. Most health care directives also have a space to write down any preferences not covered in the specific treatment questions asked.

As with the appointment of a health care representative, you don't have to fill out a living will. Having such a directive, however, lets you specify in advance which treatments make sense to you at the end of life. It is another way of extending your control over your own health care.

If you do fill out a health care directive, give a signed and witnessed copy to your primary physician, your health care representative if you have one, your hospital, and any other major health care institution or organization with which you are connected. It is also wise to share the contents of your living will with your family and close friends. Let them know what you would want. Doctors and hospitals may become uncomfortable when the family is surprised by a family member's wishes as stated in a living will, especially if family members disagree with the patient's wishes. You can make life easier for everyone by talking openly with your loved ones about what you would want.

Other Opportunities for Advance Health Care Planning

Along with advance directives, it is helpful to consider three more aspects of advance health care planning. Although not technically advance directives, they are important ways of planning ahead for choices to be made when you can't make choices for yourself.

Personal Values Statements

Personal values statements are becoming more common as a way of clarifying and supplementing a person's advance directives. Values statements provide a detailed profile of a person's views, goals, and underlying personal values concerning health care. A values statement indicates not only what kind of care a person desires, but also *why* he or she desires it. It is an expression of a person's beliefs and priorities in the person's own words. Although values statements do not have the legal weight of advance directives, when used with advanced directives, they extend a sense of clarity about what the person would want and why. A sample *Personal Values Statement* is included as Form 24.

DNR Orders and POLST Forms

A *do-not-resuscitate order* (DNR order) is an instruction a doctor puts in a patient's medical record with the informed consent of the patient or the patient's health care representative. It says, in effect, "If this person's breathing or heart stops, do not start cardio-pulmonary resuscitation (CPR) or any other measures to restart those vital functions." The legal status of DNR orders varies from state to state, so be sure to check with your doctor if you have questions.

In many states, if you wish NOT to be resuscitated, you can wear a medic-alert necklace or bracelet with that information, or you can carry a DNR card in your wallet. Another approach in many states and communities is for the physician and patient (or health care representative) to both sign a set of physician's CPR orders on a standard, brightly colored form. This form, which is sometimes called a POLST (Physician Orders for Life-Sustaining Treatment) form, can then be posted on the refrigerator at home, or it can travel with the patient. First responders to a 911 call are trained to look for this form and will follow its instructions when they find it.

Organ Donation

Organ donation is a person's voluntary gift of organs or tissues, either for transplanting to another person or for medical research. In many states, people are asked if they wish to be organ donors when they renew their driver's licenses. Many advance directive forms also have a place for a person to say whether he or she wishes to be a donor. As with other advance health care directives, if you wish to be an organ donor, it is helpful to share that information with your family or other close loved ones. This minimizes the possibility of confusion or controversy at the time of your death.

To Sum Up . . .

All of the above health care options involve the following steps:

- Thinking about your wishes and values as they apply to your health care.

- Taking steps, both legal and informal, to write down your wishes, values, and priorities.

- Making sure that health care providers and close loved ones know what you want, and have access to your health care directives.

Planning and communication are the important elements here. They will allow you to make sure your wishes are followed, even when you can't make decisions for yourself.

More Resources

- The **American Medical Association** and other medical societies provide brochures and fact sheets about advance directives and health care planning on the **Medem Medical Library** website. (*www.medem.com*)

Quick Links

>>> These web-based resources may be accessed through our website:

www.aginginstride.org

- The **American Bar Association**'s Commission on Law and Aging website includes information on advance directives and selecting a health care representative. (*www.abanet.org/aging*)

- The **NOLO Law for All** "Plain English Law Centers" includes information on health care directives and choosing a health care agent. (*www.nolo.com*)

Receiving Care in a Nursing Facility

INTRODUCTION

When it comes to providing residential care for older adults, nursing facilities (also called "nursing homes" or "skilled nursing facilities") have done it longest and for the widest variety of clientele. For many years, nursing facilities were the only alternative for seniors who couldn't live at home or with a family member. This long history as care providers gives nursing facilities a solid base of information and experience, a long track record of service to a population that until recently was too often ignored by the rest of society. However, the long history of nursing facilities also has a negative side. Many people have heard horror stories about the poorly funded and largely unregulated nursing facilities of the past. The very subject of nursing facility care evokes for many a stereotype of neglect and abandonment. When a move to a nursing facility is considered, the discussion too often raises fear in the potential resident and guilt in family members.

It's time to start over. Forget everything you've heard or think you know about nursing facility care. Much has happened in the last 20 years in how we, as a society, provide essential services to older adults. Those changes have had a tremendous, positive impact on nursing facility care.

Nursing facilities are now highly regulated and the care they give to residents closely scrutinized. Despite problems with funding and chronic staff shortages, most nursing facilities work hard to provide professional and compassionate care to their residents. Their staffs take pride in a job well done. As you begin to consider nursing facility care, your most important tool is an open mind. Don't be blinded by your preconceptions. A lot of high quality care is provided by nursing facilities, but long-term care does have its strong performers and its weaker performers. It always makes sense to do your homework.

There is a lot to think about, but we're here to help! In the following three issues, we will walk you through the process of choosing and settling into a nursing facility.

In Issue 25, we focus on deciding whether nursing facility care is the best option in your situation. If care in a nursing facility seems like the right decision, how do you choose the best facility, one that will deliver quality care and the highest possible quality of life?

In Issue 26, we take you through the process of moving into a nursing facility. What practical considerations come into play? How can friends and family help make the transition a smooth one?

In Issue 27, we outline the legally protected rights of nursing facility residents. We also offer suggestions for spotting problems and getting them resolved quickly and effectively.

There is no way to take all of the anxiety and uncertainty out of a nursing facility move. But making good choices, reducing the dislocation and stress of the move, and becoming familiar with residents' rights are reasonable, achievable goals. They will contribute greatly to you or your loved one receiving the best possible care and having an overall positive nursing facility experience.

To help you gather information and make some notes along the way, we have included these forms:

- Form 25: *Worksheet for Evaluating a Nursing Facility*
- Form 26-A: *Nursing Facility Move-in Checklist*
- Form 26-B: *Resident/Family Care Conference Worksheet*
- Form 27: *Worksheet for Questions, Concerns, and Complaints*

ISSUE 25: CHOOSING A NURSING FACILITY

Is care in a nursing facility the right decision? Many older adults and their families struggle with this question. Answering the nursing facility question for yourself is difficult. Getting everyone in a family to agree can be even tougher.

There is no magic formula here. Your best strategy is to work through the facts and options, trying to be as clear and objective as you can be. As you approach your decision, consider these practical suggestions:

- Begin by doing a candid assessment of your (or your loved one's) care needs.

  - Do you need skilled nursing care? If so, how intensively? One or two visits a week? Every day? Around the clock?

  - Do you need therapy services to speed recovery or promote function and independence?

  - Do you need personal care—help with activities of daily living, like dressing, bathing, using the toilet, eating, managing medications?

  - How is your mental attitude? Are you as physically active as possible, mentally stimulated, and connected to other people? Do you need help dealing with isolation, depression, and/or fear?

- Consider the question, "where can these needs best be met?"

  - Is care at home, with the support of an in-home helper or home health team, a possibility?

  - Would a less intensive residential care setting, such as an assisted living facility or adult family home, be a good solution?

  - If care in a nursing facility seems appropriate, do you need a skilled nursing facility that specializes in sub-acute care following hospitalization, or will a less intensive intermediate care facility meet your needs?

  - Are you in need of skilled nursing care that specializes in caring for persons who are dealing with serious chronic illness or dementia?

- If the decision still seems confusing, get some input. A doctor, hospital discharge planner, home health professional, or care manager can help you make sense of your situation. All these professionals are trained to support patients and families through exactly the kinds of questions you're facing.

- Be clear about one thing: although each care setting (at home, assisted living, adult family home, or nursing facility) has its unique characteristics, they all create new and potentially enriching opportunities for moving forward with a person's life and a family's life together. If care in a nursing facility is the right decision, it will present new challenges in terms of how you and your family remain close, but the opportunities will still be there!

Selecting a High-Quality Facility

Nothing will give you more peace of mind where a nursing facility placement is concerned than knowing you did your research. A great place to begin the selection process is by talking with your doctor, hospital discharge planner, home health nurse, or care manager. All these professionals should be able to steer you toward facilities in your area that have a reputation for quality care, provide the type of care you need, and currently have a bed available or a short waiting list.

Doing Some Basic Nursing Facility Research

Nursing facilities are usually listed in the local telephone Yellow Pages. You may also obtain a local list by contacting any Senior Information and Referral office in the country. To get started, call the nationwide Eldercare Locator line at 1-800-677-1116.

Researching Nursing Facilities on the Internet

Today, there is a wealth of information about nursing facilities available on the Web. The question is, how do you evaluate the information that's there? Here are some important starting places:

- *www.medicare.gov*—This is the official government Medicare website. It offers a variety of resources, including a guide to choosing a nursing facility, a nursing facility selection checklist, and comparative listings of all nursing facilities that participate in either Medicare or Medicaid. This site includes *Nursing Home Compare*, which offers comparative data about participating facilities, including many important "quality indicators." *Nursing Home*

Compare is not without its own limitations. As the site itself warns, the data it offers can be partial or out of date, since conditions in a nursing facility can change quickly. Nevertheless, it's a logical place to start your online research.

- **Search engines**—These services, such as Google or Yahoo, can help you locate information about particular facilities. A facility may have its own website, or your search might turn up references to that facility on other websites or in online publications.

- **For-profit listing services**—A number of commercial websites also list nursing facilities and the services they provide. Though most of these sites charge facilities a fee for their listing or for each referral or admission they generate, they can be very helpful sources for information.

Paying for Care in a Nursing Facility

Nursing facility care is costly. Depending on the service provided and the income level of the resident, there are four sources of payment for services:

- **Medicare.** Medicare, the federal government program for people 65 and over and for some who are disabled, will pay for a limited stay in a nursing facility after certain types of hospitalization. This kind of care is referred to as *sub-acute care* or *rehabilitation*. Coverage for this care is strictly limited as to the number of days and types of care covered. Medicare does not cover long-term care for managing chronic illness or dementia. Also be aware that not all nursing facilities accept Medicare patients. Issue 32, *Medicare and Medicaid*, has more information about Medicare.

- **Managed care.** Your managed care plan may include some coverage for post-hospital care in a nursing facility. As with Medicare, only certain situations are covered, and not all nursing facilities in a community have a contract to provide the care.

- **Medicaid.** Medicaid is funded jointly by the state and federal governments and administered by each state. Medicaid will pay for most of the costs of extended care in a nursing facility for persons who need the care and are unable to pay on their own. Eligibility requirements are tied to a person's income and assets and vary from state to state. Persons who do not qualify for Medicaid when they move into a nursing facility may later qualify after they have exhausted their own resources, a process called "spending down."

See Issue 32 for more on Medicaid.

- **Private Pay/Long-Term Care Insurance.** Nursing facility care that is not paid for by Medicare, Medicaid, or managed care is usually the responsibility of the resident. A growing number of older adults and those in their middle years are purchasing long-term care insurance to protect their assets from the financial risk of nursing facility care extending over months or years. Long-term care insurance is discussed in more detail in Issue 33. When paying for nursing facility care yourself, it is important to understand the fee schedule and how services are charged. Many facilities have a "basic" rate that covers a limited number of services, with additional services charged over and above the basic rate.

Location

Location is typically an important factor to consider when choosing a nursing facility. Other factors being equal, most people choose a nursing facility that would be convenient for trips to the doctor or hospital and for visits from family and friends.

An Educated Nursing Facility Visit

Based on levels of care, cost, and location, you will be able to narrow your search to two or three best prospects. Perhaps you are already down to just one promising fit. Whether your short list has one name on it or several, your next step is critical: you need to make personal visits. Ask questions. Make notes. We recommend this if you are comparing two or more possibilities, but it's the smart thing to do even if you feel you are choosing from a field of one.

Need Help with Medicare and Medicaid?

Nursing facilities that participate in the Medicare and Medicaid programs should be able to help answer your questions or put you in contact with someone who can. Another excellent resource in most states is called a SHIP program, which stands for State Health Insurance Assistance Program. You can obtain the phone number or website of the SHIP office in your state through Senior Information and Referral, the Eldercare Locator line (800-677-1116), or in the "Helpful Contacts" section of *www.medicare.gov*.

There are a variety of factors to observe, as well as many questions to ask when you visit each facility. These are all included as a checklist in Form 25, *Worksheet for Evaluating a Nursing Facility*, but are summarized here to give you a feel for what a visit should include.

Residents

Do the residents appear comfortable and well cared for? Are they appropriately dressed and well groomed? Are they engaged in activities?

Staff

Do the facility's employees seem knowledgeable and well organized in the tasks they are performing? Are they courteous and attentive to the residents? Do they know and use the residents' names? Do they knock before entering a resident's room? Are they wearing name tags to let residents and visitors know who they are? Are they groomed appropriately? Do they seem motivated and engaged in the work they are doing?

Resident Rooms

Are the residents' rooms clean and comfortable? Are lighting, ventilation, and space adequate? Are the bathrooms equipped with non-skid surfaces and grab bars? If rooms are shared by two or more people, is privacy respected as much as possible? Can residents bring any furnishings from home?

Meals

What is the atmosphere of the dining room as meals are served? Do things seem calm and organized? Is the food appealing? Is it served hot?

Social Activities

Does the facility offer a variety of activities and outings? Does it encourage residents to remain as informed, independent, and active as their physical and mental condition permit? Are calendars, posters, and photographs displayed?

Building and Grounds

Is the facility well maintained? Are quiet, comfortable spaces available for family visits? Are there walkways or a courtyard for outdoor visits in good weather? Do stairways and hallways have safety rails?

Questions to Ask

Many important characteristics of a facility are not apparent on the surface. So, we encourage you to ask some questions. Probe a little. For example, you might ask about:

Choice of Doctor

Does the potential resident's regular doctor see patients at this facility? If not, which doctors are available?

Admission Agreement

What sort of written agreement does the facility ask new residents to sign? Ask to see a copy. What are the payment schedules and fee arrangements? How are services charged?

Range of Services

What is the variety of services the facility provides? Does it offer rehabilitation services? Skilled nursing care? Special care for residents with dementia?

Family Involvement

What are the opportunities for family involvement? Is family involvement encouraged? What are the facility's policies on family participation in care planning and care conferences? If families don't live in the immediate area, is there a way they can be involved in care planning by conference call? Can they communicate with the nursing staff and administration by e-mail?

Survey Results

All long-term care facilities are regularly inspected as part of their license renewal and their participation in Medicare or Medicaid. The facility's most recent survey results are always available. Ask to take a look. Were there any major problems? If so, have they been corrected?

Facility Policies and Procedures

What does the facility ask of each resident? What are its "rules and regulations?" For example, what is the facility policy on smoking? On loud noise? On protection of resident belongings? Does the facility allow pets to visit?

To Sum Up . . .

What can you expect at the end of your nursing facility selection process? Making an informed decision won't suddenly erase all the fear and other emotions you're experiencing. But if you invest the time and effort, rather than depending on guesswork, you will feel better about your move.

One caution: don't expect to find a perfect nursing facility, one in which questions and concerns are guaranteed never to surface. Some facilities are stronger and seem to deliver quality care more consistently than others. But in every situation, you or your loved one will benefit from staying informed and involved in care and care planning. If something needs fixing, or if you have a preference that something be done differently, speak up!

Finally, don't think of nursing facility admission as an end. In some important ways it is a beginning. In Issue 26, we look at how you can help make moving to a nursing facility a positive experience.

More Resources

- For background brochures and checklists, visit the website of either the **American Association of Homes and Services for the Aging** (AAHSA) (*www.aahsa.org*), or the **American Health Care Association** (AHCA). (*www.ahca.org*)

Quick Links

>>> These web-based resources may be accessed through our website: www.aginginstride.org

- For *A Consumer Guide to Choosing a Nursing Home* visit the website of the **National Citizens' Coalition for Nursing Home Reform** (NCCNHR). (*www.nursinghomeaction.org*)

- The website for Medicare includes **Nursing Home Compare**, a searchable directory that gives information about the performance of every Medicare and Medicaid-certified nursing facility in the U.S. (*www.medicare.gov*)

ISSUE 26: MOVING TO A NURSING FACILITY

Once the decision to move to a nursing facility is made, new challenges arise. In this issue, we look at what's involved in moving, or in helping a loved one move, to a nursing facility. Beyond the move, what can be done to settle in and take full advantage of opportunities that can improve quality of care and quality of life for you or your loved one?

Any move is difficult for an older adult. Moving to a nursing facility is no exception. But family members and friends can do many things to reduce the physical and emotional stress involved. They can help plan the move, participate on the day of the move, and provide love and support afterwards. Use Form 26-A, *Nursing Facility Move-in Checklist*, to organize your efforts.

Before the Move

Nursing facility residents have the right to keep and use items of personal property to the extent space permits. But space is almost always in short supply. Choices will have to be made about what to take along and what to leave behind.

Friends and family can help by:

- Learning from the facility exactly what space limitations apply.

- Helping prepare for the move, including arranging for storage or care of items left behind.

- Marking all clothing and personal belongings with the person's name, and making a list of the resident's things.

- Anticipating and responding to special concerns, such as arranging care for a pet.

On the Day of the Move

On move-in day, a family member or friend can help reduce feelings of disorientation and dislocation by:

- Helping unpack, and making sure that pictures, personal mementos, and other similar items are placed where they will create a feeling of home.

- Sharing a meal at the new facility, getting to know staff members, and learning about the various programs, services, and activities the facility has to offer.

- Spending some quiet time after everything is unpacked to make sure your family member or friend is as comfortable, relaxed, and reassured as possible.

Settling In and Figuring Out Who's Who

You remember what it was like beginning a brand new school year or a new job. There was new information to absorb, new opportunities to learn about, new responsibilities. The first days and weeks in a care facility are like that.

One way to get your bearings is to learn about the staff and the different roles they play. Here are some brief profiles:

Ten Ways for Families and Friends to Stay in Touch

- Send flowers or balloons on a special day.

- Write cards or notes often.

- Visit as often as you can.

- Send pictures, audiotapes, or videotapes.

- Bring a card or small gift.

- Get to know the resident's new friends and care providers.

- Remember to thank members of staff whenever appropriate.

- Take another relative or friend with you.

- Help the person set up an e-mail account, then send e-mail frequently.

- Join the resident for a meal or special outing.

Medical Staff

All nursing and rehabilitative care services in a nursing facility are provided under the direction of the **resident's personal physician**. That means the facility's nursing staff will always be following the doctor's orders, and will check with the doctor when significant changes occur or new medical issues arise.

Residents have the right to choose their personal physician; but as a practical matter, the choices are limited to the doctors who agree to care for patients living in that nursing facility. It is helpful to find out in advance whether the resident's current physician can continue to provide services, or if a new physician needs to be chosen.

In addition, each facility has a **medical director** who helps establish appropriate care policies and procedures for the nursing staff and independent physicians who care for patients or residents living there.

Nursing Staff

Nursing staff play the primary role in delivering day-to-day care. The team leader is the **director of nursing**, who sets goals and standards and provides overall direction and management for delivering care. **Registered and licensed nurses** provide a wide variety of physician-prescribed treatments, including wound care, administration of medications, pain control, and catheterization. Nurses also help in assessing residents' needs, monitoring progress, and updating each resident's plan of care. **Certified nursing assistants**, also called CNAs or nurse aides, work to meet the residents' personal care needs. They support the nurses and assist with activities of daily living, such as feeding, bathing, dressing, and mobility.

Rehabilitative Services

Professionals in this department include **physical therapists**, **occupational therapists**, and **speech therapists**. They work with patients recovering from surgery or hospitalization, as well as conditions such as stroke, hip fracture, Parkinson's disease, and arthritis. The goal of rehabilitative care is to help each resident reach his or her highest level of function and, when medically feasible, prepare for discharge and return to independent living.

Social Services

Social workers help identify the emotional and social needs of each resident and provide or recommend appropriate services and support. For example, they help residents adjust to losses, chronic illness, and other challenges. They also help residents and their families understand how things work (including Medicare and Medicaid) and what opportunities and resources are available to them.

Pastoral Care

In many facilities, staff includes a **chaplain** or **pastoral care counselor**, whose job it is to support residents and their families on spiritual questions.

Dietary

Dietary staff are responsible for planning, preparing, and serving healthful, appetizing meals and snacks. They regularly review each resident's chart to make sure the prescribed diet meets the resident's nutritional needs and dietary restrictions.

Activities

Social and recreation activities are critical. They help a resident stay as physically active as possible, as well as providing important intellectual stimulation and emotional support. **Activities professionals** know that enjoying companionship and connection to others is essential for all of us. A facility's activities program is sometimes referred to as "therapeutic recreation" or "recreation therapy."

Care Planning and Care Conferences

Care planning is the way information about residents and their care needs is gathered, discussed, and reflected in a plan of care. Under the law, a resident's plan of care must be completed within 21 days of admission. It must be reviewed and updated at least quarterly. The law also requires each facility to keep residents fully informed of their health status, the plan of care, and any changes to either health status or plan of care.

The **care team** is the group that works together to create and carry out a resident's plan of care. If possible, the care team includes the resident as an active participant and decision maker. If a resident wishes, a family member or other representative is also encouraged to participate. Other team members include the resident's physician and representatives of the various disciplines involved in care, including nursing, social services, pastoral care, activities, therapy, and dietary departments.

Care conferences are one important way a resident's plan of care gets updated and

Getting Ready for a Care Conference

If you are a family member, here are some ways to get ready for a nursing facility care conference:

- When you receive word of an upcoming care conference, reply to the staff, letting them know whether or not you will be able to attend. If you can't make it in person, ask if a conference call is possible, or provide your input ahead of time by phone or e-mail.

- If you plan to attend, take some extra time to make sure you arrive on time or even a little early. Being early will let you visit with the resident and meet the caregivers, and will make things seem less rushed.

- Write down your questions or concerns. Make a note of information you wish to share with the care team. Form 26-B, *Resident/Family Care Conference Worksheet*, can be a good tool for organizing your points.

- Above all, speak up during the conference. Be constructive. Be polite. But also be assertive and clear in your views and expectations. Remember, there is no such thing as a "dumb" question.

information is shared within the care team. Every facility is unique in its approach to care conferences, the format they follow, and how often they take place. Care conferences play an important role in making sure everyone has accurate, up-to-date information about the resident, the resident's needs and wishes, and what steps and strategies the care team should be using to meet those needs.

To Sum Up . . .

Moving yourself or a loved one to a nursing facility can be a challenge. Preparation and organization will make the experience a positive one for everyone involved. The important factors, especially for family members involved in a move, are to:

- Plan ahead and be personally involved before, during, and after the move.

- Make an effort to meet the members of the care team and understand the various roles they play in a resident's care.

- If you can, take an active part in care conferences and the care planning process.

Adjusting to a nursing facility placement is rarely easy. However, you can make it easier with planning and support. You can do this, and it *can* be a positive transition in your life.

More Resources

- **The American Health Care Association**'s Long-Term Care Living website includes information about all stages of the nursing facility decision and transition. (*www.longtermcareliving.com*)

Quick Links

>>> These web-based resources may be accessed through our website:

www.aginginstride.org

ISSUE 27: YOUR RIGHTS AS A RESIDENT

Bill of Rights

Nursing facility residents have rights. And responsibilities. These have been set as governmental mandates, part of the stricter oversight of institutions that care for the frail elderly.

Most nursing facilities set their own high standards as institutions and for individual staff members. They seek to deliver high-quality care and to respect the dignity of their residents. However, even in well-run, well-intentioned nursing facilities, problems sometimes occur. Here's what you need to know about residents' rights, resident and family responsibilities, and how to manage problems that occur.

What Rights are Protected?

Facilities that participate in either Medicare or Medicaid must provide new residents and their families with detailed information about residents' rights, and about their own policies and procedures for protecting residents' rights.

In brief, these rights include:

- The right to always be treated with dignity and respect.

- The right to be informed about health status, care options, and other pertinent health information.

- The right to make one's own decisions as much as possible, and for as long as possible.

- The right to privacy during care and while visiting or speaking with others.

- The right to have health status and other personal information kept confidential.

- The right to be in contact with others.

- The right to have personal belongings kept safe, and funds and billing matters handled properly.

- The right to proper procedures on transfer, discharge, or change of room or roommate.

- The right to have complaints dealt with promptly, fairly, and without any fear of retaliation for complaining.

Residents Also Have Responsibilities

Along with their rights, residents also have some responsibilities. These include:

- Showing respect for the rights and property of others.

- Keeping the facility advised in matters of scheduling, such as appointments out of the facility and transportation needs.

- Helping to keep personal belongings safe and secure, for example, by marking clothing and other items with the resident's name.

- Paying on time for all items and services for which the resident is financially responsible.

- Taking part, as much as possible, in care planning and decision making, and considering whether or not to complete an advance health care directive.

- Treating staff with respect and courtesy.

- Informing the management promptly when a question, concern, or complaint arises.

Dealing with Concerns and Problems

Federal regulations protect your right to ask questions if there's something you don't understand and to file a complaint if a problem arises. The law, however, doesn't specify any procedures for dispute resolution. If you have a concern or complaint, you have four basic options. In most cases, you will want to begin with the most local, least formal option. If you don't receive satisfaction, proceed to the next level.

- **Voice your concern directly and informally with staff or a supervisor.** Most problems can be solved at this level. Again, most facilities and staff members want to do a good job.

- **Present a spoken or written complaint under the facility's "grievance procedure."** When residents enter a facility, they will be given written information about that institution's formal grievance process. Don't hesitate to use this process if necessary. Remember, all residents have a right to quality care and cannot be treated badly for lodging a complaint.

- **Contact the state or local long-term care ombudsman.** It is the specific job of these people to protect residents and help resolve grievances. For more information, see the box below.

- **File a complaint with the state's survey and certification agency.** If you have been unable to settle your problem at any of the previous levels, you may file a complaint with your state's accrediting and oversight agency. You can get the necessary address and phone numbers directly from the nursing facility, from your state or local long-term care ombudsman, or from the "Helpful Contacts" section of *www.medicare.gov*.

The Long-Term Care Ombudsman

The professional staff and/or trained volunteers who serve in a long-term care ombudsman program specialize in one thing: *problem-solving*. Here are some of the ways they can help:

- They listen to questions or concerns about the quality of care provided in a nursing or residential care facility.

- They investigate reported problems to discover what the situation is and recommend needed changes.

- They are an excellent source of information about long-term care in your area.

- They provide community education about long-term care.

- They get involved when needed to protect residents' rights.

- They support long-term care and assisted living facilities in promoting residents' independence and quality of life.

You can get the phone number for your area's long-term care ombudsman by calling Senior Information and Referral, or by looking it up online at *www.ltcombudsman.org*.

If you are dealing with a quality issue of some kind, use Form 27, *Worksheet for Questions, Concerns, and Complaints,* to organize your questions and concerns and let the facility know there's a problem. Most facilities also have their own complaint resolution form, so use that if you prefer.

Most nursing facilities genuinely want to know—and know as soon as possible—if a resident or family member is unhappy about a situation the facility could or should remedy. Remember, too, that expressing your concerns is your right. Every facility that participates in Medicare or Medicaid is legally required to have a procedure for receiving, investigating, and promptly acting on resident complaints. It is unlawful for a facility to discriminate or take any action against someone who exercises his or her right to express concern.

Saying "Thank You"

It's not part of any legal obligation, but if you feel that the facility and/or a staff member is particularly helpful, a written or even just a verbal "thank you" is always appreciated. Like life in a family, continuing relationships work best on a basis of goodwill, open communications, and mutual respect. Try to be as diligent in reporting your compliments as your complaints.

To Sum Up . . .

No nursing facility stay will be completely trouble-free. Where residents' rights and responsibilities are taken seriously, you can work quickly and courteously to resolve problems, and make sure that you or your loved one receives the highest quality care possible.

More Resources

- To find the phone number for your area long-term care ombudsman, check the **National Long-Term Care Ombudsman Resource Center** website. (*www.ltcombudsman.org*)

- To find your state's survey and certification agency, see the **U.S. Government's** website. (*www.medicare.gov*)

Quick Links

>>> These web-based resources may be accessed through our website:

www.aginginstride.org

Legal and Financial Concerns

INTRODUCTION

By the time most of us are ready to retire, we've had experience with understanding and solving certain kinds of legal and financial concerns. Over the years, for example, we've probably bought and sold anywhere from a few to a few dozen automobiles. We've signed dozens, maybe even hundreds, of legal documents in renting apartments, buying homes, applying for consumer credit or loans, and arranging our other business affairs.

We know that being informed, planning ahead, and making smart choices are important in legal and financial matters. A person's physical, mental, and spiritual health come first. But basic financial well-being and avoiding legal problems run close behind. If our legal and financial affairs are in order, it gives us freedom and peace of mind as we pursue life's more important goals. Therefore, it's important to focus on these issues.

In Issue 28, the topic is "taking care of business." Business in this context includes keeping track of what you own, fulfilling the obligations you have, and taking full advantage of insurance and other benefits to which you are entitled.

Issues 29 and 30 concern important legal documents: wills and other estate planning tools, guardianships, and durable powers of attorney.

In Issues 31, 32, and 33, we look at sources for payment of health care and other costs during retirement: Social Security, Medicare and Medicaid, and privately purchased long-term care insurance. How do these programs work? Who do they cover? What will they cover and not cover? In the case of long-term care insurance, should you consider purchasing this form of protection? If so, how do you go about comparing policies and making a good choice?

Finally, in Issues 34 and 35 we deal with two areas in which older adults too often become victims of unethical and illegal practices: consumer fraud and elder abuse. No one wants to be stolen from, defrauded, or intimidated at any point in their lives, least of all when they are, perhaps, feeling increasingly vulnerable.

As you address legal and financial issues in your life, you may wish to use these forms to organize your efforts:

- Form 28: *Confidential Personal Information*
- Form 33: *Checklist for Selecting Long-Term Care Insurance*

ISSUE 28: TAKING CARE OF BUSINESS

When the color of the paper in those window envelopes goes from white to pink—when the word "URGENT" is stamped on the envelope—when "CANCELLED" is typed across the bill, then we know our personal business is starting to get out of hand.

Or maybe our bills are paid on time, but a medical emergency arises and we cannot find our insurance card, Dad's Social Security number, or Mom's Medicare card. What company did we choose for that supplemental coverage? Many times, care providers and other professionals want important information from us when we are under stress, in a hurry, or confused.

Whether your goal is to regain control of a checkbook gone wild or to simply "get organized," a good first step is to complete an inventory of your personal records. Try using Form 28, *Confidential Personal Information*, to gather information. Whether you use our form or some other, your personal inventory should contain the following information:

- **Personal information**—Full legal name, address, Social Security number, driver's license number, Medicare and/or Medicaid number, Army I.D. number, or any other significant personal identification numbers.

- **Family and friends**—The names, addresses, and contact phone numbers of your children, as well as other close relatives or friends who should be notified in case of emergency.

- **Household support**—If you receive services in the home, from house cleaning to personal care or Meals On Wheels, list contact names and phone numbers.

- **Health care providers**—The names and phone numbers of your primary care physician and other physician specialists, pharmacy, hospital, and any other care facility.

- **Insurance information**—Company names, policy numbers and phone numbers for *all* health insurance, life insurance, homeowner's or renter's insurance, and automobile insurance.

- **Legal and financial**—Names and phone numbers for your lawyer, accountant, broker, financial advisor; also the institution names and account numbers of all bank and brokerage accounts, all safe deposit boxes, and all stock and bond certificates.

- **Estate planning documents**—Your will or other estate documents, health care directive, and powers of attorney, including appointment of a health care representative. Names, addresses, and phone numbers of those who hold both business and medical powers of decision-making on your behalf should be included.

- **Financial records**—The location of prior years' tax returns, this year's tax information, checkbooks and savings passbooks, all real estate documents, insurance policies, and other financial records.

Take your time, copy numbers carefully, and make sure all information is complete and up to date. Consider asking a close family member or a trusted friend to help you as you gather and record information. If you are married, you and your spouse should each fill out a form.

When you're done, make copies. Decide who should have a copy. Your son or daughter? Lawyer? Trusted friend? Accountant? Then get the copies filed, mailed and delivered. Good job! Putting together a personal inventory is a lot of work, but worth every minute of it in an emergency.

Help in Managing Business Affairs

Do you think you might need some help in managing the business of your life, but don't know where to start? You might notice that your personal business tends to fall into general categories of activity. While several of these areas will be treated in greater depth in the discussions that follow, such as long-term care insurance and Medicare, it might be helpful to think of your personal business as including the following activities.

- **Bill paying and bank records**—A range of alternatives is available to assist you, including online or electronic services from banks, bill-paying services, or just sitting down with a friend or family member on a regular basis to organize records and pay bills.

- **Taxes**—Support is available from accountants, tax preparation services, and trusted friends or family members.

- **Insurance**—Given the wide variety of insurance products marketed today, it can be confusing to assess and compare policies and coverage. We all want to be adequately—yet not overly—insured. A trustworthy insurance agent can help you evaluate your risks and policies to make certain you have what is reasonable and appropriate. For more information on long-term care insurance, see Issue 33, *Long-Term Care Insurance.*

- **Medicare and other health care bills**—Keeping track of medical paperwork can be overwhelming. You might want to set up a simple system to record your receipt and payment of medical bills. Often, the business offices of health care providers and hospitals are very helpful.

- **Investments**—Income from savings and investments such as stocks, annuities, and rental property might be part of your retirement plan. A trusted financial advisor or broker can manage your investments based on your personal financial objectives. You can be as involved or uninvolved in day-to-day decisions as you choose.

At some time in our lives, all of us are likely to need varying degrees of help with personal business. Time spent organizing papers now will ease stress levels later, when emergencies may arise. Developing patterns of talking with trusted advisors at appropriate times will help train you to seek out the right people at the right time.

If you think that day-to-day business is becoming too much for you and you either don't have close family or don't want family involved, there are a growing number of professionals who specialize in helping seniors in this way. To find a reputable business helper, try contacting:

- Your accountant.
- Your local senior center.
- Senior Information and Referral.
- Independent eldercare management professionals.

Knowing your business affairs are well-managed should bring you peace of mind and allow you to focus on those activities that give your life meaning and pleasure.

To Sum Up . . .

Staying on top of the business aspects of living is important in all stages of life. Information and paperwork have multiplied unmercifully in the past quarter century. But there is no reason to feel uneasy about getting help. Take care of the tasks you can manage, and delegate the rest. Getting help in taking care of business is not a form of giving up control, but rather a way of exercising responsibility, and making sure your business is handled properly and on time.

More Resources

- **The National Academy of Elder Law Attorneys** website features a searchable directory of attorneys specializing in elder law, as well as information on elder law issues. (*www.naela.com*)

- The American Bar Association's **Commission on Law and Aging** website includes information on a wide array of elder law issues, and a "Law and Aging Resource Guide," searchable by state. (*www.abanet.org/aging*)

- The National Council on Aging's website includes the **Benefits Checkup** calculator. (*www.benefitscheckup.org*)

- A **U.S. Government** website has a screening tool to help you find government benefits that you might be eligible to receive. (*www.govbenefits.gov*)

Quick Links

>>> These web-based resources may be accessed through our website: www.aginginstride.org

ISSUE 29: ESTATE PLANNING

Estate planning is the legal term for designating what you want to happen when you die or if you become incapacitated and unable to act for yourself. With the help of a lawyer, you create instruments such as wills, trusts, and advance directives that ensure that your wishes will be followed concerning the following questions:

- How do I want my property distributed after I die? Who do I want to be in charge of that process?

- If I lose the ability to handle my own financial affairs and act in my own best interests, who do I want to act on my behalf?

- With regard to my future health care, who do I want to make decisions for me if I can no longer make them for myself, and what specific wishes do I want to specify concerning how decisions should be made for me?

In this issue, we address the first of the three questions above: how will my property be distributed when I die, and who will be in charge of that process?

Alternatives for Transferring Assets at Death

When you die, the property you have accumulated in your lifetime—money, real estate, personal effects—will pass to others. For many older people, the process of planning and thinking about how to distribute their estate is a positive activity. It is a satisfying moment when you decide, for example, to leave your car to your daughter, money to help fund college educations to your grandchildren, and a life insurance policy or annuity to benefit your favorite charity. It honors the people and organizations that have been important to you in your lifetime.

There are five main ways of transferring property after your death:

- A will, in which you say specifically how your estate is to be distributed.

- A community property agreement in states that recognize this form of property ownership.

- Joint tenancies with right of survivorship and similar forms of property ownership.

- Trusts established during a person's lifetime that continue in effect upon death.

- If you leave no instructions or designation, then your estate will pass to your relatives according to rules spelled out in state law. If you have no relatives, your estate passes to the state itself.

Disposition According to the Terms of a Will

A person's will may be simple or complicated, depending on the size of the person's estate and the plan for distributing property. A will serves a number of purposes. It says how property is to be divided after a person dies. It also controls *when* property will pass. For example, your will might provide that your estate will pass to your spouse for his lifetime, and then be equally divided among your children.

A will also names an "executor," the person you designate to carry out the terms of your will. Powers and responsibilities of the executor are spelled out as part of the will.

For larger estates, a will and the estate planning that goes along with it might well include the following:

- Lifetime gifts of property.
- The creation of one or more trusts to ensure that specific goals and needs (for example, college education of grandchildren) are met.
- Charitable bequests.
- Steps taken to minimize or avoid tax liability.

When a person dies after making a will, the will usually has to go through "probate." This is a legal proceeding in which a court recognizes the validity of the will and approves the personal appointments (for example, executor, guardian, trustee), property transfers, and any other provisions it contains. Probate also gives creditors of the deceased an opportunity to come forward and make their claims for payment before the estate is distributed and closed.

Probate is almost always accomplished with the active involvement of a lawyer whose fee is paid from the assets of the estate. The executor and any trustees appointed under a will are also usually paid for their services. Many states have enacted probate reform laws, streamlining the court process considerably.

As you begin to think about creating or updating a will, before you meet with your lawyer, here are some questions you'll want to ask yourself:

- Who do I want to receive my property when I die? What individuals and organizations do I want to remember?

- Do I want to leave certain property in trust, rather than giving it outright? If so, who do I want to act as trustee?

- Do I want to make any religious or charitable bequests? If so, to what organizations or causes?

- Who do I want to name as my executor (and trustee, if your will creates a trust), and who should I name as my alternate choice, if my first choice is unable or unwilling to serve?

- Are there tax planning issues I should consider?

- Will probate proceedings be necessary?

Community Property Agreements

Some states recognize "community" ownership of property. Under community property laws, property acquired through the efforts of either a husband or a wife during marriage is presumed to be community property. Community property laws may also permit spouses to enter into a "community property agreement" in which both of them agree that all their property will automatically become the sole property of the surviving spouse at the moment one of them dies. A community property agreement may be useful in certain circumstances because it avoids the need for probate. Your lawyer can advise you whether community property agreements are permitted under the laws in your state and, if so, whether such an agreement would be beneficial in your situation.

Joint Tenancies with Right of Survivorship

Most states permit two or more persons to hold property as "joint tenants with right of survivorship." When property is owned this way, it passes automatically at death to the surviving joint tenant or tenants. Creating joint tenancies with right of survivorship may have tax implications, so this is another time when advice of a lawyer or other tax advisor is important.

State law specifies the steps required to create a joint tenancy with right of survivorship. In most states, for example, a joint tenancy with right of survivorship can only be created through a written document that specifically declares the intention of the owner/transferor to create a joint tenancy in which his or her interests will pass automatically on death.

Many people confuse a joint tenancy bank or investment account with simply giving another person the authority to sign checks, make deposits and withdrawals, and take other administrative actions. Under a joint tenancy with right of survivorship, the entire account balance automatically becomes the property of the surviving joint tenant or tenants when one joint tenant dies. That property is not considered part of the deceased's estate, as far as future ownership is concerned.

Authority to sign checks and make deposits and withdrawals, on the other hand, confers no ownership rights, either while the account owner is living or upon the death of the account owner.

When you set up joint accounts, it is important to be clear about your intention. If your purpose is to pass that property to another person outside your will, document your intention to create a joint tenancy with right of survivorship. If your purpose is simply to enable another person to act on your behalf in financial transactions, be equally clear in expressing your intentions, preferably by putting them in the form of a power of attorney.

Trusts

Trusts are another way you can transfer property without probate. Lawyers generally like trusts; they are very flexible estate planning tools that can be adapted to each person's unique circumstances.

Think of a trust as a three-way arrangement involving:

- A "trustor," the person who owns the property and places it in trust for the benefit of someone else.

- A "trustee," the third party who carries out the wishes of the person creating the trust.

- A "beneficiary" or "beneficiaries," who enjoy the benefit of the property according to the trustor's wishes, but who do not own or control it.

In a trust, the trustor transfers legal title to the trustee, who then has the responsibility of managing the property for the benefit of the beneficiary or beneficiaries. Trusts are different from other property transfers in that title to the property and the right to the income or other beneficial use of the property are in separate parties. The trustee has the responsibilities and burdens of property ownership and earns a fee for services rendered. The beneficiary enjoys the benefits of the property, but only to the extent provided under the terms of the trust.

Trusts are used for many purposes. For example:

- To assure professional management of property, and to relieve the beneficiary of the burdens of property management.

- To take advantage of legitimate strategies for avoiding or reducing taxes.

- To arrange for a number of beneficiaries to share in the income from or use of the trust property.

- To give a lifetime interest in property to one person (for example, to a surviving spouse), with ownership later passing to another person or group (for example, to children or grandchildren) when the first beneficiary dies.

- To provide financial security for minor children by making sure the trust assets are available for certain designated purposes, such as paying for college.

Trusts may be either "testamentary trusts" or "living trusts." Testamentary trusts are those established under the terms of a will and are put into effect upon the death of the trustor. Living trusts are created during the lifetime of the trustor and can be either revocable (subject to change) or irrevocable (not subject to change).

Living trusts can be set up so that the property included in the trust, potentially the entire estate of the trustor, passes at death according to the terms of the trust. If properly structured, a living trust can have the effect of avoiding probate as to the trust property.

Intestacy (Having No Will)

If you have no will or other arrangement for the distribution of your property when you die, it will pass under state law according to rules for "intestate succession." These rules vary from state to state. In some states, for example, the law provides that if a man dies without a will and is survived by his wife and two children, his estate, after payment of debts, taxes, and expenses of administration, goes half to his wife and one quarter to each of his children.

There are good reasons for not relying on intestacy laws to do your estate planning for you. What the law says and what you would choose for yourself are probably two different things.

To Sum Up . . .

Estate planning sounds like an expensive and intimidating process, but it will go quickly and smoothly if you take some time to map out your goals. If you have done no planning, there's no time like the present to go see a lawyer who will help you decide what planning tools and documents work best for you. If you did your estate planning several years ago, it could be out of date. You should review your estate planning with your lawyer every five to 10 years. It is just one more way of staying in control of your life.

More Resources

- The **American Bar Association** website contains articles and information about estate planning, including the online "ABA Guide to Wills and Estates." It also features the searchable "Lawyer Referral Service." (*www.abanet.org*)

- The **Lawyer Locator** is a service of the Martindale Hubbell Legal Network. The website offers a searchable database of attorneys, as well as legal articles and other resources. (*www.martindale.com*)

- The **NOLO Law for All** "Plain English Law Centers" website includes estate planning information covering wills, trusts and probate, and many other legal subjects. (*www.nolo.com*)

- The **National Institute on Aging Agepages** website features fact sheets on various aspects of estate planning. (*www.nia.nih.gov*)

Quick Links

>>> These web-based resources may be accessed through our website:
www.aginginstride.org

ISSUE 30: DURABLE POWERS OF ATTORNEY AND GUARDIANSHIPS

In Issue 24, we discussed planning for future health care decisions, specifically the use of a health care power of attorney to give another person the authority to act on your behalf. Now, we turn to a very similar concern: "If I become incapacitated and can no longer manage my own financial and personal affairs—say, because of a stroke, head injury or Alzheimer's disease—who will manage them for me?"

When a person loses the ability to act independently, someone else must step in to act for that person until the person either regains the ability to act or dies. From a legal perspective, there are two ways to designate that person: through a durable power of attorney or by a court-created guardianship.

Durable Power of Attorney

A durable power of attorney is a legal document where one person, the "maker," appoints someone else to act as "attorney in fact" or "agent" in case of the maker's incapacity. Powers of attorney are called "durable" when the maker clearly states that this appointment is to continue in effect even in case of incapacity.

Ordinarily a power of attorney is a temporary document. For example, you might want to give someone temporary authority to sign documents and pay bills while you are away on a trip. Under the law, an ordinary power of attorney comes to an end automatically on the death or incapacity of the person who created it.

In contrast, a durable power of attorney is intended to be permanent. The document can be written in such a way that it takes effect immediately, or it can provide that the agent's power only begins once the maker has lost the ability to understand and make decisions. A durable power of attorney that takes effect right away has the advantage that the agent can act immediately in case of an emergency. Conversely, a durable power of attorney that first requires a determination of incapacity has a built-in check-and-balance provision: activation depends on a judgment call by one or more people other than or in addition to the designated agent. The procedures for determining incapacity must be spelled out in the document itself.

There are other checks and balances that tend to prevent abuse and protect someone who signs a durable power of attorney. For example:

- You don't have to appoint just one representative; you may, if you prefer, name a panel of two or three persons to take actions on your behalf.

- You retain the power to revoke (cancel) your durable power of attorney at any time up to the point of incapacity.

- You may include in your durable power of attorney specific instructions and conditions that will limit and guide your agent in the actions taken on your behalf.

A durable power of attorney is an important, powerful, and flexible tool in estate planning. It gives you control over who will act for you if you are incapacitated. In its absence, if you become incapacitated, the alternative is a guardianship.

Guardianship

A guardianship is a legal proceeding in which a court-supervised guardian is appointed to administer the affairs of a "ward," someone who is incapable of acting on his or her own.

A legal guardian occupies a position of trust and responsibility, and is empowered to make essential decisions for the person who is incapacitated. The laws of guardianship have evolved over the years, with most states now recognizing two different types: *full* and *limited*.

The law aims to protect as much of a person's freedom and autonomy as possible. If a person is incapable of making any personal, medical, or financial decisions, a full guardianship will be established. But if the person only needs help in some areas but not in others, a guardianship with more limited powers may be appropriate.

How Do You Know When Someone Needs a Guardian?

In most cases, this is not an easy question to answer. Here are some factors to consider if you face the issue for a spouse or other loved one:

- Can the person keep track of important documents, remember to pay bills on time, and manage a checkbook?

- Is the person able to follow conversations about important financial or medical matters and make informed, thoughtful decisions?

- Is the person able to communicate his or her wishes clearly?

How a Guardianship Works

The process of setting up a guardianship begins when someone, usually a member of the family, asks the court to name a guardian. An attorney is almost always involved in drawing up the papers and presenting them in court.

The judge looks at the situation and decides three things:

- Is a guardian needed?
- Who should be appointed as the guardian?
- What powers and duties will the guardian have?

If the prospective ward has stated his or her wishes ahead of time, the judge will usually take those wishes into account. For example, a person might include in an advance directive or other legal document language such as: "If it ever becomes necessary to have a guardian appointed for me, it is my wish that my son John be appointed."

Who Should Serve as Guardian?

Usually, the person appointed as guardian is a family member or close friend.

Before agreeing to serve as guardian, a person should:

- Understand what the responsibilities will be.
- Try to learn about the person he or she will be acting for, including any wishes the person has made known while still able.
- Realize that a guardian is always expected to act with honesty, promptness, and respect for the ward's best interests.

Acting as a person's guardian is a very important way of caring for a loved one. It is a big responsibility, but also a rewarding one. If you take on this job for a loved one, you will know that loving, kind, and prudent decisions are being made on that person's behalf.

How Much Will it Cost?

The expenses in setting up a guardianship usually include:

- Attorney's fees.
- Court filing fees.
- The cost of any independent evaluations.
- The guardian's bond and compensation, if any.

Check with your attorney concerning these and other possible expenses, and to find out whether public funds or the assets of the person involved might be available to pay these costs.

How To Get Started

If your concern is for the future and completing a durable power of attorney is still an option, that's the place to start. Talk things over, make sure wishes are clearly understood, and make sure the person being appointed is willing and able to serve.

If a durable power of attorney is no longer an option, discuss your loved one's situation with the doctor and the attorney. If your loved one is incapacitated in one or more areas, the attorney can help you evaluate the need for a guardianship and decide how to proceed.

To Sum Up . . .

Losing the ability to understand and decide things for ourselves is a risk we all face. The longer we live, the greater the risk becomes. A durable power of attorney is the best way to say ahead of time who we want to manage our financial and personal affairs if we can't do it for ourselves.

If an individual has already become mentally incapacitated, it is too late for a durable power of attorney. In that situation, a court-appointed guardian will take over decision making.

Once again, planning ahead helps! If you make a durable power of attorney, you will retain control of your affairs even when you are unable to act for yourself.

More Resources

Quick Links

>>> These web-based resources may be accessed through our website:

www.aginginstride.org

- The **American Bar Association** website contains articles and information about selecting and working with an attorney, as well as the "Lawyer Referral Service." (*www.abanet.org*)

- The **Lawyer Locator** is a service of the Martindale Hubbell Legal Network. The website offers a searchable database of attorneys, as well as legal articles and other resources. (*www.martindale.com*)

- The **NOLO Law for All** "Plain English Law Centers" website includes estate planning information covering guardianships and durable powers of attorney. (*www.nolo.com*)

ISSUE 31: SOCIAL SECURITY

The Social Security System is the U.S. government's "safety net," a program to help provide a continuing income for people who are retired or disabled, their dependents, and dependent survivors. Almost all workers pay Social Security taxes throughout their working lives. Employers pay a matching amount. Social Security retirement benefits are not charity; retired persons who receive Social Security benefits earned that benefit through payroll taxes.

Social Security income is not intended to be the only source of income for retired persons. It is intended to supplement money saved through pension plans, savings, and investments.

How Do I Qualify?

Social Security benefits are available if you:

- Have retired and reached at least age 62 or are totally disabled; and
- Have earned enough credits towards eligibility (10 years of paying Social Security taxes); or
- Are a dependent survivor of a worker.

Some people who have not worked for pay, such as homemakers, or who worked for limited years, can still receive benefits as dependents of workers.

How Much Will I Receive?

The amount of your monthly Social Security check depends on several factors, especially these two:

Your Earnings

The Social Security Administration figures your benefit amount using a formula that takes into account your average annual earnings since you began working. Both the Social Security taxes you pay while working and the benefits you receive after retirement depend on your income level.

People who earn a higher salary pay higher Social Security taxes and also receive higher benefits. However, there is a limit to the amount a person pays and receives. Lower income workers actually receive a proportionally higher amount of Social Security income.

Your Age When You Begin Receiving Benefits

The earliest possible age to receive retirement benefits is 62. If you begin then, your benefit will be significantly lower than if you wait until you are a little older. You will receive the largest possible amount if you begin at "full retirement age." Your full retirement age depends on the year in which you were born. If you were born in 1937 or before, your full retirement age is 65; for those born after 1937, full retirement age increases a bit. (For example, full retirement age for a person born in 1939 is 65 plus four months; for someone born between 1943 and 1954, it is now 66.)

Once you reach full retirement age, there is no limit to the amount you can earn and still be collecting your Social Security benefits. Before you have reached full retirement age, however, your benefits may be reduced based on how much you are earning by continuing to work.

If you take early retirement, the amount of your benefit checks will be permanently lower, depending on how early you retire. If, however, medical disability is your reason for retirement, you might qualify for Social Security disability benefits. In that case, you will receive the full amount of retirement benefits when you reach retirement age.

Give Yourself a "Benefits Checkup"

BenefitsCheckUp is a web-based program for older Americans and their families and caregivers. This program, a service of the National Council on the Aging, lets you know quickly and confidentially the benefits for which you qualify and how to go about claiming them. It covers, for example, Social Security, Medicaid, food stamps, government-supported weatherization programs, as well as state-administered programs like pharmacy assistance, property tax relief, vocational rehabilitation, and in-home services. To check out your own benefits picture, go to *www.benefitscheckup.org* and follow the instructions.

Other conditions do apply, so be sure to find out about your own case as you plan your retirement. You can request a *Personal Earnings and Benefit Estimate Statement* from the Social Security Administration at any time. Start there, and if you have questions, call the number listed on the statement for further information.

How to Sign Up for Social Security

Start planning early! In the years before you plan to retire, you should talk to a Social Security representative. Have your most current *Personal Earnings and Benefit Estimate Statement* in front of you. Remember that the benefit estimate in that statement is based on the norm. In fact, a number of factors contribute to determining your actual benefit amount, so get the information you need in order to receive the maximum benefit.

When you are ready to apply to receive Social Security benefits, you can do it by phone at 1-800-772-1213. Or, call that number to make an appointment to visit your local Social Security office.

For More Information

If you have questions about Social Security, to sign up for Social Security, or to find out how much Social Security income you can expect to receive:

- Call 1-800-772-1213 with questions.
- Make an appointment to visit your local Social Security office.
- Visit the Social Security website on the Internet at *www.ssa.gov*.

To Sum Up . . .

Social Security is an important source of retirement income for most older Americans. How much you receive under Social Security will depend on several factors, including how much you've earned over the years you have paid into the system and how old you are when you retire. If you are at an age when you are doing some pre-retirement planning, you can obtain information on how much you can expect to receive each month from the Social Security Administration and then plan from that information.

More Resources

Quick Links

>>> These web-based resources may be accessed through our website: www.aginginstride.org

- The U.S. Government's **Social Security Administration** website includes information about the Social Security program, including retirement planning, contact information and a benefits calculator. (*www.ssa.gov*)

- The online consumer information column, **"Ask Mary Jane,"** contains useful insights to the ins and outs of Social Security benefits. (*www.ncpssm.org*)

- The National Council on the Aging's website includes the **Benefits Checkup** calculator. (*www.benefitscheckup.org*)

- *www.GovBenefits.gov* is a screening tool to help you find government benefits that you may be eligible to receive.

- The **NOLO Law for All** website includes a series of articles about social security. (*www.nolo.com*)

ISSUE 32: MEDICARE AND MEDICAID

Understanding Medicare

Medicare is the U.S. government's health insurance program. Medicare provides health care coverage for most American adults age 65 and over, for people of any age with permanent kidney failure, and for certain people under age 65 who are disabled. Medicare is the largest purchaser of health care services in the United States.

Health care costs in the United States continue to soar. In order to provide coverage to the growing number of people who need it, Medicare must contain the cost of care provided. It's a complicated and controversial system; you have probably read about it often in the news. Every year there are changes to Medicare funding and benefits, with the promise (or threat) of more extensive changes in the future.

Here is a basic picture of how Medicare works: Medicare lets you choose the way that you will receive your benefits. The original Medicare plan is the traditional fee-for-service arrangement, meaning you go to your choice of doctors and Medicare pays a designated amount for every office visit or procedure. Other choices, such as Medicare Managed Care Plans, Health Maintenance Organizations, Preferred Provider Organizations, or Provider Sponsored Organizations, may also be available in your area. Call 1-800-633-4227 or visit the Medicare website (*www.medicare.gov*) to find out what Medicare options exist in your community. Your local library or senior center may also be able to help you find this information.

Medicare has two parts: Part A–Hospital Insurance; and Part B–Medical Insurance.

Medicare Part A—Hospital Insurance

Most people get Part A coverage automatically when they turn age 65. They pay no premium for Part A, because they (or their spouse) paid Medicare taxes while they were working.

People who did not pay Medicare taxes while working may be able to buy Part A coverage. Contact the Social Security Administration toll-free at 1-800-772-1213 for information.

Medicare Part A covers most services provided by institutional health care providers. If you are enrolled, here is what is covered:

Hospital Inpatient Services

If you need to go to the hospital for medical services or surgery, Medicare will pay that hospital a set sum based on your diagnosis. The amount is based on the average cost of care for persons with the same diagnosis in the same region. The Medicare payment to the hospital covers charges for inpatient hospital care, including:

- A semi-private room.
- Meals.
- Treatments and testing procedures.
- Intensive care.
- Medications.
- Equipment.
- Nursing care.

Certain limitations apply:

- **Number of days coverage**—Medicare will pay for up to 90 days in the hospital during any benefit period. A benefit period begins when you start receiving care covered by Medicare, and ends 60 days after you are finally discharged. There is no limit to the number of benefit periods you can have. Each person covered by Medicare is also entitled to a lifetime "reserve" of up to 60 days hospitalization. Care in a psychiatric hospital is covered by Medicare, but subject to a 190-day lifetime limitation.

- **Deductible expenses**—"Deductible" means the amount of health care expenses you must pay every year before Medicare begins to pay. The amount of the deductible is adjusted from year to year. In 2004, for example, a person covered by Medicare pays the first $876 of hospital charges.

- **Beneficiary co-payment**—If you are covered under Medicare Part A, you must also pay an amount (a co-payment or co-insurance) for each hospitalization that extends beyond 60 days. In 2004, the charge is $219 per day for the 61st through the 90th day of hospitalization, and $438 per reserve day (91st through 150th day).

Skilled Nursing Facility Care

Because of the high cost of care, the Medicare program exerts considerable pressure on hospitals to discharge patients as soon as possible. In many cases, this means that patients will be well enough to leave the hospital, but not well enough to return home. Therefore, Medicare covers the costs of care in a skilled nursing facility, a nursing home, or sub-acute care or rehabilitation facility, on a limited basis (up to 100 days). All charges are paid for the first 20 days; a required co-insurance amount begins if you have to stay longer.

Covered services include semi-private room, meals, skilled nursing services, rehabilitation services, medications, and medical supplies. Skilled nursing facility coverage is subject to various conditions. For example:

- Admission to a skilled nursing facility must follow a period of at least three consecutive days of hospitalization.

- The stay must be for further treatment of the same condition for which the person was hospitalized, and must begin within 30 days after hospital discharge.

- The patient must require skilled nursing or rehabilitation services on a daily basis.

- After 20 days, the patient is responsible for a co-payment for each day's charges (up to $109.50 per day in 2004).

Medicare does not cover skilled nursing facility care as a long-term or custodial care alternative. If you need non-medical services, such as meal preparation, housekeeping, or help with personal grooming, you must pay for it privately, or the costs may be covered by Medicaid.

Hospice Care for the Terminally Ill

The Medicare Hospice Benefit pays for hospice care for people who wish it and who have been diagnosed with a terminal illness. For a patient to receive this benefit, his or her physician must certify that he or she is expected to live less than six months. There are no deductibles to the hospice benefit, but the patient pays some limited costs.

Not all hospice providers are licensed to receive the Medicare Hospice Benefit, so it is important to check with your preferred hospice provider to see if it qualifies. Even if your hospice provider cannot receive the Medicare hospice benefit, Medicare may pay for some aspects of your hospice care under home health care benefits.

Home Health Care

Medicare covers home health care services for people who are essentially confined to their homes, who need occasional skilled medical and nursing care, but who do not need to be in an institutional setting.

This includes persons recently released from a hospital or skilled nursing facility and those with chronic health problems that require ongoing treatment. Medicare covers:

- Part-time or intermittent nursing care.
- Physical, occupational, and speech therapy.
- Medical social services.
- Limited home health aide services.
- Medical supplies and durable medical equipment.

These services are paid in full, except for a 20 percent co-payment for medical equipment such as wheelchairs, walkers, and commodes.

2003 Medicare Reform Act

In late 2003, Congress passed and the President signed into law major changes to Medicare. Here are some of the highlights of the new law:

Prescription Drug Benefit

Interim Drug Card. For the years 2004 and 2005, Medicare recipients will be able to purchase a drug discount card. The hope is that these cards will save participating seniors 15 percent or more on their prescription drug costs.

Coverage for Prescription Drugs. Starting in 2006, Medicare beneficiaries will be able to sign up for an optional Medicare drug plan or join a private health plan that includes drug coverage. Under the Medicare plan, the premium is expected to average $35 per month, or $420 a year. How much the plan will pay toward drug costs will vary depending on how much those costs are in a given year.

The various coverage percentages are shown in the following table:

	Annual Drug Costs	Medicare Pays	Beneficiary Pays
Deductible:	First $250	0%	100%
Basic Coverage:	From $251 up to $2,250	75%	25%
Coverage Gap:	From $2,251 to $5,100	0%	100%
Catastrophic Coverage:	Above $5,101	95%	5%

Help for Low-Income Beneficiaries. In 2004 and 2005, low-income Medicare beneficiaries will receive an annual subsidy of $600 to help cover the cost of drugs purchased with one of the new drug discount cards. Then, beginning in 2006, the premium, deductible, and coverage gap will be waived completely for people with incomes below $12,123 per year and partially waived for incomes up to $13,500 per year. Limitations based on the assets a person owns also apply.

Retiree Coverage. The new law includes more than $70 billion over 10 years in incentives to employers who continue providing a private drug benefit to retirees after the Medicare drug benefit begins in 2006.

Generic Drugs and Imports from Canada. The law is expected to speed up the process of making generic drugs available for purchase in place of more expensive brand-name drugs. The new law also contains provisions that may remove the ban on importing certain drugs from Canada, where they are less expensive.

Part B Deductible and Premium Increases

Beginning in 2005, the Part B deductible (see next section) will increase from $100 to $110, and it will be adjusted each year thereafter to keep pace with growth in Medicare spending for doctors' services and outpatient care. The Medicare Part B premium will also increase for people with incomes over $80,000 per year.

New Coverage for Physicals and Screenings

The new law adds some new Medicare benefits, including coverage for an initial physical examination for beneficiaries and screenings for diabetes and cardiovascular disease.

Medicare Part B—Medical Insurance

Medicare Part B is an optional part of the Medicare program. When you enter the Medicare program, you must decide whether or not to subscribe to Part B services. If you do elect Part B coverage, there is a premium to pay, which is deducted from your Social Security check. (In 2003, for example, the monthly premium was $58.70.)

For most seniors, it makes sense to pay the Part B premium for the coverage it offers. The services Medicare Part B covers include:

- Physician services.
- Outpatient hospital services.
- Physical and occupational therapy.
- Speech pathology services.
- X-rays, laboratory charges, and other diagnostic tests.

- Durable medical equipment such as wheelchairs, crutches, special beds.
- Ambulance service.
- Prosthetic devices.
- Outpatient surgical and rehabilitation services.
- Certain medications.

Medicare Part B does *not* pay for:

- Most prescription drugs.
- Routine physical exams.
- Services not related to the treatment of illness or injury.
- Dental care.
- Dentures.

- Cosmetic surgery.
- Routine foot care.
- Hearing aids.
- Eye examinations.
- Eyeglasses.

The limitations on coverage through Medicare Part B include an annual deductible of $100 and a co-pay of 20 percent of the Medicare-approved charge.

The phrase "Medicare-approved charge" is important. Medicare has a formula it uses to approve payment of a certain amount, even if this is less than the actual charge. For example: Mrs. Johnson goes to see her doctor. Her doctor charges $90 for the visit. When Medicare receives the bill, it decides through its formula that the approved charge for this type of visit is $70. Medicare will then pay the physician 80 percent of that $70, or $56 (if the patient has already paid the annual

$100 co-payment). Mrs. Johnson must pay the balance, or $34.

Some health care providers "*accept assignment.*" This means they are willing to settle for only the payment that Medicare allows. The benefit to doctors is that if they accept assignment, Medicare pays them directly. The benefit to the patient is a lower charge. If you have a choice of doctors, do not hesitate to ask if they accept assignment. It can mean a significant savings for you.

How to Enroll in Medicare

If you are already receiving Social Security benefits by the month of your 65th birthday, you will automatically be enrolled in Medicare Part A and Part B. If you do not want Part B, follow the instructions that come with your Medicare card.

If you are approaching age 65, you may apply for Social Security and Medicare at the same time. You should apply three months before your birthday.

If you did not opt for Medicare Part B when you first signed up, you may enroll during the General Enrollment Period of January 1–April 1 of each year. Note: if you don't enroll in Part B during your first possible enrollment period, your premium may be higher later. To find out about that and other special cases (such as having other insurance through a working spouse), call the toll-free number, or visit the Medicare web site.

To enroll in Medicare, visit your local Social Security office, or call Social Security at 1-800-772-1213. If you are also applying for Social Security, you may be able to apply on the Internet at *www.ssa.gov*.

Organizing and Paying Your Medical Bills

Medicare is a wonderful resource for older adults, but the bookkeeping task can be a challenge! Even an ordinary illness can result in a mass of confusing paperwork. It helps to have a system to keep track of your medical bills.

As you organize and pay your share of medical bills, two things will be helpful. First, all Medicare "Explanations of Benefits" are referenced by the date the service was provided, so keep track of the service dates on the bills. Second, remember the distinction between the Medicare-approved charge and the actual charge for service.

Because dealing with medical bills under Medicare can be so cumbersome and intimidating, many older adults fail to take full advantage of benefits for which they have paid through a lifetime of contributions. Understanding the process can improve the quality of your health care and save you money. Don't be afraid to ask for help. Those who work in the billing departments of doctors' offices, hospitals, and other health care providers are skilled in answering questions about Medicare and straightening out claim problems. Generally they are happy to help you.

If You Have a Question About Your Medicare Benefits

If you have questions about what Medicare has and has not covered, call the phone number on the "Explanation of Benefits" form. That form also explains the process for having your Medicare benefit officially reviewed. A call to the hospital or doctor's office may show that the doctor made an error in his or her Medicare paperwork (doctors are human too!) or that a processing error has been made. It is easy to have the claim resubmitted properly. If you have questions about why any procedure or office visit was not covered, don't just assume it's a coverage problem. Ask questions until you get satisfactory answers.

If you have any questions or would like to order informative booklets, call the Medicare toll-free number: 1-800-633-4227. For the most up-to-date information about Medicare policies and benefits, go to the Medicare website at *www.medicare.gov*.

Supplemental or "Medigap" Insurance

Medicare will not cover all of your health care costs. Deductibles, co-payments, and medical charges beyond Medicare's approved limits can add up quickly. That is why approximately two-thirds of all Medicare recipients purchase a supplemental or "Medigap" policy. "Medigap" means that these health insurance policies are intended to fill in the "gaps" in Medicare coverage—the charges you would have to pay out of pocket.

Medigap policies are standardized in most states, so you can easily compare policies and prices as you shop. (Policies are categorized as Plans A through J—from least to most comprehensive.) Insurance companies must follow federal guidelines that require each policy to include certain core benefits, such as co-payments and extended hospital coverage. For a higher premium, you can purchase more comprehensive coverage for such items as prescription drugs, preventative care, and the amount of your deductible. In some states, you can also choose a "Medicare Select" policy, costing less than standard policies, but including a restricted choice of physicians and hospitals. Medigap coverage is parallel to Medicare—that is, if an item is not covered at all by Medicare, Medigap policies won't cover it either. For example, Medigap policies do not cover long-term care, vision or dental care, hearing aids, or private duty nursing.

Before deciding to purchase a Medigap policy, it is important to assess your needs and to decide which features are right for you. Read each policy carefully to be certain what is covered, as well as what restrictions or exclusions exist. For example, not all plans cover home health care or emergency health care during travel in a foreign country. For a convenient comparison of policies in your state, go to "Medigap Compare" on the U.S. Government's *www.medicare.gov* website.

Not everyone needs Medigap insurance. If you are enrolled in the Medicare Managed Plan, you do not need a Medigap policy, and it is illegal for a company to sell you one. If you meet (or are close to meeting) the financial criteria for Medicaid, you also do not need a supplemental policy.

Medigap policies are guaranteed renewable, which means they cannot be cancelled unless you fail to pay the premium. The best time to purchase a Medigap supplemental policy is within six months of enrolling in Medicare Part B. During this time period, you cannot be denied coverage due to pre-existing health conditions. If you do not purchase a policy during the initial enrollment period, you may not be accepted later by the company you choose, or you may have to pay more.

That said, don't be pressured into rushing as you select a plan. Weigh the benefits of various policies; be clear on what is covered and what the premiums will be. Work with an agent who comes highly recommended and who is familiar with Medigap policies.

For more information about Medicare supplemental insurance, or for help selecting a policy, contact your state's Health Insurance Counseling and Advocacy Project office or State Health Insurance Assistance Program. These agencies provide free, confidential advice to Medicare beneficiaries and their families. You can locate your state's insurance assistance program by calling the Eldercare Locator at 1-800-677-1116 or online at *www.eldercare.gov*.

Understanding Medicaid

The Social Security Act of 1965 created two major health care programs for Americans. One was Medicare. The other was Medicaid (or, in California, "MediCal").

Eligibility for Medicare is determined by how old you are. In contrast, Medicaid eligibility depends on your economic situation, the income and/or resources you have.

Today, over 40 million Americans, many of them seniors, receive health care services paid for by the Medicaid program.

In the sections that follow, we discuss some typical Medicaid questions. Medicaid is administered by state governments, so eligibility and coverage vary from state to state. Be sure you follow up on this general information by looking into the specific program benefits and requirements of your state. We'll try to get you pointed in the right direction.

Can I Give My "Resources" Away in Order to Qualify for Medicaid?

This is a question many people ask. They want to know whether they can give their non-exempt property to their children, rather than "spending it down." The answer to this question is complicated and needs to be discussed with a knowledgeable lawyer or other advisor who knows the rules in your state. Generally speaking, though, a person will be considered **ineligible** for nursing facility Medicaid coverage if all of the following are true:

- The property is transferred to someone other than a spouse.

- It is given away or sold for less than its true value.

- The transfer is within 30 months of when the person applies for Medicaid.

- The purpose of the transfer (as judged by the state) was to qualify for Medicaid.

What is Medicaid?

Medicaid is a joint federal- and state-funded program to help pay the cost of medical expenses for the poor. Each state designs and administers its own Medicaid program, and there is great variety among the states as to how Medicaid is organized, who is eligible, and what specifically is covered. All states provide some coverage for low-income older adults for:

- Payment of Medicare Part B premiums.
- Payment of Medicare co-payments and deductibles.
- Extended nursing facility care.

Of these covered items, and other items such as prescription drugs, eyeglasses, and hearing aids, which are covered in some states, by far the most crucial and most expensive is Medicaid's coverage of long-term care in a nursing facility. Each year Medicaid pays for about half of the nursing facility care delivered in this country. Older people who need long-term care and who have modest assets quickly find their personal assets depleted, and thus become Medicaid-eligible some time after they have entered a nursing home.

Medicaid and Nursing Facilities

Income Limits

Unlike Medicare, Medicaid is not automatically available to people. To qualify for Medicaid, a person's monthly income and overall resources must be below a specific amount.

For purposes of the Medicaid program, the word "income" includes all monthly or periodic money received from sources such as Social Security, pensions, the military, or annuities. Medicaid does not consider money generated from property owned, such as stock dividends, rents, or real estate contract payments, to be income. Instead, property generating a monthly income is treated as a resource. Resources are discussed in the section below.

States vary in deciding how much income a Medicaid applicant is allowed to have and still qualify for benefits. Some states only provide benefits for people with income below a specified amount. Other states have no specific income limit but instead allow participation on a sliding scale basis.

For a married couple where one spouse needs nursing home care, Medicaid will usually consider only the income of the spouse in the nursing home in determining income eligibility. So, if your spouse is in a nursing home and his or her only income is $500 from Social Security, only that amount would be considered in determining Medicaid eligibility. Your own income would be disregarded.

Check with your local Medicaid agency to see how income limits are set in your state.

Resource Limits

For Medicaid eligibility purposes, "resources" typically include everything a person owns, except income. For example, that would include a home, bank accounts, individual retirement accounts (IRAs), insurance policy cash surrender values, and vehicles.

Federal and state laws determine the maximum amount of resources a Medicaid-eligible person in a nursing facility may keep. However, some kinds of resources are typically disregarded in this calculation—in other words, you can keep them and still qualify for Medicaid. Examples include the family home, if a spouse or dependent relative is still living in it; one car; household furnishings and personal effects; a certain amount of life insurance; a certain amount for a burial fund.

Medicaid will also exclude (allow to be kept) certain resources if a person in a nursing home is married to a spouse who doesn't live in the nursing facility. Medicaid refers to this person as the "community spouse."

Check with the Medicaid agency in your state to learn what resource limits and exceptions would apply in your situation.

Applying for Medicaid

If you think you or your loved one may qualify for Medicaid, you should contact the Medicaid agency in your state—or your loved one's state—to learn about its application procedure. If the person applying is already in a hospital or nursing facility, there may be a social worker or discharge planner on staff who can help with the application process. Start by getting a clear picture of the state's eligibility rules relating to income and resources.

A Medicaid applicant has the right to request a hearing if the application for Medicaid is denied. Pay close attention to the time deadlines for filing an appeal.

The procedures and filing deadlines are included in or attached to any denial notice. A person appealing a Medicaid application denial may be eligible for free legal services to work on the appeal through their local legal aid office.

Medicaid is a complex and sometimes frustrating government program. However, it provides necessary resources for health care for many older adults, especially those needing long-term care. If you think you or your loved one may be nearing the point of Medicaid eligibility, contact the state Medicaid office and get all the pertinent information.

To Sum Up . . .

Medicare and Medicaid, despite their difficulties and political battles, provide many necessary services to older adults, the disabled, and the poor. Working with these large government agencies is not easy. The rules are endless, and the paperwork often frustrating. However, if you take the time to understand the rules and work with the system, these programs can provide significant benefits for you and those you love.

More Resources

- The U.S. government's **Medicare** website contains information on all aspects of the Medicare program. (*www.medicare.gov*)

Quick Links

>>> These web-based resources may be accessed through our website: www.aginginstride.org

- **Medigap Compare**, the "Medicare Personal Plan Finder," is a tool on the Medicare.gov website that allows you to easily compare Medigap policies in your state. (*www.medicare.gov/mgcompare/home.asp*)

- The U.S. government's **Centers for Medicare and Medicaid Services** includes information about Medicaid and links to state programs. (*www.cms.gov*)

- The **NOLO Law for All** "Plain English Law Centers" website has information on Medicare, Medicaid, and Medigap insurance. (*www.nolo.com*)

ISSUE 33: LONG-TERM CARE INSURANCE

You may never need care in a nursing facility, but consider the following information:

- Around 6 percent of all Americans over the age of 65 live in a nursing facility.

- By the age of 85, that percentage rises to over 20 percent.

- Half of all people 85 and over need help with the activities of daily living.

Many Americans assume that if they ever develop a chronic, long-term disability, their health insurance, Medicare, or Medicaid will pay for their care. The reality is that private health insurance and Medicare cover only limited nursing facility costs, and Medicaid pays only under certain conditions. Supplemental (Medigap) insurance, likewise, covers only minimal, short-term nursing facility stays. Purchasing long-term care insurance is a wise choice for many people.

What is Long-Term Care Insurance?

As with any form of insurance, when you purchase long-term care insurance, you are regularly paying a relatively small sum (or premium) to protect against the risk that you might someday have to pay a much larger amount—in this case, the potentially huge cost of extended care in a nursing facility. Most long-term care insurance policies cover not only nursing facility care, but also some types of home care and other care options.

Who Should Have It?

Financial planning can be complicated; it may not be a simple decision for you whether or not to purchase long-term care insurance. Your financial advisor or insurance agent can help you weigh the advantages and disadvantages.

One thing to consider is your age. The best time to buy insurance is when you don't need it yet. Certain existing health conditions that are more common as we grow older normally cause an applicant to be turned down. These include Alzheimer's disease or other dementias, muscular dystrophy, Parkinson's disease, or severe osteoporosis. People who already need help with several activities of daily living, such as bathing, dressing, or going to the toilet, would also in most cases be denied. Other health conditions, such as high blood pressure, diabetes, emphysema, or history of stroke, might also disqualify you. Even if you aren't denied outright, the premium in your case might be prohibitively expensive. As with most insurance, "buy it before you need it" holds true.

Another consideration when thinking about long-term care insurance is your financial status. Once you begin paying the premium on your policy, you must continue to do so in order to retain your coverage. Is this a realistic expectation, given your current and/or projected income? Even if the premium seems like a lot of money, weigh this against the cost of a year's care in a nursing home. It is not uncommon for a person's life savings to be quickly wiped out by a catastrophic illness, leaving the spouse in a difficult financial position.

How Much Will It Cost?

The cost of long-term care insurance depends on several factors:

- **Your age when you purchase the policy**—The younger you are when you purchase your policy, the lower the annual premium will be. Once you have purchased the policy, your premium will not be raised just because you grow older; you lock into a rate that will not change, except when it is raised for all policyholders, or you change your coverage.

- **Your current health and health history**—As mentioned above, certain health conditions, if they don't cause you to be disqualified entirely, make it impossible to purchase a policy at the normal price or with full coverage. A *rated* or *modified* policy, which restricts coverage and costs more, might be an option, but not all companies offer them.

- **The particular benefits the policy will pay**—See the following "Questions to Ask When Shopping for a Policy" for a more detailed list of these considerations. Remember: in general, you get what you pay for. The lowest-priced policy might not be the best choice if the coverage will not be adequate to meet potential future needs.

How to Shop for Long-Term Care Insurance

As with any insurance, it's important to know the exact details and options of the policy you're considering. Comparison shop, and read the fine print. Avoid high-pressure sales, and don't rely on marketing materials or general descriptions. Instead, request that the company provide you with a sample policy and outline of coverage. Your insurance agent or financial advisor can help you decide which policy is best for you.

Questions to Ask When Shopping for a Policy

- **Is the company reputable and in good financial health?**

  It's important to purchase your policy from a company that will still be around if you need to collect benefits. Your insurance agent or financial advisor can help you learn which companies have a good reputation, are highly rated, and have a good track record for policyholder service.

- **What is the benefit amount and time period of coverage?**

  What is the maximum daily dollar amount the policy will pay? For how long a period of time? Some policies offer lifetime coverage, others are for a limited period of years.

- **What is the elimination period?**

  The deductible in long-term care is measured by days, not dollars, and is called the *elimination period*. This means the number of days you must pay for your own long-term care during a particular illness before your insurance will pay—normally between 20 and 100 days. In general, the shorter the elimination period, the higher the premium. You should also find out the details about what is considered a "separate spell of illness." Will the waiting period start over if you experience a temporary improvement of condition?

- **What is covered?**

  Though a few policies cover nursing facility stays exclusively, most long-term care policies today are *comprehensive*, covering not only nursing facility care, but also home care services, such as nurse or home health aide visits. Many also cover assisted living and other residential care settings, adult day care services, respite care, and hospice. Of those that cover home care, some pay only for home *health* care provided by a licensed agency. Others include chore services, such as cooking, grocery shopping, home modification, and other tasks. Ask to see a detailed description of coverage.

- **In what circumstances can you make a claim?**

  Be sure to find out what it takes to qualify for benefits. Are any levels of prior care required before benefits begin? Must you have been hospitalized first? How many activities of daily living (ADLs) must a policyholder need help with to trigger a claim?

- **Are pre-existing conditions an issue?**

  Some policies require a wait, typically six months, before you can receive benefits for a health condition you already had when you obtained the policy.

- **Does the policy restrict where and from whom care can be received?**

  Some long-term care insurance policies include the same types of limitations as preferred provider-type health insurance. The company contracts with a list of providers and facilities, and will only pay benefits if the policyholder chooses those providers. The company may pay a smaller amount if the policyholder goes outside the list of approved providers.

- **Are there any other limitations?**

  Most of today's long-term care policies cover Alzheimer's disease and other dementias, but, as Alzheimer's is a leading cause for nursing facility admission, be certain that it is included in the policy you select. Other limitations may typically apply: for example, many policies specifically exclude coverage for alcoholism, drug abuse, or the effects of self-injury.

- **Are benefits adjusted for inflation?**

  This is a very important consideration. The cost of long-term care is rising faster than the cost of living, and a daily benefit amount that is appropriate today will be inadequate to cover costs in future years. About 5 percent per year is the typical increase. Some policies also allow you to purchase increased coverage later on.

- **How much are the premiums expected to increase?**

    Companies can raise their premiums from time to time, as permitted by state insurance commissions. Ask to see a rate increase history for policies you are considering and compare them. Some companies have a record of frequent, large increases; others have fewer and smaller increases.

- **Is the policy renewable?**

    Under federal law, long-term care policies are renewable so long as the premium is paid on time. Be sure to check your policy to see what conditions might cause your policy not to be renewed.

- **What about group policies?**

    Your employer or professional group may offer long-term care insurance as part of its benefits package. These policies are often less expensive than those you buy individually, and some companies will also let you enroll family members, including parents. Be sure you have all the facts before you sign up. Find out what happens if you leave your employer: can you continue the policy on your own? Would the premium be higher? Are benefits different?

To decide whether long-term care insurance is right for you, and which policy best meets your needs, consult with a reputable insurance agent. Discuss the policy with a trusted person, such as your health care provider, financial advisor, or knowledgeable friend or relative. Locating the best policy for your needs takes time and effort, but it can pay off by protecting your assets and giving you greater choice, should you need long-term care in the future.

To Sum Up . . .

Nursing facility care these days is expensive. That means most middle-income Americans are at risk; we could have our life savings eaten away if we ever need long-term care in a nursing facility. Long-term care insurance is a way of protecting against that risk. It is a financial planning *product*, though, which simply means that buyers need to beware. Purchasing long-term care insurance can make very good sense. But it also makes good sense to be sure to you're dealing with a reputable source, comparing several competing long-term care insurance options before making your selection.

More Resources

- The **State Health Insurance Counseling and Assistance Program (SHIP)** offers seniors free counseling and information about long-term care insurance. A directory of websites for each state's SHIP program can be found on the Medicare website. (*www.medicare.gov*)

Quick Links

>>> These web-based resources may be accessed through our website:

www.aginginstride.org

- The **AARP** website includes information about long-term care insurance. (*www.aarp.org*)

- You can also find this information by calling **The Eldercare Locator** at 1-800-677-1116, or at *www.eldercare.gov*.

ISSUE 34: CONSUMER FRAUD

"You have won...!" "Your name has been selected...!" "Here is your opportunity to buy at a fraction of the cost...!" "Earn thousands a year at home...!"

We are bombarded by pitches like these. They come in the mail, by phone, at the front door, in magazines, and via e-mail. Honest companies and charities sometimes use these sales methods, but so do dishonest businesses and con artists. They cheat consumers of billions of dollars every year! Sad to say, many of their victims are older people.

Why do these crooks target seniors? There are several reasons:

- Retirees typically have money in the bank and a steady income.

- Older people tend to be home more during the day, with more time to listen to sales calls.

- Anyone who seems lonely and isolated looks like an easy mark for a "friendly stranger."

- Many older people are extremely polite and find it hard to just hang up on a salesperson. Some even feel pressured into buying something just to get the salesperson off the phone.

- Those who suffer from confusion or are physically frail can be more vulnerable to high-pressure pitches.

Because older adults are such frequent targets, even seniors who are physically healthy and mentally acute need to be wary. Some of these con artists are very, very good at what they do.

Scams, Frauds, and Swindles

Scams and unethical sales methods aimed at older people can cause serious financial loss. Abusive practices range all the way from petty overcharges or "hard sells" for unneeded items to outright frauds and swindles.

Here are just a few examples of common types of shady business practices and scams:

- High-pressure sales (vitamins, magazine subscriptions, etc.).
- Worthless investments.
- "Work at home" schemes.
- So-called sweepstakes and contests that require the "winner" to buy something or make an expensive 900-number call.
- Dishonest contractors or service providers.
- Phony charities.
- Credit card schemes.
- Quack medical devices or treatments.

Protecting Yourself: Common Sense and Rules to Live By

With all the con artists out there, how can you protect yourself or your family member? To reduce the risk of loss:

- Always comparison shop for price and quality before you decide on a purchase. Get several bids for home repairs or improvement work.

- When dealing with contractors, ask to see their license. Check the license number with the state licensing agency, or call your local builders association.

- Deal only with reputable merchants; they have a long-term interest in satisfying their customers.

- Avoid sellers who resort to high-pressure sales tactics. Hang up on them or close the door in their faces!

- Read and understand any written contracts before you sign. Never rely on spoken promises; get it in writing! Ask a friend or family member to look over low-value contracts before you sign. If signing a contract for thousands or tens of thousands of dollars, have your lawyer review the contract.

- Never give out your credit card, bank account, or Social Security numbers.

Warning Signs of Frauds and Scams

It's impossible to anticipate every scheme that crooks might devise. A healthy skepticism and cautious buying habits are good protection. Here are some warning signs to watch for:

- You are offered "something for nothing."

- A salesperson is overly friendly, wants to know about your personal life, and engages you in conversation that has nothing to do with the product or service being sold.

- A salesperson pressures you to make up your mind right now.

- A company wants to give you a free prize or gift if you buy something. They may ask that you pay shipping charges, gift taxes, or a handling charge.

- A home improvement contractor comes to your door and "just happens to be in the neighborhood."

- A salesperson asks you to give out your credit card number or bank account number.

- Someone asks you to dial a 1-900 number.

- A home-business opportunity offers big money working at home.

- A salesperson hesitates or refuses to provide information, a phone number, or written materials about the company or charity; an organization only has a post office box for an address.

- You've never heard of the charity, or their name is similar to, but not the same as, a reputable organization.

- An ad promises miracle cures.

- A stranger or an "official" approaches you or calls you on the phone and asks you to get involved with some lost property, a "bank examination," or some other far-fetched scheme.

- Before you donate to a charity, be sure it is real. Find out what percent of your money will go to the charity itself, and how much will go to the fundraiser. Ask a friend or family member for a second opinion before making a major donation.

- Don't be fooled by impressive-looking brochures or glowing testimonials.

- Check with your health care provider before you buy medical devices or undergo any treatment. Deal only with trained health care providers and reputable pharmacies.

- Don't call expensive 900 numbers.

- Read everything carefully. Sweepstakes notifications often try to fool you into thinking you have won a prize.

- Never buy something just to get a free gift.

- Remember, just because someone wants you to buy something or donate doesn't mean you are obligated! To end a pitch, just say, "No thank you," and hang up. That's right, hang up!

- If solicitors are pestering you or a family member, put your name on the Federal Trade Commission's national do-not-call registry. Go to *www.donotcall.gov* for more information and to sign up.

- Above all, be aware. Be cautious. Be skeptical. Be realistic. Be assertive. Maintain your independence and use common sense.

If You've Been Cheated

If you think you or a family member has been cheated, here are steps you can take:

- Find out your legal rights. Many federal, state, and local laws exist to help protect consumers from dishonest business practices.

- The Consumer Protection Division of your state's Attorney General's Office is a good place to start. This office should be able to advise you on specific situations, or direct you to another agency for help.

- Contact the Federal Trade Commission (FTC). This is the agency with responsibility for federal laws on door-to-door sales and unfair credit practices.

- Contact the Postal Inspector of the United States. This agency polices fraud committed through the mail.

- Check to see whether your community has a victim assistance program.

- Above all, prevent future problems by educating yourself and your family members about fraud. This not only makes it less likely that you will be victimized again, but also helps restore self-confidence.

For many older people, being cheated can be an embarrassing experience, and one you would just as soon forget. Don't let embarrassment get in the way of reporting what's happened. If something doesn't seem right, call the authorities right away. You'll be helping protect others as well as yourself.

Lightning Can Strike Twice!

If a person has been victimized before, he or she is actually a more likely target! Con artists sell mailing lists of "easy marks." They don't hesitate to approach a person again and again, using a different company name or a different scheme. If you've been cheated, you need to be on your guard more than ever.

To Sum Up . . .

Reading about consumer fraud against seniors can be pretty discouraging. It's a sad fact of life that there are people out there who make it their business to cheat older people out of their savings.

It need not happen to you—and it won't if you keep your guard up. Play things safe. If you're tempted to take advantage of some proposition, force yourself to slow down long enough to talk things over with a trusted relative or friend. It's rare that you will have regrets by saying no. Saying yes to a salesman too quickly is what gets people into trouble.

More Resources

- The U.S. government's **Bureau of Consumer Protection**, part of the Federal Trade Commission, offers information on a wide range of consumer-related topics, including those of particular interest to older adults. (*www.ftc.gov*)

- The U.S. government's **FirstGov for Consumers** website also includes links and information on scams and swindles, and general consumer information. (*www.consumer.gov*)

- Information about health fraud can be found on the sites of the **U.S. Food and Drug Administration** (*www.fda.gov*), as well as from **Quackwatch**. (*www.quackwatch.org*)

- The **U.S. Postal Inspection Service** displays a list of consumer fraud and schemes on their website. (*www.usps.com/postalinspectors*)

Quick Links

>>> These web-based resources may be accessed through our website:
www.aginginstride.org

ISSUE 35: ELDER ABUSE

Elder abuse is mistreatment of an older adult. It can happen in any residential or care setting, from the person's own home to a nursing facility or the home of a relative.

Unfortunately, mistreatment of older persons takes many forms. Here are the four major categories of abuse:

- **Physical abuse**—causing pain or harm by hitting, slapping, pushing, or any behavior that inflicts pain or injury.

- **Psychological or emotional abuse**—actions that humiliate, intimidate, threaten, or harass an older person.

- **Financial abuse**—any situation in which a caregiver or other person takes an older person's money or property, or uses his/her position as caregiver, guest, or family member to get at the person's money or belongings.

- **Neglect**—not providing some type of basic care, such as adequate food, clothing, hygiene, or medical attention.

Knowing What Is Abuse and What Isn't

These four categories of elder abuse have one thing in common: *someone is mistreating an older adult.* The person doing the mistreating might be a paid caregiver, a family member, a visitor, or another older adult living in the same home or care facility. In some cases, an older adult's own behavior is a threat to his or her welfare; this is referred to as *self-neglect.*

Legal definitions of what is and is not elder abuse vary from state to state. There is a clear trend toward holding caregivers, and others in a position of trust and responsibility, strictly accountable when they injure an older person through abuse or neglect.

Elder Abuse vs. the Right to Refuse Care

Sometimes elder abuse is easy to spot. Other times the situation is more complicated. The law protects the right of an older person to be free from abuse and neglect, but if the person is able to make informed decisions, the law also protects his or her right to refuse care. For example, if an older person in an adult foster home has voluntarily stopped eating, he or she may be losing weight and looking frail, but the home is not guilty of neglect. In fact, it has been argued that *forcing* older adults to eat can be perceived by them as abusive. It is a question of their choice. If you see an older person in a care setting who is not eating or taking medication that would be beneficial, don't jump to a conclusion of abuse without getting the facts first.

Elder Abuse Is Against the Law!

Federal laws and regulations that protect nursing facility residents are very clear: every resident has a legal right to be free from harsh or abusive treatment of any kind. Facilities that participate in Medicare or Medicaid must take steps to prevent abuse and to intervene immediately if they find it.

Other laws protecting older adults in all settings—at home, in an assisted living community, or at an adult family home—vary by state. If you are dealing with a possible elder abuse situation, you will need to learn more about the standards of conduct, reporting requirements, and remedies in your state. If you have questions about what constitutes abuse, call your local Senior Information and Referral program, senior center, or the police.

Preventing Elder Abuse

Care facilities and home care agencies are legally required to protect the rights of the older persons they serve, including the right to be free from abuse or neglect. All these organizations should have policies and procedures to help stop elder abuse, and to respond quickly if they suspect abuse or neglect is occurring.

Agencies' responsibilities for prevention and intervention include:

- Checking out or screening job applicants before they are hired.

- Adopting clear guidelines for protecting patients or residents during care.

- Spelling out how situations will be investigated and resolved, including reporting and documentation as legally required.

- Educating staff, so they will recognize elder abuse and know what to do if they see it happening.

Reporting Elder Abuse

Here are some things you should know about reporting suspected elder abuse:

Good Judgment, Common Sense

Use the same kind of good judgment and common sense you would in reporting other serious situations. If the behavior you see creates an immediate threat of serious injury or loss of property, you should get help right away.

On the other hand, if this isn't an emergency, you'll probably want to check things out to be sure you are perceiving the situation correctly. Remember, sometimes a family member or professional caregiver wants to give more help, but the older person refuses. If you suspect abuse in an institutional setting, get in touch with a member of the care team, a supervisor, or someone else in a position of authority and report what you've seen and the concerns you have. Ask them to help you understand exactly what's happening and why. Check to see whether other family members or friends share your perception. Then, if you still have concerns, it's time to report them.

If you suspect elder abuse in a home setting, it may be more difficult to check. Try to spend more time observing the dynamic of the home. Ask other family members and friends what they have observed. Try to get more information.

Whom Should I Call?

If you're dealing with an emergency situation, such as domestic violence or other obvious criminal activity, call the police. For other situations involving suspected abuse or neglect, you may call your state's elder abuse hotline. Numbers are listed at *www.elderabusecenter.org*, or you can get the number by calling your local Senior Information and Referral, listed in the White Pages, or the National Center on Elder Abuse, 202-898-2586. If you are concerned about abuse in a long-term care facility, your state's long-term care ombudsman can help.

Caregivers Have a Special Responsibility

If you are a caregiver, whether paid or volunteer, your job description includes: *understanding what elder abuse is, helping to prevent it, and reporting situations so they can be investigated and stopped.* This is a legal obligation. Being alert to the possibility of elder abuse and responding appropriately to suspected cases of elder abuse are important responsibilities. Here are some tips to help you:

Mandatory reporting—Many states have laws that require health care providers and professionals to report and document incidents of elder abuse. If these laws apply to you, make sure you have a clear understanding of your personal responsibilities. If you are unsure of something, ask questions. If you feel your training on elder abuse has been inadequate, say so.

Avoid isolation—Caregiving is stressful. If you are a caregiver, it's always a good idea to stay connected to other people. Don't try to do it alone. By making your caregiving part of a team effort, you will experience less stress. When you have questions or need backup, others can help. If you're feeling isolated as a family caregiver, call Senior Information and Referral to tap into the eldercare support network in your community. You'll likely be pleasantly surprised by the level of support available to persons in your situation.

Control your feelings and behavior—Remember your role. As a caregiver, it's part of your job to stay in control of your own feelings and behavior, even when being a caregiver includes dealing with difficult behavior on the part of those in your care. Be honest with yourself. If you begin to feel like you are losing your patience, take a short break. If you can, move on to another task and then return when you can make a fresh start. If coping with the stress of being a caregiver in your particular situation is a chronic challenge for you, ask for help in the form of education, counseling, a support group—whatever it takes to get you back into a safe zone as a caregiver.

If You Personally are Being Abused

Many older people are afraid to report abuse. Especially when the abuser is another family member, older people fear that they will not be listened to, that the reporting will result in reprisal, or that reporting will have serious negative consequences to the family.

It is difficult to report abusive behavior by those who are close to you. However, you have the right to live your life free of the fear of harm and intimidation. It's not your "fault" if your abuser suffers the consequence of his or her actions. Explain your situation to your doctor, lawyer, or a close friend whom you trust. Get the support you need to confront and change the situation. You do not need to be a victim.

To Sum Up . . .

Recognizing and responding appropriately to elder abuse situations is serious business. There is a clear and growing trend in our laws to protect seniors and to impose reporting requirements on those involved in their care. However, these laws do vary from state to state. If you are in the role of a caregiver, you need to know the rules that apply to you.

We can all play a role in stopping elder abuse. This means being more sensitive to the problem. It means knowing how to recognize the signs of possible abuse. Above all, it means knowing what to do, *and then doing it,* when we see an older person being mistreated.

More Resources

Quick Links

>>> These web-based resources may be accessed through our website: www.aginginstride.org

- The **National Center on Elder Abuse** website has information and contact numbers for older adults and their families. (*www.elderabusecenter.org*)

- The **Office of the Inspector General** website includes information on Medicaid provider fraud and patient abuse and neglect. (*www.oig.hhs.gov*)

- The **U.S. Administration on Aging** website includes information and resources on elder abuse prevention and treatment. (*www.aoa.gov*)

- The **National Long-Term Care Ombudsman Resource Center** has information and contact information if you suspect abuse in an eldercare facility. (*www.ltcombudsman.org*)

Issues Near the End of Life

INTRODUCTION

Death occurs for everyone. No matter how hard we have worked to age gracefully and successfully, we cannot escape our mortality. So, it's important—many would say crucial—to include issues near the end of life as we go about the business of aging in stride.

Some of what we are about to cover may seem unsettling and uncomfortable. Talking openly and honestly about death and dying is difficult for many. But read on. As you'll quickly see, in this part of life, as in others, there is much to be gained by honest assessment, planning, and open communication.

In Issue 36, we try to put the universal experience of dying—our own, as well as that of a person we love—into some perspective. Thinking and talking about death isn't easy, but there are ways to make it easier. There are many benefits to gain from straightforward and timely conversation.

Issue 37 covers special types of care available to those who know they have only a limited life expectancy. You've probably heard about hospice care, and you may also have heard of palliative care. Not nearly enough people, however, fully appreciate how valuable these types of care can be to the person and the family during the final stages of life.

When a person dies, there are some practical questions that need to be answered and things that will need doing. These practical concerns are the focus of Issue 38.

Issue 39 discusses something that goes with the territory of being human: experiencing grief and loss. It can be helpful—and healthful—to step back a bit and look at what normal, healthy grieving involves.

In the forms section, you will find a pair of tools to help you in this area:

- Form 37: *Checklist for Selecting a Hospice or Palliative Care Provider*
- Form 38: *Funeral or Memorial Service Planner*

ISSUE 36: A GOOD DEATH

In this death-denying society, the phrase "a good death" may seem jarring at first. But all of us will die at some point. Many people have ideas about the way they would like to die. Some would wish a sudden death. Others would prefer time to plan, to say good-bye, to get ready. While each person's vision is different, most adults do have some feelings about how they wish to die, and as we grow older, our preferences grow stronger.

None of us has complete control over the moment or means of our dying. However, as death draws near, there are often choices that can be made to support a person who is dying in a manner close to their vision of a good death.

Facing Up to Death and Dying

Some people know that death is coming relatively soon because they have been diagnosed with a terminal disease or medical condition and told they have only a year or two of life before them. For others as they age, there is no clear indicator of where they are in relation to the end of life. Individuals know or guess that their body is slowing down and working less well, and simple arithmetic tells them that it is unlikely they will live many years longer. It is a good idea for all older adults to periodically think about the possibility of dying, and to address the concerns laid out in this issue. Have you made decisions about or arrangements for organ donation and what will happen to your body after death? Are your legal and financial affairs in a state where someone can easily access the information and documents necessary to ensure a smooth transition of your estate? Do you have a living will and/or health care representative? What do you want to accomplish with the rest of your life? As early as your forties, you should be asking these questions with some regularity and acting on your answers.

As individuals grow older, the questions take on greater urgency. As with all the other transitions that come with advancing years, we urge you to face the prospect of death honestly, to think about what is most important for you to accomplish in the time you have left, and to spend your energy doing those things you want to do. There is so much that can bring closure, peace, and a sense of accomplishment to the last stage of life. Even if your health condition is uncertain or poor, there are things you can do to take control and give you satisfaction.

Many people isolate themselves and grow reclusive as they realize their health and abilities are failing. They may not want to be seen as "less" than they once were. But in reality, your friends and family most likely prefer to be with you as you *are*, rather than not with you at all. Don't let embarrassment and false pride interfere with relationships and activities that are important to you. Life is uncertain for everyone. There are things you can accomplish and people you want to see. So live your life as fully as you can!

Talking About Death and Dying

Too often, we are hesitant to talk about death directly, or even indirectly. A conspiracy of silence prevails. Family and friends are reluctant to bring up the subject of death because they don't want to distress the dying person; the dying person remains silent to avoid causing pain to family and friends. Too often, all parties live in a kind of verbal denial, limiting or completely cutting off the possibility for conversations that are healing, life-affirming, or even essential.

Initiating the Discussion

The best time to begin talking about the emotional, practical, and spiritual issues clustered around dying is well before the onset of life-threatening disease or disability. Consider it a gift to your family and friends to initiate such discussions.

Probably the first, most vital information to convey to those who are close to you is your values and preferences concerning life-sustaining and life-prolonging care in a medical emergency. Ideally, choose a time when those close to you are relaxed, not in a hurry. Let them know you wish this to be an open and ongoing conversation. It's often easiest to begin with the kinds of questions contained in a living will: "This is what I would like done if I am incapacitated and my heart stops, or I need to be put on a ventilator." Directly address questions that concern disposition of your body after death: "You know, I would prefer burial to cremation." Most family members, especially those who will be responsible for making decisions when the time comes, will welcome the chance to listen and to ask questions. These simple questions often lead to further discussion. More importantly, early conversations like these set a precedent that these hard issues are OK to talk about in the future.

Sometimes it happens that there is no opportunity to discuss issues around dying in the absence of serious illness, but it is never too late to open the conversation. Again, it usually falls to the person who is dying to give permission, by example, for such talk to occur. Let your family and friends know you want to talk; encourage them to ask questions, to express their feelings. Tell them honestly what you are thinking, what concerns you have, what details are important to you. If there are subjects you would prefer not to discuss, you can make that clear as well.

If Your Family Does Not Want To Talk

There can be a variety of reasons why your family or close friends may not want to talk about your dying. They may not want to face the pain of loss; they may wish not to become emotional; your health crisis may bring unwelcome thoughts about their own possible death. It is usually not helpful to try to force another person to have a conversation they are not ready to have. Be honest. Let them know why this conversation is important to you. Try again later.

Concerns of the Dying

In some ways, those who know their life expectancy is limited live their lives the same way and have the same concerns as all of us who are focused on the business of living. Maintaining a sense of normalcy is important. However, there are special concerns, questions, and tasks that take on a particular relevance in the last stages of life. What does it mean to be ready for the end of life? What is the spiritual reality of death? Many of us don't want to think about such questions. However, those who know that life's end is near often need to reflect on their own personal experience of living and dying. It can seem a lonely, difficult task. But it doesn't have to be.

Questions About Living

When there is only a short time left in life, there are choices to make about how best to use one's remaining time. The following questions are important to consider:

- What do you still want to accomplish, and what help do you need to achieve those goals?

- What do you need to do to get your business and financial affairs in order?

- Who are the people with whom you want to spend time, and how can you schedule that time?

How To Be a Friend To Someone Who Is Dying

- Let the dying person decide what you will talk about and when. Indicate your openness to whatever your friend wishes to discuss.

- In discussions of spiritual beliefs concerning life and death, be honest. However, do not challenge or discourage the expressed feelings or beliefs of the dying person. We all have the right to chart our own spiritual journey!

- If you cannot be present in person, call or write letters or e-mail. Those at the end of life need to know you are thinking of them.

- Don't be afraid to cry or to laugh. Real emotion can bring healing and peace.

- When a person is too tired or weak to talk, he or she may still appreciate having someone near. Some people like to be read to or to listen to music. Touching—for example, holding a hand or giving a foot rub—can be an important way of communicating care.

- Cards, flowers, and small gifts help the receiver remember your visit after you are gone.

- Keep your visits to an appropriate length.

- Doing something fun together is often as helpful as serious conversation.

- Be willing to change your plans for your visit, based on how your friend is feeling at the moment. Be flexible.

- Let those you love know what you treasure about them, why they are important to you, and what memories you especially cherish.

- Are there letters you need to write, conversations you'd like to have, matters you need to resolve?

- What will bring pleasure to this part of your life?

It is good and healthy to think about these questions, and to talk about them with family and friends. Those who know they are soon going to die often achieve a very high quality of life for the very reason that they are determined to focus their energy on what is truly important to them.

Questions About Dying

Death is a mysterious journey for us all. It makes sense to have questions about the process of dying and what it means. Such questions may include:

- What do I believe about what happens to a person during and after death?

- Are there ways to prepare spiritually for dying?

- How do I sum up my life, make peace with who I have been and who I am?

- What kind of funeral, memorial service, or other remembrance do I want after my death?

- Who do I want with me at the end of my life?

These questions and others like them can be difficult, but they can also bring great joy and a sense of inner peace. Each of us is different, of course. Most people who are at the end of life need and welcome friends and family who do not close off such conversations, but instead encourage them, listen supportively, and offer to share their own ideas and life experience when that is helpful. Along with friends and family, caring professionals can also be of emotional and spiritual help during this time. They include ministers, priests, rabbis, and other leaders of spiritual communities; chaplains, spiritual directors, and pastoral counselors; private therapists and support groups. Each person's path is different, but it is important to find people who can be good friends and companions to you as you face the last challenges of your life.

To Sum Up . . .

The end of life can contain some of life's richest moments and its greatest personal growth. This ending is not something to fear, but rather a time to be lived with heightened awareness and appreciation. The best companions to the dying are those who are willing to go the distance of the journey, to be supportive and helpful, to laugh and cry and talk and be still. Most important to both the dying and their friends is to live each day as it comes, and to treasure the opportunities for love, for friendship, and for growth with each day's particular challenges and gifts.

More Resources

- The **National Hospice and Palliative Care Organization** (*www.nhpco.org*) and their companion foundation, the **National Hospice Foundation** (*www.hospiceinfo.org*) offer articles on a number of end-of-life issues.

Quick Links

>>> These web-based resources may be accessed through our website:

www.aginginstride.org

- The **Public Broadcasting System's** *On Our Own Terms* series of videotapes may be available from your library. The series' companion website features resources and tools for developing one's own end-of-life philosophy. (*www.pbs.org/wnet/onourownterms*)

ISSUE 37: HOSPICE AND PALLIATIVE CARE

During the Middle Ages, the term "hospice" was used to signify a place where weary travelers could stop, rest, and refresh themselves before continuing their journey. In 1967, a British physician, Dr. Cicely Saunders, began using the term to symbolize a new kind of care for the dying. In a London suburb, she founded St. Christopher's Hospice, which cared for its patients by offering supportive care and pain control. The patients at St. Christopher's came there because they had reached a point in their various illnesses where they were no longer looking for a cure. Instead, they wanted to make the most of the time left to them, to live out their lives at the highest level of quality possible, even if that compromised how long they would live.

Since its beginnings in 1967, the hospice movement has spread quickly throughout the world. In the United States alone, there are now over 1,500 hospice programs affiliated with the National Hospice Organization. Each year these programs serve over 100,000 patients and their families, and are recognized by patients, physicians, and insurance carriers as providing high quality, cost-effective, compassionate care for people with limited life expectancies.

What Services Does Hospice Care Include?

Hospice organizations vary greatly in size, but their philosophy and the services they offer remain basically the same. Hospice care is provided by a multi-disciplinary team of professionals and trained volunteers. The professionals on the care team usually include the patient's personal physician, nurses, social workers, physical and occupational therapists, chaplains, and home health aides. Working closely with both the patient and the patient's family, the hospice team provides:

- Training and assistance for the primary caregiver, so that he or she feels confident and supported in the caregiver role.

- Regularly scheduled nursing and supportive care visits.

- Nursing care and consultation available for patients on an on-call basis 24 hours a day, seven days a week.

- Care focused on the emotional, social, and spiritual needs of a dying person and that person's family, as well as on physical and medical needs.

- Care directed as much as possible by the patient, working together with family and hospice staff.

- Care directed at effective symptom management and at enhancing quality of life, promoting interaction with family and other loved ones.

- Care that considers pain control a primary goal of treatment.

- Home-based care if possible; but if a patient's symptoms cannot be managed at home, then inpatient care provided in as pleasant and homelike an atmosphere as possible, where family and friends are encouraged to be present. Hospice care can often be provided in nursing homes.

- Bereavement support for close family and friends of the patient.

What is Palliative Care?

Medical care can be divided roughly into three categories:

- **Preventive care**—designed to improve and maintain a good state of health.

- **Curative care**—therapies, interventions, and medications designed to cure diseases and conditions that threaten health.

- **Palliative care**—care designed not to cure disease or halt adverse medical conditions, but to minimize symptoms and control pain.

Typically as people grow older, they are more likely to experience chronic diseases and conditions for which medicine today has no effective cure. In recent years, doctors and researchers have given significant attention to developing a range of effective therapies in palliative medicine. These advances have allowed many people increased mobility and function and decreased pain levels, despite living with chronic or terminal illnesses and conditions.

To be eligible for hospice care, three things are necessary:

1. The patient understands that he or she has a terminal illness, and has reached the point in that illness where he or she is no longer seeking a cure. Hospice provides supportive care and symptom management, but does not offer procedures or care focused on curative medicine.

2. The patient's physician is willing to work with the hospice team to provide care, and usually must certify that, in the physician's judgment, the patient has an incurable disease and six months or less of life expectancy.

3. A family member or close friend must usually be willing to act as the primary caregiver to the patient, especially if hospice care is provided at home.

The patient must also understand and consent to the kind of care he or she will be receiving. The physician must be willing to support this kind of care. There must be a caregiver who will be with the patient through the dying process.

Paying for Hospice Care

If you have Medicare Part A or certain categories of Medicaid coverage, you may be eligible for the Medicare (or in some states, Medicaid) Hospice Benefit. A hospice staff person will help you determine your eligibility. If you elect the Medicare (or Medicaid, if available) Hospice Benefit, the following services will be covered:

- Home visits by the hospice staff.
- Medications.
- Supplies.
- Medical equipment.
- Short-term respite care.
- Laboratory tests.
- Outpatient procedures to alleviate symptoms.
- Hospitalization for symptom management.

If you decide to change your approach to treatment from supportive care to a more aggressive or curative approach, you may revoke the Medicare or Medicaid Hospice Benefit and your regular Medicare/Medicaid benefits will be resumed.

If you have private insurance, a hospice staff member will research the availability and scope of your coverage. Many private insurance providers do provide hospice benefits. If you have limited or no insurance coverage, most hospices will work with you to set up a reasonable payment schedule or to provide financial assistance.

The Benefits of Hospice

Imagine the following scene: you are in a private home; a dying person is lying in his own room on a hospital bed covered by his favorite quilt; family and friends are with him in the room, talking, laughing, telling stories. Sometimes the patient enters in; sometimes he sleeps. The hospice nurse comes by on her daily visit

Timing is Important!

Here are two pieces of very practical advice:

First, for most of us, talking about end-of-life care becomes more difficult and emotional the closer we get to the reality of it all. So, to the extent you can, discuss your preferences earlier, rather than later.

Second, don't make the common mistake of waiting until near the very end to make arrangements for hospice or palliative care. The single biggest regret many families have following a hospice care experience is that they didn't begin hospice care a bit earlier.

How do you know when the time is right for hospice or palliative care? Talk with your doctor. Make sure he or she knows that you understand the benefits hospice has to offer under the right circumstances, and that you want to avoid being either too early or too late in getting a hospice or palliative care program involved. If your doctor seems unwilling or unable to make a timely referral, get the name of a local hospice and palliative care provider from a friend or Senior Information and Referral, and give them a call yourself.

and checks with the primary caregiver. Some changes in medication are suggested. The nurse examines the patient and listens carefully to his concerns. She offers to call the doctor for advice. Later that night, a volunteer is coming to read to the patient so that the primary caregiver can attend the birthday party of a friend. Yes, there is death in this room, but there is also life, and love, and companionship.

To Sum Up . . .

Hospice is a special kind of caring for those in a special time of life. By definition, it isn't for everyone. However, for those who know they are in the last six months of their life, it can be an enormous comfort and blessing for both patient and family. If you or someone you love is diagnosed with a terminal illness, hospice is an important option you will want to consider.

More Resources

- The **National Hospice and Palliative Care Organization** offers a directory of hospices (searchable by city and ZIP code) and consumer information about hospice and the grieving process. (*www.nhpco.org*)

- The **NHPCO's National Hospice Foundation** has information about hospice care, selecting a hospice program, and the Medicaid benefit. (*www.hospiceinfo.org*)

Quick Links

>>> These web-based resources may be accessed through our website: www.aginginstride.org

ISSUE 38: PRACTICAL ISSUES AT THE TIME OF DEATH

When a person dies, a number of practical issues need to be addressed. Some of these details need to be considered almost immediately. Others can wait for days or even weeks. The most important tasks are outlined in this section.

Notifying Others That Your Loved One Has Died

When a loved one dies, some names will come to you immediately as people who should be contacted: close family, good friends, the doctor, the lawyer, the person's priest, rabbi, or other clergy person. Make a list of calls you will want to make yourself. Other calls have to be made, but your friends and your loved one's friends, as well as other family members, can make them for you. In order to avoid duplication or important calls falling through the cracks, it is always a good idea to make a written list and check off those who have been notified.

Working With the Funeral Home

Normally, within 24 hours of your loved one's death, you should be in contact with the funeral home to set up an appointment with the funeral director. Funeral homes offer a wide range of services at the time of death. These usually include:

- Transporting the body from the place of death to the funeral home.

- Preparing the body for burial, arranging for a casket and other necessary items for burial, or arranging for cremation.

- Working with the family and, if desired, a religious professional in arranging for a funeral or memorial service.

- Assisting in the preparation of an obituary and funeral notice, and arranging for those to be published in the newspapers of your choice. (Some newspapers charge for obituaries, so be sure to ask.)

- Transporting the body and family members (if desired) to the funeral or memorial service and/or to the cemetery.

- Completing the necessary paperwork for the death certificate, and obtaining certified copies of the death certificate for the family. It's helpful to ask for an adequate number of certified death certificates. They are more expensive if you order them later. You will need one for the Social Security Administration; one for each bank account, life insurance policy, or pension; and several more for processing the person's estate and other financial business. A good rule of thumb is to request at least 10 copies.

Some funeral homes also offer support groups and bereavement counseling for family members of the person who has died.

Most funeral directors are professionals who provide their services with integrity and compassion. The role they play in a community is a necessary one, and most do their work sensitively. However, it is important to realize that funeral directors deal with people who are in an especially vulnerable state. When someone you love has just died, if prearrangements have not been made, you need to make quick decisions on painful issues. These issues include whether the person will be buried or cremated, what kind of casket or cremation container to buy, where to buy a burial plot, and what kind of funeral or memorial service to have. Some of these decisions may involve the outlay of significant amounts of money and may also be emotionally charged, so they become more complicated. The following suggestions will minimize the risk of making decisions about which you later feel angry or regretful.

- Never send one family member alone to make funeral arrangements. Have two or three family members go, or maybe take a good friend, pastor, or neighbor who is more detached from the pain of the loss.

- Most funeral homes offer a basic minimum service package. Additional services are charged individually. Make sure you understand the charges. The funeral director should give you an itemized list. If you have questions about certain services, ask for time to think, then arrange to meet later or call back with your answer. Unless any particular service is required by law, feel comfortable in saying that you don't want it.

- Money does not equal love. Some people think they must buy an expensive casket or provide a lavish funeral to show their love for the one who has died. This is not true. Buy only those goods or services that seem reasonable to you.

Many people dread the appointment with the funeral director, but remember that he or she is there to help you and will make your time as easy as possible. If you have taken time to consider what you want, and you take someone with you, this visit will probably be less difficult than you fear.

Planning a Funeral or Memorial Service

After one they love has died, most people find it helpful to participate in some structured ritual of remembrance, celebration, and letting go of the person who has died. Depending on religious traditions and individual tastes, this ritual might range from a Requiem Mass followed by an elaborate reception, to setting a time for family members and friends to gather in a home to talk about the one who has died. Such services, both formal and informal, can be a source of comfort and strength, gathering together the community of grief to remember, cry, and even laugh together.

The following is a list of questions that will help you in planning a funeral or memorial service for a close friend or relative who has died. You can also use Form 38 to help you.

- Did your loved one leave any specific instructions about the kind of service he or she wanted? Did those instructions include specific requests for readings, music, a person to preside, or a place where the service is to be held?

Memorial Societies and Other Prepaid Funeral Plans

In many areas of the country, there are Memorial Societies that charge a nominal fee for membership and then contract with chosen funeral homes to arrange simple cremation services. Often, funeral homes offer individuals the opportunity to choose and pay for the goods and services they prefer while they are still alive. These prearrangements can provide great peace of mind for families. They know their loved one's final arrangements reflect that loved one's desires and preferences. Most people let their family know when such prearrangements have been made. However, it is usually wise to check with local funeral homes if you are in doubt as to whether your loved one has made such decisions in advance.

- Where will the service take place and who will officiate? Are there musicians or others who need to be involved?

- When will it be convenient for the service to take place? Do family members, friends, the service location, or the presider have schedules that need to be taken into account?

- Are there readings, music, pictures, or any other elements you think would be especially meaningful for you or others as part of the ceremony?

- Do you want to choose someone to deliver a formal eulogy? Do you or others wish to offer some personal words of remembrance?

- Do you wish to have a visitation (a time when people can see the body, say good-bye, and speak with the family) before the service? This custom varies among communities and religious traditions.

- Will there be any kind of reception or other gathering of friends and family before or after the service? Where will it be held? What kind of food service do you want and who will provide it?

If you are part of a church or other religious community, your contact in that community will undoubtedly have other questions to ask you about the service. However, it is best to think about the questions outlined above before you meet with whomever will be in charge so that you have some idea what you want.

Other Practical Tasks

Along with the immediate issues of dealing with a death, there are other practical tasks that should be addressed in the days and weeks following your loved one's death.

- Contact the person's lawyer regarding the content of the will, if one exists, and any other legal business.

- You, or whomever has been appointed in the person's will as the personal representative of the estate, should contact the person's bank, brokerage houses, financial advisor, pension administrator, life insurance company, Social Security, and any others with whom the person had significant financial dealings. Many of these persons and institutions will want certified copies of the death certificate.

- Outstanding bills need to be collected and paid, but this should be coordinated with other aspects of handling the estate.

- Club and association memberships (e.g., the golf club, a trade association, or professional organization) need to be cancelled or transferred; the same applies to magazine subscriptions and mail delivery.

- For many families, it is difficult to go through a loved one's personal possessions—clothing, papers, mementos, furniture—in order to sort them, and to decide what the family wishes to keep, and what they want to sell or give away. Like visiting the funeral home, this task is easier if shared among several family members.

To Sum Up . . .

Taking care of all that needs to be done after a death can take months, depending on how the person's affairs were organized and how complicated they were. It is tiring and emotionally draining work. If you can, share the responsibilities among family members, do difficult tasks with another person, and don't take on too much at any one time. It is normal to feel overwhelmed at times. However, taking care of these practical matters is an important part of the grieving process. Performing these tasks well and carefully brings its own sense of satisfaction and helps in the crucial work of saying good-bye to the loved one. As with all aspects of the dying process, even in the midst of hard decisions and actions, there will be times of joy and good remembrance and companionship.

More Resources

- The **Public Broadcasting System's** *On Our Own Terms* series of videotapes may be available from your library. The series' companion website features resources and tools for funeral planning and other end-of-life issues. (*www.pbs.org/wnet/onourownterms*)

- "Funerals: a Consumer Guide," an online factsheet, can be found on **The Federal Trade Commission** website. (*www.ftc.gov/ftc/consumer.htm*)

- The **National Funeral Directors Association** website offers consumer information on funeral planning. (*www.nfda.org*)

- The **Funeral Consumers Alliance** website includes information on funeral planning and avoiding fraud. (*www.funerals.org*)

Quick Links

>>> These web-based resources may be accessed through our website:

www.aginginstride.org

ISSUE 39: EXPERIENCING GRIEF AND LOSS

Grief is the way in which one person lets go of another. Though every person grieves differently, there are some common characteristics. First comes a sense of numbness or unreality that can last from several hours to several days. The numbness is replaced with a profound sense of loss. To grieve is to feel that loss and come to terms with it. This stage of acute grief for a close loved one can last from a few days to many months, depending on the relationship. It is common for those suffering acute grief to exhibit signs of depression: loss of appetite, difficulty sleeping, sadness, restlessness, lack of interest in normally enjoyed activities.

Especially if the one who has died lived with you or was someone with whom you had daily contact, many outside "triggers" bring on a sense of loss in those early days. A time of day comes around when you and that person were always together; his or her favorite song plays on the radio; you cook your loved one's favorite foods; Christmas, birthdays, other holidays come and go. It is normal for these environmental cues to trigger your grief. It is normal to want to talk about both your loved one and your feelings about the death. You tell stories and you laugh. You tell stories and you cry. The talking, laughing, and crying are all part of the healing process. Healing is accomplished by releasing feelings, working through them, and letting them go. Healing also comes from slowly replacing old life patterns with new ones, simply growing accustomed to life without this person you loved.

What is Normal Grief?

It is normal to experience a whole range of emotions and behaviors following a loved one's death. There is sometimes sorrow, although that may come later. If the dying has been sudden, then shock and a sense of unreality linger. If the dying has been long or painful, or if you have given much time to the care of the one who has died, an initial feeling of relief or freedom is common. So is fatigue. So are anger, apathy, restlessness, vulnerability, guilt, and anxiety. Some people's grief is characterized by swift and frequent mood changes. The experience varies from person to person. The following suggestions are ways to help you successfully navigate the work of grief.

- **Allow yourself to feel all you are feeling, and express those feelings.**

  Some people find that writing helps, especially with thoughts and emotions that seem too personal to share. Start a journal. Write a letter to your loved one. The process of getting your feelings out moves forward the grief process.

- **Access your support system.**

  Use your family and friends. Those who love you want to be helpful in this time. One of the most important roles they can play is listening. If they have known the person who died, often they too find it helpful to talk. If you are afraid that you are asking too much of family and friends, or if they don't seem to understand, try a support group. Many hospitals, hospice organizations, and senior centers sponsor such groups, and sometimes it is helpful to surround yourself with people going through the same kind of loss as you. Religious leaders are also trained to help people through the work of grief. There is help out there; you are not alone. Though some people believe that they should not "burden" others with their problems or sorrows, research shows that those who use the resources available to help them through their grieving move through the process faster, and with a healthier outlook.

- **Educate yourself.**

  There is much good literature out there to help you understand what you are experiencing. Most bookstores contain an entire section of books concerning grief. They range from "how-to" texts that give you concrete suggestions for addressing the problems encountered in grieving, to personal narratives of people who have been where you are.

- **Take care of yourself physically.**

  Emotional state is affected by physical state. Eat balanced meals, get adequate sleep, and do some form of physical activity every day. The inertia of grief often makes it difficult to want to prepare food, or to get out in the yard, or take a walk. But forcing yourself to make the effort is worth it. Eating regularly increases your energy level. Getting exercise releases the endorphins into your system that promote a greater sense of well-being and also helps you sleep better. These elements of self-care are fundamental to navigating the grief process.

- **Avoid alcohol and other substances not prescribed by your doctor.**

  Although they may initially numb emotional pain, drugs and alcohol may prolong, complicate, and delay your grief.

- **Give yourself permission to say no.**

  Do not rush to take on new responsibilities. Say no to social engagements that make you feel uncomfortable. There is a fine line here, though. On the one hand, it's OK to take the time you need. On the other hand, isolating yourself can prolong your grieving and keep you from making the adjustments you need to make. Try to monitor yourself. Most of us know when we really should be saying yes to a job or an invitation, and it is simply inertia or fear that keeps us saying no.

- **Be patient and gentle with yourself.**

  Healing from grief takes time. Often, people outside do not understand how much time it takes. Even those grieving are often surprised by what a long and complex process it is. Respect your own way of grieving. We are all individuals. Some people talk more; some talk less. One person finds release from grief in physical labor; another finds it holding babies in the church nursery; still another uses writing as a primary tool. As long as you are making progress, then the strategies you are using work for you.

How Do You Know When Your Grief Is Not Normal?

Occasionally, for a number of reasons, people get stuck in the grieving process. The block may have to do with the particulars of the relationship between you and the one who has died. It may be caused by other stresses in your life. Whatever the cause, if you are having trouble dealing with the death of someone close to you, get help. A variety of help is available in most communities. Check your community's resources and use them.

There is no absolute divide that separates normal and abnormal grief. Most people grieving the loss of someone close to them report periods of "feeling crazy." However, most people get better over time. For some, the sadness diminishes gradually; for others, the time between painful episodes grows longer. There is no constant, no ideal standard by which to measure your experience. However, some guidelines are helpful:

- If you experience significant physical symptoms of depression after the first few months following the death, you should seek help. Physical symptoms to watch for include sleeplessness, lack of appetite, constant fatigue, irritability, lack of concentration. A good place to start with any of these symptoms is your primary care physician. Have a checkup. Your doctor may prescribe medication or refer you to a trained grief counselor.

- If, after a period of several months, your grief significantly disrupts the patterns of your life, your ability to work, your other relationships, or your regular pastimes, you will want to seek help.

- If your friends, family, or others you trust suggest that you need help, listen to them. Sometimes those on the outside can see more clearly than you.

Where to Find Help

Many sources of help are available to those suffering from unresolved grief. Choose the kind of counseling or group experience that feels most comfortable and that you would find valuable.

- **Individual counselors**—Many psychiatrists, psychologists, social workers, pastoral counselors, and other therapists work with people who are grieving. You can get referrals from your physician, clergyperson, or a local health provider (such as a hospital or hospice organization). Check your health insurance to see whether counseling is an included benefit and if you are limited to certain providers.

- **Support groups**—Many people find it helpful to join or form a group to share the grieving process and provide mutual understanding and support. For some, such a community experience is available informally within a circle of friends and acquaintances. However, most people who want such a group must seek it out. Many social service agencies and health care providers offer or sponsor bereavement groups on an ongoing basis, or can make a referral to a program in your community.

The most important consideration when choosing a setting in which to address issues of unresolved grief is to find an environment that is comfortable and safe so you can enter into the experience, deal with the issues that are troubling you, and allow healing to take place. The goal of grief work is not to banish sadness. The goal is to come to an acceptable sense of closure and go on with your own life.

The Particular Problems of Sudden Death

Up to this point, we have been talking about grief as a general process. However, if the one you love dies suddenly, the death can catch you unprepared, both emotionally and practically. Though you might feel grateful that your loved one has not suffered, there has been no opportunity for closure. Business and financial affairs are often not in order. Many people who have experienced the sudden death of a loved one remain in a seeming state of unreality for days or even weeks. They worry about words left unsaid and things left undone.

Going through the practical and logistical tasks that must be done is an important part of facing the reality of the death. If you are worried about emotional closure, if you feel there are things that should have been said that you had no opportunity to say, it is often helpful to write a letter to the one you loved, saying all that you wish you might have said. Alternately, you might say those things to another person. It is important that you get those thoughts and feelings—and whatever grief or anger you feel because they were unsaid—outside of yourself. You need to forgive yourself and let go of whatever was left dangling. Remember that a long-time relationship speaks for itself. Although there might have been particular issues left unresolved, there was a long history of good things between you. Trust that. Allow yourself to be at rest. It is an important part of your healing.

Death After a Long Illness

Just as there are issues particular to sudden death, there are particular feelings and concerns that accompany death after a chronic and terminal illness. In such cases, the immediate death is often followed by a sense of relief. It is understandable to feel grateful that one you love is released from suffering. If you have been a primary caregiver, it is also natural to feel relief that the burden of caregiving has been lifted. Some people feel guilty about this sense of release, but that guilt is misplaced. It is normal and right to feel relief. It does not mean you don't care, that you loved the person any less. You have experienced what is called "anticipatory grief" in journeying with another towards death. By the time your loved one dies, you have already grieved the loss of much of your relationship with that person. This does not mean you will not grieve after the death itself; it only means that the circumstances of serious illness gave you a head start.

One of the gifts of life-threatening illness is that it usually allows time to do both the emotional and practical work of closure. That is something for which to be thankful. There are still practical issues to be resolved and feelings that are difficult, but much less is left incomplete than with sudden death. In fact, many who have cared for a loved one during a long illness find their major challenge is a sense of not having enough to do. Affairs are in order and the work of caregiving, which has been so emotionally and physically demanding, is over. The absence of that work can leave a large hole in their lives. Go cautiously. Though you may not know it, you are probably exhausted in body and spirit. Caregiving is enormously demanding, using up emotional and physical reserves. Caregivers need some time to rest, to heal, before taking on major new commitments. Give yourself that time to shore up your reserves, and then go about deciding what to do with the time that has been freed up. It is important enough to say this again: when you have been a primary caregiver, pay particular attention to eating well and exercising so that your sleep is improved and your body can heal itself.

The Gift of Remembering

Although acute grief does end, there will always be moments when remembering will be easy and other moments when it is painful. Celebrating a grandchild's birthday or graduation, you wish your spouse could be there. Christmas comes, and a place at the table seems empty. If you have loved, there will always be times when the reality of your loved one's death will be hard for you.

Part of letting go is learning to find comfort and joy in your memories, in the stories you can remember of those you love. Memory is a wonderful gift. It keeps your relationships with loved ones alive even when the people themselves have died. Savor your memories. Share your stories with others. Those recollections are a treasure, both for you and for your family. They are the cord that links generations and gives strength and continuity to family life.

To Sum Up . . .

Everyone's experience is different. The stages of grieving do not pass overnight. The time needed to get over a major loss can be as short as a few weeks—or as long as many months or even years. If you are concerned about yourself or a friend, don't look so much to the time involved, as to what is happening physically and emotionally during that time.

More Resources

- The **National Hospice and Palliative Care Organization** website includes information on grief and bereavement for family, co-workers and management. (*www.nhpco.org*)

- The **Public Broadcasting System's** *On Our Own Terms* series of videotapes may be available from your library. The series' companion website features information about the grieving process. (*www.pbs.org/wnet/onourownterms*)

- The **Department of Health and Human Services'** Federal Occupational Health website offers "A Lifecare Guide to Grief and Bereavement." (*www.foh.dhhs.gov*)

- **AARP**'s website includes a section on grief and loss. (*www.aarp.org*)

The Support of Family and Friends

INTRODUCTION

Up until this point, this book has been addressed primarily to older adults, with the hope that family and friends will also find the topics helpful and interesting. But the next group of issues is addressed primarily to family and friends who are involved in being loving and helpful to the older adults in their lives. Our focus is the primary issues involved in being a supportive and effective helper, friend, caregiver, and advocate.

The desire to be of help and support to an older adult is a good thing. For most of us, that desire is grounded in love and concern. We see our parents, neighbors, or older friends having difficulty managing housework or personal care and it makes us sad or worried. We notice that Aunt Ellie is becoming socially isolated, or that a dear friend's failing eyesight is impacting his driving and personal grooming, and we are troubled. A work colleague's mother falls and breaks her hip, and suddenly we are aware of our own parents' increasing frailty, and wish they lived nearer to us.

It is a positive impulse to want to be helpful to the older adults in our lives. The challenge is translating the desire to help into words and actions that respect and honor, as much as possible, the ability of seniors to control their own lives and make the choices that seem best for them. It is so easy for a well-meaning son, niece, or friend to move unintentionally from the desire to help to an attitude of knowing best what should be done for their loved one. In "taking charge" of the situation, the person who attempts to be helpful instead diminishes the older person's confidence, self-respect, and ability to manage affairs.

The best kind of support family and friends can offer blends qualities of communication, respect, compromise, flexibility, and common sense. In most situations, rushing in with a sweeping "quick fix" is not the best approach. Any would-be helper must honor the older person's need and right to think and act independently for as long as possible. Sometimes this means standing by while an older loved one makes decisions that are quite different from the decisions you would make. Most often, it means negotiating compromise solutions where all parties give a little to reach a plan that is workable, if not ideal, for everyone.

The issues in this section are intended to offer guidance to family members, friends, and older adults as you talk and work together. Remember that you share a common goal: that the individual for whom you are planning lives life as fully and joyfully as possible.

In Issue 40, we begin by looking at what it takes to get everyone working together toward a shared set of goals, rather than at cross purposes. "Being on the same page" starts with a look at family dynamics, good communication, and the development of a plan.

Then, in Issue 41, we look at the special challenges you face if you want to stay involved as a caregiver or source of support for your loved one, but live far away. Long-distance caregiving poses special challenges, but because so many people find themselves in that position, there are good resources available to help you out.

One of the resources families often use as they sort through senior care issues is a private geriatric care manager, an eldercare professional, usually a nurse or social worker, who can do assessments, give guidance, and help families develop and implement a plan of care for frail older adults. Issue 42 will introduce you to the range of services care managers provide and give you guidance in choosing and developing a positive relationship with a care manager.

Issue 43 explores the subject of sharing your home with an older relative or friend. What should you consider before entering such an arrangement? What can you do to make sure that sharing your home works for all parties?

Despite the growing number of assisted living facilities, nursing facilities and adult foster homes, the majority of older adults needing care still receive that care at home from a family member. Issue 44 looks at the concerns of being a primary caregiver. Taking care of a loved one can be rewarding and result in a level of personalized care for your loved one that no institutional care facility can match. Caregiving is demanding, however. This issue will help you move into the relationship with realistic expectations and give you practical advice on taking care of both the recipient and the giver of care.

Finally, in Issue 45, we take a look at one special role in taking care of a loved one: serving as that person's health care representative. What is a health care representative? What is the scope of your responsibilities? How can you best prepare for this role? If you have to make life and death decisions for your loved one, how should you approach these decisions? What resources exist to help you?

In the forms section you will find the following tools to help you in your role as caregiver, friend, advocate, and representative:

- Form 40: *Family Meeting Planner*
- Form 42: *Checklist for Selecting and Working with a Geriatric Care Manager*
- Form 45: *Health Care Representative's Discussion Checklist*

ISSUE 40: EVERYONE ON THE SAME PAGE

Many older adults live independently well into their 80s and 90s. They enjoy good health, remain active and involved, are able to take care of their business and legal affairs. We all wish we could live out that scenario—and, as we've seen, there is much we can do to help keep the mind and body sharp and functioning well. However, sudden or chronic illness, decreasing energy, a fall, or failing memory may make it difficult if not impossible for an older person to live safely and comfortably alone or to manage his or her business affairs. Help of one kind or another becomes necessary. Usually those involved in helping are immediate or extended family; sometimes friends and neighbors also play a role. For every person needing help, there is a particular team or support network: the group of family, friends, and professionals who work together with that person to provide assistance for the present and plan for the future.

Getting Started

Families get involved in two ways to provide care for an aging family member. Sometimes, the need for help comes on incrementally. Here's a common scenario:

It started out that sister Mary, who lives closest to Dad, helped him balance his checkbook every month because his failing eyesight made reading the bank statements difficult. But as his vision continued to fail, Dad gave up driving and Mary started coming by twice a week to take Dad on errands and to bell choir rehearsal at church. After a bill was incorrectly paid, she took over all Dad's business affairs. During Dad's bout of bronchitis last winter, she started coming over every day, taking over meal preparation, housekeeping, and an increasing amount of personal care. After three months of this, Mary was exhausted; her husband resented the amount of time she spent away; and finally in a phone call to her sister, she fell apart.

It's a pretty common story: one family member providing an increasing amount of care almost without noticing it until it becomes too much. Then the rest of the team is called in.

The second trigger for family involvement is a sudden illness or traumatic event—a broken hip, the death of a spouse, a heart attack, or stroke. Almost overnight, a person who had been living independently can no longer do so. The family gathers to help figure out what will happen next.

Whenever family comes together, there are family issues. Every family has them. Old patterns of behavior, competing loyalties, hurts, insecurities, jealousies, angers. Families aren't simple. As the team gathers in love and concern to take care of an older family member, there will be the primary agenda—"How do we best take care of Dad?"—and then, often just beneath the surface of discussion, there will be the secondary agendas of old family business—"Mom always loved you best!"

The old business will always be there. In the stress of having to make decisions for an ailing family member, it is easy for that "residue" to take over, making teamwork impossible. The best way to minimize that possibility is to be aware of the problem and decide as a group to either keep other family issues in the background, or, if that is impossible, to get those issues out on the table and deal with them *before* you tackle the problem of care for your loved one. You want to avoid entangling the present problem in old family issues. Does that sound impossible? It may be for some families. But it is worth trying, both for the well-being of the person needing care and the well-being of the whole family.

Holding a Family Meeting

When faced with the challenge of figuring out a care plan, many families find it helpful to hold a family meeting. Depending on your family's style, this meeting may either be very formal or relatively informal. Family meetings are often an excellent way to share information, mobilize resources, and agree on a game plan. A structured family meeting also tends to minimize the inward creep of old family business. If you wish to plan a family meeting, consider these suggestions:

- Prepare ahead to give structure to your discussions. Write out and send an agenda to those who will be attending. Make sure assignments and responsibilities are clearly detailed on the agenda. It's helpful to divide the work among team members. One person can be assigned to talk with the doctor, another to explore various home care services, and a third to provide companionship and information to the person needing care. Form 40, *Family Meeting Planner,* is available as a suggested guide.

- If one family member is already more actively involved as a caregiver or advocate, you need to honor that role. Should that caregiver be the one to organize and plan the family meeting? Would it be more considerate to have that person *not* plan the meeting, letting someone else take that job, leaving the caregiver to simply report what has happened and how he or she sees the current situation? Remember that "thank you" can be the two most powerful words in the English language.

- Whenever possible, the loved one for whose life you are planning should attend and participate in the meeting. None of us likes to think that others are plotting behind our backs! From the very beginning, find out what help your loved one thinks that he/she needs. Listen closely. Learn as much as possible about your loved one's goals and priorities. No matter what that person's physical or mental status, acknowledge and respect his or her presence, and the views and feelings they bring to the discussion. Never talk about *anyone* in the third person as though he or she were not in the room.

- Finally, if you know absolutely or are "pretty sure" that a family meeting will be difficult, consider asking a trusted friend, mediator, or a professional care manager to attend and help focus the discussion. Asking a third party to facilitate will usually cost money and it will make the meeting more formal, but in difficult family situations, both those considerations may prove to be advantages. Most family members work harder at being tactful and cooperative with an outside person in the room, and knowing that the meeting is costing money may serve to keep people focused on the business at hand!

Setting the Tone

Those who do research on group dynamics and what makes a successful meeting tell us that setting a positive tone and making sure every person knows his or her presence is important almost assures you of a productive meeting.

Begin your family meeting with family time. Let each person have a turn to speak about how they're feeling, what their questions and concerns are. Acknowledge the contributions that have been and are being made. There will always be imbalances in the contributions of various team members, based on geography, financial resources, skills, and time. Look for practical ways to share responsibilities. To the extent that work can't be spread evenly, make sure you recognize and appreciate those who are taking on major roles or tasks.

Developing a Team Strategy for Helping

What is the goal of your family meeting? Or if you elect not to have a formal family meeting, what is your goal as care team? For most families, the goal can be simply articulated: develop a plan of care for your loved one that meets essential needs, is acceptable to him or her, and allows family members to be less worried. Again, if your parent or other relative is able, he or she should be the central player in developing a plan. You, as the support team, are the implementation squad! Sometimes illness, confusion, or trauma make it impossible for a person to participate in the planning. Usually the reality lies somewhere in the middle of those two opposing poles. The person receiving care and the support team need to work together to make a plan. It is always important, as much as possible, that the plan reflect the values, life goals, and priorities of the person for whom it is being made, even if those goals, priorities, and values are not shared by other family members.

Most care plans involve a mix of contributors. Family members who live close by agree to certain responsibilities. Family members farther away do whatever jobs can be done long distance, providing support, encouragement, and back-up so that the primary caregivers can have some respite. Some responsibilities are delegated to paid providers. These can include everything from bill paying to yard maintenance to assistance in daily grooming. Beyond the essential jobs accomplished by the core team, many families depend on an expanded team that includes neighbors and friends who provide a range of helpful services, from transportation and grocery shopping to a daily or weekly check-in and simple companionship.

If no family members live close to the person needing care, this poses special challenges to the care plan. Issue 41, *Staying Involved When You Don't Live Nearby*, will be important for you to read. Someone locally should be designated the "official" emergency contact person. Sometimes this can be a friend or neighbor. However, you might also want to look into the services of a paid geriatric care manager. Read Issue 42, *Working with a Geriatric Care Manager*, for more information to help you decide if this option is right for you. If you think a care manager might be of help in your family situation, it is always an advantage to choose this person and establish a relationship *before* a crisis occurs.

At the end of all your deliberations, you should have a plan. The plan has to pass four tests to be approved:

- Most importantly, it has to be acceptable to the person for whom it has been formulated.

- It has to address, in a meaningful way, as many of the needs you're dealing with as possible. But don't expect your plan to be perfect or solve all problems. The plan that does everything does not exist! Be realistic in your expectations.

- The plan has to be financially sound. No plan can depend on financial resources that aren't available.

- All the members of the team need to agree to the plan, even if it wasn't their first choice, even if they have some reservations. The responsibility for the plan must be shared by all.

So now you have your plan. It has passed all four tests. Before you go out and celebrate, take time to write down what you have decided. Include as much detail as necessary about who has taken on what responsibilities and assignments. Include timelines and pathways of responsibility when necessary (e.g., Sally will get investment information to Allen by next Friday). Make sure that every member of the team has a copy of the plan. Also make sure that there is a contact list so that all team members know how to reach each other. The next step is to stay in touch and monitor how the plan is working.

Developing Good Communications Skills

If your family already has good communication skills, chances are that you developed your plan with relatively little difficulty. But families with a history of communication problems experience more difficulty working together. Almost everyone, though, needs to be reminded occasionally of the basic skills that make *all* interactions easier.

- **When having an important conversation, think about what you will say in advance, be careful with your words, make sure the other person is understanding you.** If you have something important to say, treat it as if it were important. Just as you prepare for important business meetings or festive family dinners, take care that the conversation goes well.

- **Learn to tell and to accept the truth.** Honesty is vital in working with any team. It is crucial as you work together to plan and implement care for a loved one.

- **Think of family communications as an opportunity for personal and family growth.** If your family history has been difficult in the past, take advantage of this new challenge as an opportunity to turn the page and make a fresh start in *good* communication.

- **Be inclusive.** Make sure that everyone is invited to talk, to share their opinions and perspective. Don't let one or two family members dominate the discussion and the decision-making.

- **Stick with it.** Work on a model of consensus decision-making. Reaching consensus usually takes some work. Be willing to give it the time and effort it requires.

- **Be open to both asking for and accepting help.** The whole idea in bringing together the team is to not "go it alone."

- **Share the load.** Try to develop a fair balance in terms of sharing responsibilities within your family. If there's some rebalancing to be done, or some disproportionate efforts to be acknowledged, make sure that happens.

- **Know when to say "no."** If the "fairness" message is not getting through, or if you are simply stretched beyond your capacity, it may be time to say no. It's also important to let others know that "no" is an acceptable response, as long as they are willing to help you work out an alternative.

When Reaching Consensus Doesn't Work

So far in this issue, we have presented a scenario where family members, despite whatever other business is going on, are able to come to a workable plan for taking care of a loved one needing care. Sometimes it's not that simple. There are times when family members, especially those of different generations, see a problem in an entirely different way and so see entirely different solutions. For example:

> Helen is a woman in her 80s living alone. In the past five years, her energy for housework has decreased, and her house has gotten away from her. Most of her friends have moved out of the neighborhood, so she has whole days with no social interaction. On those days, she doesn't bother to get dressed or to bathe. Helen's only daughter, Marie, lives 50 miles away. She tries to visit her mother once or twice a week.

> As the level of her mother's housekeeping and grooming has declined, Marie has grown more worried about her mother's living situation. A week ago, when she came to visit her mother, Marie found her on the floor, where she had fallen an hour before. That mobilized Marie. Certain that her mother could live alone no longer, Marie took two days off from work to visit assisted living facilities. Having found two she really liked, she came enthusiastically to her mother. But Helen refused even to go see them, insisting she did not want to move, that it was too expensive, and she didn't want to live with old people. Marie offered the compromise that her mother would stay at home, but Marie would arrange a cleaning service to come in and help with the house, making falls less likely. Her mother refused; it was too expensive. Marie offered to pay. Again, Helen refused.

The story of Marie and Helen follows an all too common script. Marie obviously didn't handle the subject of moving very well when she talked with her mother. Helen was unprepared, and upset that Marie had done research "behind her back." Marie made some mistakes, but her actions were all motivated out of genuine concern for her mother's well-being, fueled by her shock at having found her mother on the floor. Helen also made some mistakes. She was being stubbornly independent. In fact, the condition of her house did make living there unsafe. She was unwilling to admit to herself the truth about that, or to let Marie help her find solutions.

The problem now is that both Helen and Marie are feeling hurt, angry, and as if their feelings are not being considered. Nothing has changed in the mother's living situation, but their relationship has taken a turn for the worse.

What is to be done here? If Marie's mother is legally competent, she has the right as an adult to make the significant decisions of her life, even if she makes bad decisions for herself. It is the most difficult lesson that would-be caring family members have to face. If an older adult can still reason for himself or herself, then he or she is the ultimate decision maker. Family members have to accept those decisions, even when they see the possibility for serious consequences.

If you have been in Marie's shoes in this situation, you know the range and depth of emotions stirred by such an impasse. It's hard to watch someone you love make mistakes, especially when you're afraid that eventually you will be picking up the pieces. But at the end, it is that person's life, and that person's choice. If you find yourself in this position, make sure you have support. Good friends or other family members are helpful for venting and sharing your concerns; use them. If you find yourself upset over time, seek counseling. It is a genuinely hard situation.

If you have been in Helen's shoes, we counsel you to think hard about your choices. Yes, you are entitled to make your own decisions, but part of that is being honest in your assessments of what's needed. When your family "gangs up on you" because they're worried, it's time to recheck your honesty meter. Sometimes families are pushy and alarmist; sometimes, however, older family members are stubborn and not weighing their options realistically.

Nobody wins when family conflicts come to a stalemate. The best outcome will be that all parties retreat to their own corners, think things through, and try again, having learned something from the first encounter.

To Sum Up . . .

Working together as a family or support network to take care of a loved one can be tricky. Try not to get bogged down in old family business. Focus on planning, sharing the load, identifying resources, and communicating effectively. Be sure your loved one is involved to the fullest extent possible, in a way that respects and promotes independence, autonomy, dignity, and life goals. In most situations, families can come to a solution that is workable, if not perfect, and brings peace of mind to the family.

More Resources

- The **Family Caregiver Alliance** offers resources and decision-making information about elder care, including the fact sheets "Helping Families Make Everyday Care Choices" and "Holding a Family Meeting." (*www.caregiver.org*)

- **AARP's** website includes resources and information about making caregiving decisions as a family. (*www.aarp.org*)

- The **National Family Caregivers Association** website features information, support and tips. (*www.nfcacares.org*)

Quick Links

>>> These web-based resources may be accessed through our website: www.aginginstride.org

ISSUE 41: STAYING INVOLVED WHEN YOU DON'T LIVE NEARBY

In earlier times, it was common for families to live in the same community generation after generation. Shorter distances made it easier for families to stay close. They could share the responsibilities that go along with caring for older family members.

Today, we live in a much more mobile society. Families are often spread out from one end of the country to the other. They still stay in touch, but they do it by phone, e-mail, and occasional visits.

This arrangement works until a parent, grandparent, or other close relative needs care and support, or when a care crisis occurs. Then you come face to face with the challenge of long-distance caregiving. It is troubling when someone you love is in difficulty and you are far away. It's complicated to know where to go for information, how to arrange for necessary help.

We can't make your worrying go away. However, be assured that many people before you have faced the same challenge. There are systems and service providers available to help you out. And there *are* ways to stay emotionally close and give support in these times. Here are some practical suggestions for understanding your loved one's needs and working with friends, relatives, and professional service providers to make sure those needs are met.

Assessing Your Situation

The first step for staying involved as a caregiver, even from a distance, is to be well informed about the issues and concerns your loved one is facing and the resources available to deal with them. You need to talk with those who are on the scene. Ask lots of questions. Listen to what people are telling you. Make notes as you go along, so you can refer back to them later.

The information you gather will play an important role in planning and managing care. Discuss what you learn with other family members and the professionals who are involved.

Your sources of information might include:

- The person about whom you are concerned.

- Family members, friends and neighbors living close by.

- Apartment or other residential manager.

- The person's doctor or other health care provider.

- The person's clergy, lawyer, accountant, or other advisor.

- A social worker or care manager familiar with the person's situation and care plan.

Remember, too, that information needs to flow in both directions. Make a note of the names, phone numbers, and e-mail addresses of anyone who can help keep you informed. Be sure to let them know how to contact you if something happens.

Making a Plan

Once you have a feel for the issues, it's time to begin determining what your role can and should be. Here are some points to keep in mind as you do this planning:

- Unless he or she is completely incapacitated, the person you're planning for must be centrally involved in developing the plan. You are trying to help Mom arrange her life, not arrange her life for her! It's a subtle but important difference. Other people who should be consulted include other local family members and any professionals who are involved, such as social workers, a care manager, or your loved one's lawyer.

- Your goal is to support your family member's maximum level of independence. Self-esteem, dignity, and health status are all best served by remaining as active and involved as possible.

- Set priorities for your involvement. You can't do everything! Decide what's most important, and what you can, in fact, do.

- Be realistic in your goals and expectations. Some issues can be quickly and easily resolved. Others persist, despite your best efforts to make them go away.

- Remember, caregiving responsibilities call for teamwork whenever possible. If other family members live closer and are doing more than you are able to do, find ways to acknowledge the greater role they are playing. Ask their help in finding concrete ways that you, too, can be helpful. Say "thank you" and find other ways to express your appreciation often.

Resources Available to Help

As you prepare to get involved in caregiving from a distance, it's reassuring to know that an entire network of eldercare support services is out there to help. Here are three key resources you can tap:

- If the person is already in an institutional care setting, coordinate with the professionals on the facility's team. Ask whether it's appropriate, given your relationship to the person and his or her wishes concerning confidentiality, for you to receive and give input to the person's plan of care. Try to schedule your next visit to coincide with a care conference at which the person's needs and care plan will be discussed.

- If community-based eldercare services are needed, contact the local Area Agency on Aging. You can find a phone number in the Yellow Pages, or by phoning the National Eldercare Locator number, 1-800-677-1116.

- A growing number of long distance caregivers find it helpful to work with a geriatric care manager. These eldercare professionals can be of great value in assessing caregiving needs and coordinating needed services. Care managers can be consulted to help solve a one-time problem, such as arranging for an alternate living situation and coordinating the move. They can also develop an ongoing relationship with your family in which the care manager stays involved as local advocate and care coordinator. To lean more about finding and working with a geriatric care manager, turn to Issue 42.

Staying Close, Despite the Distance

Providing needed services for your parent or other relative is only one part of the care equation. For that person's sake and your own, you will probably want to find ways to maintain and strengthen your emotional connection. Sometimes small things contribute in a big way to a sense of being in touch. For example:

- Old-fashioned letter writing is never out of style. Take the time to bring your loved one up to date in this way. Encourage others in the family, including grandchildren, to write letters, make audio or video cassettes, or send photos.

- Make it easier for your relative to write back by pre-addressing and stamping envelopes to yourself and other family members. Why not provide a supply of greeting cards for all occasions and a calendar identifying major celebrations within the family?

- Get in the habit of calling or having your relative call you on a regular basis. If you can afford it, encourage calling collect. Perhaps a pre-paid phone card can be a monthly or annual gift.

- Find out whether your relative has e-mail access or would be open to learning. If so, make sure friends and family know the person's e-mail address, and encourage them to use it.

- Fax machines have become relatively inexpensive. Some older adults find them less intimidating than e-mail. Communicating via fax allows you and your loved one to share items of interest on the spot: a great-nephew's graduation announcement, a newspaper clipping about a promotion at work, etc. When one of you has a question about a medical bill, for example, it can be faxed so you both have a copy in hand when you discuss it.

To Sum Up . . .

It's distressing to be far away when problems arise. But you can do what needs doing! Work with the available network of family, friends, and service providers. Find ways to stay in touch. And remember, caregiving, even from a distance, is stressful to the caregiver. Be extra kind to yourself.

More Resources

- The **AARP** website offers information on long-distance caregiving and other aspects of caring for aging parents. (*www.aarp.org*)

- The **Family Caregiver Alliance** website includes articles about long-distance caregiving. (*www.caregiver.org*)

- The **National Family Caregivers Association** website features information, support and tips. (*www.nfcacares.org*)

Quick Links

>>> These web-based resources may be accessed through our website:

www.aginginstride.org

ISSUE 42: WORKING WITH A GERIATRIC CARE MANAGER

Geriatric care managers provide assessment and coordination services for older adults and their families. These services can be of great value, especially when family members live at a distance, or when a needs assessment is necessary. Private care management services are largely unregulated. The qualifications of groups or individuals offering to act as private geriatric care managers vary widely, so be careful whom you select for this role. Ask lots of questions. Check references carefully.

What Does a Care Manager Do?

Care management services for older adults have developed in response to the growing population of elderly persons and the range and complexity of the programs available to serve their needs.

When it becomes clear that an older person is no longer able to live alone entirely unassisted, the person and family members may be unsure of what services are available in the community to help. They may wonder how best to take advantage of those services. A care manager can help.

Most professional care managers have experience in either nursing or social work. Many have special training in issues involving eldercare. Their job is to assess a client's individual needs, then match those needs with services available in the community.

Many care managers also provide follow-up care and monitoring to see that necessary services are being effectively and professionally delivered, and to make sure that the client's needs are being met over an extended period of time. If moving to an assisted living or nursing facility is appropriate, a care manager can help in identifying and evaluating the various options available.

A care manager will usually begin a client relationship by doing an assessment of the client's health status, living situation, and needs. In the course of an extensive interview, the older adult's physical and mental condition, social situation, and daily activities are evaluated. Usually a written report of this assessment is provided, with suggestions as to services available to meet perceived needs.

If the client and family wish, the care manager can then arrange for the needed services and see they are delivered.

When caregiving starts to get complicated, especially in situations of long distances between families, care managers are a wonderful resource to manage and balance several concerns. They can schedule assistance and keep multiple family members informed.

How Do I Find a Care Manager?

Private geriatric care managers who are members of the National Association of Professional Geriatric Care Managers are listed at its website, *www.caremanager.org*. Your local Senior Information and Referral may also be able to provide referrals.

How to Choose a Care Management Professional

Because care management is a largely unregulated profession, it is important to do your homework when choosing a care manager. This means asking questions before making your selection. Things to ask include:

- What are the person's qualifications and experience?

- Will the person provide references? Ask for two or three references from past or current clients. If that's not possible because of confidentiality, ask for the names of professionals in the community who are referring new clients to this person. Then, call the references you've been given and gather as much information as you can about the care manager and the services provided.

- Is this person or firm affiliated with a particular organization? If so, what are that organization's values and commitment to service? Will the care manager be able to be objective in making recommendations?

- What is the range of services provided?

- What are the charges, and what particular services are covered by the charges?

- Are the charges competitive with other services in the community?

Use Form 42, *Checklist for Selecting and Working With a Geriatric Care Manager*, as a guide in gathering information and making your choice.

Paying for Care Management Services

Check first with your health insurance plan to see whether it covers care management or case management services. If it does, that's probably the place to start. Many care managers work as part of a governmental or charitable program serving older adults, and their services either come free or on a sliding scale. Others charge a flat fee for an initial assessment, then charge by the hour after that. Hourly charges vary greatly, but are usually between $50 and $100 per hour. Some forms of long-term care insurance reimburse for care management services. However, clients and families most often pay the costs out-of-pocket. For low-income seniors, some care management services may be available through Medicaid or other government programs.

To Sum Up . . .

It is often difficult to juggle caregiving responsibilities in already complicated lives. The emergence of a new group of service providers—geriatric care managers—is a welcome development for busy family members, especially those living far away. Carefully screened, care managers can evaluate care needs and coordinate services, making sure that your loved one's care needs are met on a one-time or ongoing basis.

More Resources

- The **National Association of Professional Geriatric Care Managers** offers information, a directory and other resources. (*www.caremanager.org*)

- The U.S. **Administration on Aging** website contains information and resources about the services of geriatric care managers. (*www.aoa.gov*)

Quick Links

>>> These web-based resources may be accessed through our website:

www.aginginstride.org

ISSUE 43: SHARING YOUR HOME

As your parent or other close friend or relative gets older, you may become concerned about his or her ability to continue to live independently. Safety hazards in the home, inability to drive, a changing neighborhood, declining health, loneliness, or other factors may cause the person, and you, to consider other options. As one of those options, you may want to offer to share your home with your loved one.

Sharing your home can be a delightful, enriching experience for everyone involved, or it can become a very difficult situation, with everyone diminished by the experience. Living in a multi-generational household can be wonderful, but is not for everyone. Sometimes it may be better to say no and work toward another more satisfactory living alternative, than to struggle with a situation that simply doesn't fit the person's or your needs and limitations.

Making the Decision to Share Your Home

Sharing your home will have an impact on everyone in the household: you, your spouse, children, other people living in the household, and, of course, the older person for whom you'll be caring. Everyone will have to make adjustments and take part in making the newly configured household work smoothly. So, everyone needs to be a part of the decision-making process. Together, the family must determine whether this will be a good idea.

If your family currently has its own significant problems with health, family relations, or other stressful situations, adding another member to the household may make things harder, no matter how much you and your family love that person. You need to decide as a group whether or not you have the emotional energy to take in another person. Of course, you will not be able to anticipate all that the future may hold, but careful thinking and planning before you commit yourself may help you avoid a painful or unworkable situation.

As you think through your ability and willingness to have your loved one live with you, he or she should be going through a similar evaluation process. This is not a decision to be made in haste. Both you and your older relative should understand and be able to articulate in advance why you think this would be a mutually beneficial arrangement, what you expect from each other, and what you expect from yourselves. In that way, if you decide to live together, each of you knows the other's feelings.

Here are some of the more important factors to keep in mind as you make this decision.

Family Stability and Attitude

Ask yourself and other family members these questions:

- Is your spouse (or other adult living in the home) willing to have your loved one living in your home?

- How strong is your marriage or other primary relationship?

- If you have children living at home, how are they doing generally? Do they enjoy this person? What accommodations will they be expected to make in a homesharing arrangement? What benefits will they gain?

- Are there unresolved family grievances and disagreements?

- Do you find it easy to talk with this person? Can you talk about problems that may occur between you without undue tension?

- What kinds of things do you disagree about? Will those disagreements be a source of tension in the household?

- Do you enjoy spending time with your loved one? Does he/she enjoy time spent with you and your family?

- Do you or your loved one have any habits that are unacceptable to each other, such as smoking or drinking?

- How strongly does the person *want* to come to live with you? Is this option a last resort or a first choice?

- How much work will having a new household member add to the household tasks? Who will do that additional work? How do other family members feel about sharing the extra work load?

- What kinds of personal care needs does the person have? How do you and other family members feel about performing those needed services? How does the person feel about receiving that kind of personal help from family?

- What is your reason for inviting your loved one to live with you? What is your mix of personal, family, historical, and financial reasons?

These are difficult questions to answer for everyone involved. There are no standard right answers that will assure you all of a successful living relationship. Be aware also that there are no ideal solutions. The purpose of such questions is not to scare you off, but to help you identify concerns in advance of a new situation.

Your Home and Neighborhood

One of the major considerations in having an older person who needs care move in with you is the size and layout of your home. Issues of safety, privacy, and convenience need to be considered. Here are some questions to ask:

- Is there a private bedroom available for your loved one? If not, how will you deal with everyone's need for privacy?

- Is the available bedroom easily accessible? Can the person get to it without climbing stairs? Is there an outside entrance?

- What will you do with the person's furniture and belongings? Might all of them, or some of them, be incorporated into your household to add a sense of familiarity for the person? What arrangements for storage or disposal of unnecessary household goods can be made?

- Is your home safe for an older person? Use Form 6-A, *Home Safety Inspection Checklist*, to see what changes you'll need to make.

- Even if the person has no mobility problems now, is your home adaptable to canes, walkers, or wheelchairs if the need should arise in the future?

- Is the house in a relatively safe neighborhood, so that your loved one can take walks, get to the bus stop, or visit neighbors?

Finances and Household Chores

It is often difficult to talk about money issues. These are some of the questions to ask:

- What do you expect from this person in return for sharing your home? Will he or she have regular household chores or services to be performed as part of the household responsibilities?

- Do you expect him or her to pay room and board? To pay for some expenses? Can you afford to have a permanent guest?

- Will any other family members help out financially?

Remember, if you provide more than half the financial support for your parent, you may be able to claim an additional personal exemption on your federal and state income tax returns.

Family Lifestyle

The way your family lives its common life is an important consideration in deciding whether to share your home. Consider questions like these:

- What effect will having this person living with you have on your social life?

- Does he or she have friends near where you live? Will the person expect to entertain friends in your home?

- Will you include this person in all your outings and vacations? Which ones will be suitable?

- Is your loved one accustomed to a schedule like your household's? Is he or she willing and able to adapt to the family schedule for mealtimes and other important routine household events, or will changes need to be made?

- Is the person willing and able to cook on occasion? Does he or she have any special dietary needs or restrictions that would affect the household?

- Does the person drive? Have a car? Is he or she willing and able to use public transportation? If not, will he or she depend on you for transportation to the doctor, the store, to see friends? Is that compatible with your schedule?

The Future

It is a very different thing to share a home with a loved one who is active and independent than to live with the same person when he or she is confused and needs extensive personal and nursing care. Think about these questions:

- How long are you envisioning your loved one living with you? Does he or she share that assumption? From the beginning, is this understood to be a limited or an open-ended arrangement?

- What will you do if the person becomes ill or disabled and needs more of your time and care? How will you decide if the person needs more care than you can provide at home? What if you and your loved one disagree about this?

- What will happen if one or more members of your household is unhappy with the homesharing arrangement?

- If you have children living in your home, what effect will their growing up and leaving home have on your arrangement? Will having this person living with you significantly affect your plans?

- If you become ill, or need a break, what resources would be available for respite care?

How to Make It Work

There is no magic formula for making a home run smoothly with two, three, or four generations under its roof. There are, however, several strategies that can help.

- **Identify and follow a set of rules.** Decide how members of the family will share household chores, bathroom facilities, limited transportation resources, and time. Trades and rotations may be appropriate. When you work out reasonable allocations or schedules, put them in writing and post them. Press everyone to get in the habit of respecting the plan.

- **Establish a family habit of effective communication.** Let people know what is coming up. If your mother has scheduled minor outpatient surgery and is looking forward to a quiet weekend to recover, your teenage son will appreciate knowing this ahead of time, before he invites friends over. If you and your spouse are hosting a party that will last late into the evening and perhaps disturb your parent's rest, he or she might want to spend the night with a friend.

  Two simple approaches to ensuring good communication are periodic family meetings and a common family calendar posted in a conspicuous place. If yours is a large or active family, you may want to go to the extreme of copying the family calendar for each family member each week, and having weekly family meetings.

- **Work out appropriate financial tradeoffs.** Having a parent or other relative or friend live with you can both save that person money and increase the costs of running your household. Specific tradeoffs aimed at balancing these costs and benefits can help everyone. It might be reasonable, for example, to ask siblings who would otherwise be helping to pay for a parent's care to contribute to your increased household expenses.

- **Develop and follow a plan.** If possible, adopt and follow a plan that places limitations on the commitment by both sides. For example, you, your loved one, and your family may agree to a six-month trial period. Or you, your relative, and your siblings may work out a rotation system that meets everyone's needs and limitations. Know ahead of time that there are limits to what you and others are willing or able to do, and realize what those limits are.

- **Help your loved one stay active and involved.** Perhaps the most important commitment you can make is the resolve to help your relative remain active and involved in a wide range of activities and relationships. This means making arrangements for transportation to outside events, as well as actively encouraging him/her to invite friends into your home for meals or visits.

To Sum Up . . .

While sharing your home can be an enriching experience, the decision should not be made lightly—and not alone. Since adjustments and impact can be significant, make certain you start off with open discussions and careful thinking and planning.

More Resources

- The **U.S. Administration on Aging**'s online booklet "Because We Care" offers information on home caregiving. (*www.aoa.gov*)

- The **Family Caregiver Alliance** offers information on caring for a family member at home, including online booklets "Home Away from Home" and "Work and Eldercare." (*www.caregiver.org*)

- The **National Family Caregivers Association** website features information, support, and tips. (*www.nfcacares.org*)

- The **Easter Seal** website includes a variety of resources for caregivers. (*www.easterseals.com*)

Quick Links

>>> These web-based resources may be accessed through our website: www.aginginstride.org

ISSUE 44: BEING A CAREGIVER FOR SOMEONE YOU LOVE

You are a caregiver if you provide social or physical support to an aging relative or friend, or to a person who is disabled. Caregivers may make weekly visits to a sick mother still living on her own. They may bring a frail father into their home for care. They may arrange for services for a relative who lives hundreds of miles away.

What caregivers share in common is the fact that they take time and energy from their lives to care for someone who needs their help.

Reactions to Being a Caregiver

Caring for someone on a regular basis is a mixed experience. There are the positive feelings associated with helping others. If you're caring for your mother, father, or spouse, there is the satisfaction of knowing you are, in some way, returning the support they once provided you.

Caring for a frail relative also has its difficulties. Most caregivers experience some of these feelings:

- A sense of isolation, of being alone with a huge responsibility.
- Worry or doubt about the quality of the care they are providing.
- Guilt that they are not doing enough.
- Resentment toward the person cared for.
- Anger at the lack of time they have for themselves and their families.
- Frustration that this is not what they had planned for this time in their lives.
- Fear about how much longer they can keep this up, given all of the other demands on their time.
- Confusion about where to turn for help.
- A sense of loss because the person they love has changed so much.
- Physical fatigue.

Any of these responses, either alone or in combination, can lead to a sense of being overwhelmed. This is both common and understandable. It is important to monitor yourself and be alert to signs of caregiver exhaustion:

- Feeling drained of time and energy.

- Loss of sleep.

- Bottled up feelings of anger or frustration.

- Feeling trapped.

- Being reluctant to seek outside help.

- Being focused excessively on caregiving.

Taking Care of Yourself

There are steps you can take to avoid or reverse caregiver exhaustion. Remember: taking care of yourself *is* taking care of the person who depends on you. Try some of these ideas drawn from the experiences of many caregivers like yourself:

- **Share decision-making.** As long as the person you are caring for is able, involve him or her in the decisions that go along with care; try to be active partners. It will help your loved one retain a sense of independence, while taking some of the burden off of you.

- **Remember your needs.** You need time to get away from your role as caregiver, to relax and to get additional support. These needs may create feelings of conflict or guilt, but again remember: you are taking care of the person who needs you by taking care of yourself.

- **Anticipate needs.** The earlier you discuss needs, the more time you have to explore possibilities. Then you will feel better about the choices you need to make in the future.

- **Understand what you are dealing with.** Gather information about the specific disease or conditions of the person you're caring for. The more you know, the better you'll be able to plan for the future.

- **Involve others.** Ask other family members and friends for help. People usually are willing and pleased to be asked; they just may not volunteer.

Consider a family meeting to brainstorm ideas and to see how to share responsibilities.

- **Talk.** Share with someone outside the family about your reactions to caregiving. Use a friend who isn't close to the situation as a sounding-board.

- **Be flexible.** Just when you think you are in control, something will change. Being thrown off balance is frustrating; try to be ready for change.

Help is Available

As a caregiver, you are never alone. There are many people—family, friends, health care professionals, community services and others—who can help:

- **Adult day care** provides daytime care and social activities for older adults. Programs will vary as to amount and type of care available. Some provide transportation. See Issue 12, *Adult Day Programs*, for a fuller discussion of what adult day programs have to offer.

- **Home care** offers services that take place in the home. They can include: health care provided by professionals, such as nurses and nurse aides; help with baths, dressing, and eating; housekeeping; and social visits.

- **Hospice care** provides support and care for terminally ill persons who choose to remain at home in the care of a relative or friend.

- **Legal and financial services** include help with preparing a durable power of attorney or other type of health care appointment, a living will, or assistance with financial planning, public benefits, taxes, Social Security, and disability benefits. These services can be provided by skilled volunteers or paid professionals.

- **Long-term care** is available through nursing homes and sub-acute care facilities for temporary or permanent care, especially during periods of acute illness.

- **Meal programs** offer a full range of services, including Meals On Wheels-type programs that deliver meals to older adults at home, as well as group meals served at senior centers, churches, synagogues, or schools.

- **Reassurance programs** provide regular phone calls to check in on elderly persons who live alone, or electronic monitoring devices that signal when help is needed.

- **Rehabilitation programs** provide occupational, physical, and speech therapies through hospitals and long-term care and day-care facilities.

- **Respite care** programs provide temporary relief for caregivers. A person comes into the home for prearranged periods of time, while the regular caregiver takes a break. Some hospitals and nursing homes have short-term, overnight onsite programs.

- **Support groups** provide emotional support, information sharing, and companionship for caregivers. Some groups are condition-specific, such as Alzheimer's support groups.

- **Transportation programs** provide rides to and from medical appointments, day care, and other destinations.

To Sum Up . . .

You may think that you just do not have the time, talent or resources to be a caregiver. But what it really comes down to is simply "being present" for another. While many aspects to caregiving call upon a wide range of skills—cooking, cleaning, bill paying, etc.—the starting, and ending, point is focusing on another person. We may find at times that we are short on funds, skills, or time, but when caring for another, we need to be long on attention. Holding someone's hand, pulling the chair closer to the bed, putting everything else aside—that's the heart of being a caregiver for someone you love.

More Resources

Quick Links

>>> These web-based resources may be accessed through our website: www.aginginstride.org

- **Care Planner**, the Centers for Medicare and Medicaid Services online care decision support tool, helps assess and access support services and options. (*www.careplanner.org*)

- The **U.S. Administration on Aging** offers fact sheets as well as an online booklet entitled "Because We Care" with suggestions, resources, and contact information for people who are caring for an older or disabled family member at home. (*www.aoa.gov*)

- The **National Family Caregivers Association**'s website offers tips, information, and support for people who are serving as a caregiver for aged, chronically ill, and disabled loved ones. (*www.nfcacares.org*)

- The **Easter Seals** website includes a variety of resources for caregivers. (*www.easterseals.com*)

- The **Alzheimer's Association** website is a good source for information on care strategies for people with Alzheimer's and related dementias. Sections on day-to-day care, caregiver challenges and coping strategies offer valuable suggestions. (*www.alz.org*)

The Association also offers a 24-Hour Contact Center, staffed by professionals who understand dementia and its impact. Call (800) 272-3900 with questions or concerns about memory problems, dementia or Alzheimer's disease.

ISSUE 45: SERVING AS A PERSON'S HEALTH CARE REPRESENTATIVE

A *health care representative* or *proxy* is a person who steps in to make health care decisions for someone who can't make them alone. The reason could be Alzheimer's disease, a bad accident, or anything else that makes the other person "incapacitated." A person is incapacitated if he or she has lost the ability to understand options and make decisions.

How Do You Become a Health Care Representative?

A person can become someone else's health care representative in three ways:

- You can be appointed by the other person. This is called a "durable power of attorney for health care" or "health care proxy." Someone who is appointed in this way is called the person's "agent," "proxy," "surrogate," or "attorney-in-fact." (But you don't have to be a lawyer to do this.)

- You can also be appointed by a court as the person's "guardian" or "conservator."

- Or, you might be serving informally under a law or custom that lets a close family member step in if needed.

Your Rights and Responsibilities

As a health care representative, you exercise the rights of the person you're acting for. These include:

- The right to be well informed about the person's medical condition and care options.

- The right to participate in planning the person's care.

- The right to accept or refuse specific forms of care.

- The right to have medical records and other aspects of care kept private.

Your responsibilities involve exercising these rights in a caring, responsible way.

This means:

- Getting to know the wishes of the person you may have to act for, if that information is available.

- Making decisions the way the person would make them, if able.

- If the person's own preferences and views are unknown, making decisions for the person based on the person's best interests.

Getting to Know the Person's Wishes

If you have the opportunity to sit down with the person and talk things over, it is a good idea to do so. This is the time to learn about the person's wishes and personal values. You may have to step in on the person's behalf. If you do, the more you know, the more confident you'll be, and the easier your job will be. To get started, try using the checklist of discussion points included in Form 45, *Health Care Representative's Discussion Checklist*.

More About Your Role

You may play only a small role at first. A person's ability to act alone isn't always clear cut. He or she may be able to understand some things, but need help on others.

As time goes on, your role may grow. This usually means working with the care team—those providing care—to figure out what the person needs and how best to provide it.

It will help if you...

- **Prepare for meetings and phone calls**—Make a note of the questions you want to ask and the concerns you have.

- **Listen carefully**—Take your time; if you don't understand a point, ask to go over it again.

- **Speak up**—If there is something you don't agree with, say so. Better to deal with it now than later, when it's a problem.

Most health care decisions are routine; the doctor or other provider makes a recommendation based on training and experience, which you accept. But sometimes there's no clear or easy choice. That's when you, as the health care representative, must decide. The decision rests with you.

How do you decide when things aren't clear? Here are two simple—but important—guidelines:

- Follow the person's wishes, if you know them. Is there an advance directive or values statement that says what care the person would or would not want? Did the person explain in conversation what approach or types of treatment he/she would choose?

- If no one knows for sure the person's wishes, you should decide based on what is in the person's best interests. That means getting all the facts, taking a close look at the "pros and cons," and then using your own good judgment.

If You Need Help

When difficult choices come up, it's nice to know there's help available. If you're concerned about how things are going, check with:

- The person's doctor or other health care provider. It's their job to explain all the options, risks and benefits, and do it in terms you understand. Usually, they will also make a recommendation based on years of experience.

- The person's religious advisor, who may be able to help you understand the person's beliefs and values.

- An ethicist, chaplain, or social worker available through one of the person's health care providers.

To Sum Up . . .

Stepping in for a loved one and making significant health care decisions on their behalf is a big responsibility. Perhaps the best advice is still the Golden Rule: "Treat others as you yourself would want to be treated."

More Resources

- The **NOLO Law for All** "Plain English Law Centers" website includes information on health care directives and powers of attorney. (*www.nolo.com*)

- The **American Bar Association**'s Commission on Law and Aging website includes information on serving as a health care representative and other elder care issues. (*www.abanet.org/aging*)

Quick Links

>>> These web-based resources may be accessed through our website:
www.aginginstride.org

Conclusion

Life is a journey, all of it. For every person, the path is different—different skills and abilities, different life stories, different challenges. The road ahead may look hard and rocky, or, for the moment, it may look pretty good. All of us, however, have no choice but to go forward from the place where we are right now.

As we end this book, we would close with just a few reminders for you. They are reminders that you have heard over and over again in the book, but we repeat them because they can't be said too often!

- **You have the skills you need to walk this road**. Don't let yourself be discouraged by the challenges and choices ahead of you. You have faced hard news before and worked through it. You have met challenge after challenge in getting this far in your life; you can do it again. Wisdom, honesty, and knowledge of your priorities are the gifts of older age. Use them every day to make the choices that result in the highest possible quality of life for you. Be kind to yourself and know that your life's experience is a gift that is of value both to you and to others.

- **Planning is the best way to ensure that your values and choices will be known and honored.** Planning takes work; it involves looking ahead into an uncertain future and grappling with issues that may be scary or painful. However, the more time you spend in honest and realistic planning, the greater your chances of living though to the end of your life in a way that is consistent with your desires and priorities. Don't delay in looking ahead. Share your planning with those close to you. Take control of your life.

- **Physical activity and staying connected to others will improve your quality of life.** For over 99 percent of the population, these words are absolutely true. There are few people so sick or disabled that they cannot benefit from exercise. Appropriate physical activity will make you feel better, help fight anxiety and depression, and reduce your vulnerability to disease and disability. It improves cognition, and can reduce your dependance on medication. Interacting with other people—as a friend, as a volunteer, as the keeper of the family history—also improves your emotional state of mind and your ability to think clearly. It's also fun. It makes your life fuller. So what are you waiting for? These two basic prescriptions are inexpensive; they can bring you pleasure, and they will make your life better. Make them priorities in your life.

• **You are a person of value with gifts yet to give in your life.** Too many older people forget this most essential truth. Write it in big letters on a piece of paper and attach that paper to your refrigerator, your bathroom mirror, your bedside table—somewhere you will see it every day. The gifts you have to give may be simple or complex. Find your own path, from holding the hand of a grieving friend; to cleaning out your house and giving your extra furniture to someone in your family or neighborhood who's just starting out; to just sharing your love, encouragement, and perspective with others. Maybe the greatest gift you can give is being an attentive listener or reconciling a breach in your family. It is documented that those who live their lives from a perspective of gratitude and self-giving live happier, healthier lives. What are the gifts that you have to give? Find a way to give them.

If you remember and pay attention to these four basic concepts, you will live a better life. You will live the best life possible for you. Congratulations! That's the most that any of us can do.

Some of you reading this book are family or friend to an older adult who is special to you. Good for you for doing your homework! It is an important act of love and friendship to help an older adult live the life he or she desires. Especially if you are involved in caregiving for one or more older adults, it can be a challenging role. But few jobs in life are more important. To meet another person's vulnerability with respect, concern, presence, and caring is a significant gift. Never forget that! And also don't forget that it shouldn't be done alone. Use the resources available to you to lighten your load.

Each of us, as we age, will come to some challenging terrain. We can't choose the challenges it will bring or the manner of its approach. However, each one of us can make a commitment to ourselves and our loved ones to take our aging in stride, to make our lives the very best they can be. We who have written this book hope we have given you some resources to help you on your way. The rest is up to you.

Forms

THESE *AGING IN STRIDE* FORMS ARE ORGANIZED BY CORRESPONDING ISSUE NUMBER

Form 1: Successful Aging Checkup

Form 5: Checklist for Reducing Your Risk of Falling

Form 6-A: Home Safety Inspection Checklist

Form 6-B: Home Repairs and Home Modifications Checklist

Form 7: Checklist for Older Drivers

Form 9: Needs Assessment for Living on Your Own

Form 10: Worksheet for Hiring a Home Helper

Form 11: Checklist for Choosing a Home Health Agency

Form 13: "Is It Time to Move?" Retirement Housing Planning Sheet

Form 14: Worksheet for Evaluating a Senior Living Community

Form 15: Retirement Living Move-in Guide

Form 17: Checklist for Communicating Clearly with Your Doctor

Form 18-A: List of Current Medications

Form 18-B: Medications Check-off List

Form 24: Personal Values Statement

Form 25: Worksheet for Evaluating a Nursing Facility

Form 26-A: Nursing Facility Move-in Checklist

Form 26-B: Resident/Family Care Conference Worksheet

Form 27: Worksheet for Questions, Concerns, and Complaints

Form 28: Confidential Personal Information

Form 33: Checklist for Selecting Long-Term Care Insurance

Form 37: Checklist for Selecting a Hospice or Palliative Care Provider

Form 38: Funeral or Memorial Service Planner

Form 40: Family Meeting Planner

Form 42: Checklist for Selecting and Working with a Geriatric Care Manager

Form 45: Health Care Representative's Discussion Checklist

Successful Aging Checkup

This is an easy four-part self-assessment exercise. Give yourself this personal "checkup" to understand better how you are doing on the four building blocks that can help anyone age more successfully.

For each category, give yourself a grade of "A," "B" or "C":

> *A — You're doing just fine.*
>
> *B — You still have room to improve.*
>
> *C — You're really not where you need to be.*

Name: _____

	First-time Checkup Date: _____	3-month Re-check Date: _____
Part I: Planning ahead and making important decisions		
✔ I go to the trouble of gathering the facts I need, before making key decisions.	_____	_____
✔ I am open to accepting support and input from those close to me.	_____	_____
✔ I have taken time to think about my personal priorities and what my goals are for the rest of my life.	_____	_____
✔ My life planning is flexible enough to allow for different circumstances and the unexpected.	_____	_____
Part II: Staying physically active		
✔ I make staying physically active a priority in my life.	_____	_____
✔ I get the exercise I need, including:	_____	_____
✔ Aerobic activity.	_____	_____
✔ Exercises to strengthen muscles.	_____	_____
✔ Exercises to promote joint flexibility.	_____	_____
✔ Exercises to help with balance.	_____	_____

	First-time Checkup Date:	3-month Re-check Date:
	_____	_____

Part III: Activities and Social Connections

✔ I look for chances to combine physical activity and social interaction — for example, by exercising with a friend or group.   _____   _____

✔ I keep up old friendships and work at making new ones.   _____   _____

✔ I give back to my community by doing some kind of volunteer work.   _____   _____

Part IV: Spiritual and Mental Well-being

✔ I honor the role spiritual and mental well-being can play in a person's life.   _____   _____

✔ I make a conscious effort to choose the spiritual or religious path that feels right for me.   _____   _____

✔ In dealing with fears, questions, or dilemmas, I don't try to go it alone, but instead I make the effort to find support and guidance.   _____   _____

✔ I know the value of positive thinking . . .   _____   _____

   ✔ So, I honor my own strengths and successes.   _____   _____

   ✔ I look for the good in other people and situations.   _____   _____

✔ I accept with grace the things in life I'd like to change, but can't.   _____   _____

✔ I manage the stresses in my life.   _____   _____

Notes: _____

_____

_____

_____

_____

_____

_____

Checklist for Reducing Your Risk of Falling

Here's a list of steps for you to consider as part of a conscious effort to reduce your risk of falling. Next to each item, make notes to help remind you of things you need to do to follow up. Then, recheck yourself again after two or three months to see how you're doing.

Name: _____ Today's Date: _____

Get enough exercise!

❑ If you have an active exercise program, stick with it.

❑ If you don't have one, talk with your doctor or other health care provider about starting one.

❑ If you are in physical or occupational therapy, make falls and how to prevent them one of the things you talk about.

Check with your doctor . . .

❑ If you have experienced episodes of dizziness.

❑ If you think you may have problems with balance, vision, or side effects from medications.

❑ To have balance problems tested, diagnosed, and treated.

Eat right and drink enough water!

❑ Are you eating regular, healthy meals?

❑ Are you drinking enough water each day?

❑ Do you limit your use of alcohol?

Be aware of your surroundings!

❑ Plan your steps a little more carefully than you used to.

❑ Be especially alert when in new surroundings and while traveling.

Notes: _____
_____
_____
_____
_____
_____
_____
_____
_____
_____
_____
_____
_____
_____
_____
_____
_____
_____
_____
_____
_____
_____
_____
_____
_____
_____

If you've become unsteady in walking . . .

❑ Ask your doctor about getting a cane, walker, or other assistive device.

❑ If you buy one, get professional help learning how to use it properly.

Give your home a careful safety check, and get rid of hazards, such as . . .

❑ Rough floor surfaces.

❑ Throw rugs.

❑ Poor lighting.

❑ Exposed extension cords.

❑ Cluttered walkways and stairs.

Consider installing . . .

❑ Grab bars beside toilet and in bath and shower.

❑ Hand rails on stairs.

❑ Nightlights.

❑ Bedside phone.

Discuss your concerns about falling . . .

❑ With your doctor or physical therapist.

❑ During a care conference.

❑ With close family and friends.

If you know you have a higher risk of falling . . .

❑ Ask whether your doctor recommends wearing hip protectors.

❑ Consider subscribing to an emergency response program.

Notes: _____

_____

_____

_____

_____

_____

_____

_____

_____

_____

_____

_____

_____

_____

_____

_____

_____

_____

_____

_____

_____

_____

_____

_____

_____

_____

_____

_____

_____

Home Safety Inspection Checklist

This three-part form includes checklist items that should be part of any home safety inspection. On the right margin, make notes to help you follow up. Be sure to do another inspection in three or six months to note your progress in making your home safer.

Name: _____   Today's Date: _____

Part I: Preventing Accidents

In the bathroom . . .

❑ Grab bars have been installed next to toilet and in bath and/or shower.

❑ Bath and shower have non-skid surfaces.

❑ There is a nightlight.

❑ The hot water temperature is set to 120° or below.

❑ Floor surfaces are kept dry and clean.

In the bedroom . . .

❑ Furniture is placed where you won't trip over it.

❑ Night lighting is adequate.

❑ You have a flashlight for emergency use.

Interior stairs and landings . . .

❑ Have handrails on both sides.

❑ Have adequate lighting.

❑ Have floor coverings in good repair.

❑ Are free of clutter.

In the kitchen . . .

❑ Floors are in good repair and kept dry.

❑ Sharp edges on appliances or countertops have been removed or padded.

❑ Things you need are stored in easily reached drawers and cupboards.

Notes: _____

In other living spaces...

❏ Throw rugs have been removed or safely taped.

❏ All other floor coverings are in good shape.

❏ Traffic areas are well-lit and free of clutter.

Outside...

❏ Lighting is good.

❏ Walkways and stairs are clutter free.

Part II: Fire Safety

❏ Hazardous materials have been removed or properly stored.

❏ All electrical appliances have been checked and are in good order.

❏ Outlets are not overloaded.

❏ Extension cords are used properly.

❏ Chimneys and flues, if used heavily, have been checked and cleaned.

❏ Only light bulbs of the right size and wattage are used.

❏ Space heaters are used correctly.

❏ Smoke detectors/alarms have been installed and are in good working order.

❏ Everyone understands escape procedures and how to report a fire.

Part III: Home Security

❏ Locks on all doors and windows are in good working order.

❏ Outside areas are well-lit and free of unnecessary vegetation.

❏ You have a bedside phone.

❏ Emergency numbers are plainly visible next to every phone.

Notes: _____

Home Repairs and Home Modifications Checklist

*This is a two-part form. Use **Part I** to check for ways you can make your home safer and more functional. (Remember that not all of these items will apply to you.) Then, if you decide to hire a contractor or handyman, use **Part II** as a guide in making a smart selection.*

Part I: Check for Ways to Make Your Home Safer and More Functional

	High Priority	*Low Priority*	*Doesn't Apply*
Basic home upkeep:			
Repair or upgrade . . .			
✓ roof, gutters			
✓ stairs, railings			
✓ plumbing			
✓ electrical system			
✓ heating and air conditioning			
✓ appliances			
Safety improvements:			
Reset water heater to 120° or less			
Install or upgrade . . .			
✓ non-slip, non-glare flooring			
✓ low-pile carpeting			
✓ handrails on stairs			
✓ grab bars in bathroom			
✓ lighting, task-lighting, nightlights			
✓ view-hole in front door			
✓ locks or deadbolts on doors and windows			
Accessibility and independence:			
Add . . .			
✓ kitchen easy-grip knobs, pulls			
✓ rocker or touch-type switches			
✓ wheelchair or walker access			
Rearrange things for one-story living			

Comfort and convenience: Add . . .	*High Priority*	*Low Priority*	*Doesn't Apply*
✓ low-upkeep landscaping			
✓ cordless phone			
✓ automatic garage door opener			
Energy efficiency: Install . . .			
✓ storm windows, double-paned windows			
✓ weather-stripping and other insulation			
✓ more efficient heating, air conditioning			
✓ insulation on water heater, pipes			
✓ more efficient appliances			

Part II: Checklist for Hiring a Contractor

If you're planning to hire a contractor or handyman, be sure to do your homework first!

❑ Get recommendations from friends, family, reputable local merchants.

❑ Make certain the contractor is bonded and licensed.

❑ Ask for at least three recent customer references, then call each one.

❑ Check with the Better Business Bureau to make sure the record is clean.

❑ Get the price, completion date, scope of work, and other details in writing.

❑ If appropriate, ask for two or more bids, then compare "apples to apples."

Notes: _____

_____

_____

_____

_____

_____

_____

Checklist for Older Drivers

This checklist covers safety considerations for older drivers.

- *Part I lists points seniors should review when considering continued driving.*

- *Part II covers points seniors should evaluate when considering reduced driving.*

Part I: Checkpoints for Continued Driving   *Notes:* _____

❑ Driver license current?

❑ Vision and corrective lenses adequate for driving, including night driving?

❑ Hearing adequate?

❑ Senior safe driver course completed within prior 24 months?

❑ Insurance coverage adequate?

❑ Insurance premiums paid?

❑ Car(s) properly licensed?

❑ Car(s) in good working order?

   ❑ brakes

   ❑ engine idle

   ❑ accelerator linkage

   ❑ seatbelts

   ❑ tires

   ❑ brake pedal, accelerator pedal, and floor mats

   ❑ mirrors properly adjusted?

❑ Possible additional safety equipment:

   ❑ center-mounted brake light

   ❑ backup warning buzzer

   ❑ emergency kit

❑ Automobile club membership?

Part II: Checkpoints for Reduced Use of Car

Notes: _____

❏ Driver comfort—do physical limitations make driving uncomfortable or unsafe?

❏ Driver stress—are you anxious or confused while driving?

❏ Driver performance—have there been recent moving violations or accidents?

❏ Car costs—do total automobile expenses (insurance, license, upkeep, gas, parking) exceed costs of other alternatives?

❏ Possible driving modifications:

  ❏ no night driving

  ❏ no rush hour driving

  ❏ no freeway driving

  ❏ no driving in snow or dangerous conditions

  ❏ combine use of car and bus (park-and-ride)

  ❏ ride sharing

❏ Alternatives to continued driving:

  ❏ senior transit pass

  ❏ community vans

  ❏ taxi coupons

  ❏ home delivered products—groceries, prescriptions, etc.

  ❏ increased use of telephone and e-mail

  ❏ use of chore service workers or volunteers for errands

Needs Assessment for Living on Your Own

This is an easy-to-use worksheet for figuring out those areas in which you need—or may in the future need—some help. For each category:

- *Make an honest assesssment of need (left column).*
- *Decide who could help fill that need (center column).*
- *Make notes to help you follow up (right column).*

Transportation to and from doctor's office, church, shopping, etc.

❑ a definite need now   ❑ Family or friend   *Notes:* _____

❑ might be helpful   ❑ Senior services agency   _____

❑ possibly in the future   ❑ Paid helper   _____

❑ not needed   ❑ Volunteer   _____

    ❑ Other   _____

Doing laundry and keeping up with other housekeeping chores

❑ a definite need now   ❑ Family or friend   *Notes:* _____

❑ might be helpful   ❑ Senior services agency   _____

❑ possibly in the future   ❑ Paid helper   _____

❑ not needed   ❑ Volunteer   _____

    ❑ Other   _____

Preparing nutritious meals

❑ a definite need now   ❑ Family or friend   *Notes:* _____

❑ might be helpful   ❑ Senior services agency   _____

❑ possibly in the future   ❑ Paid helper   _____

❑ not needed   ❑ Volunteer   _____

    ❑ Other   _____

Help with activities of daily living, such as dressing, grooming, mobility

❑ a definite need now   ❑ Family or friend   *Notes:* _____

❑ might be helpful   ❑ Senior services agency   _____

❑ possibly in the future   ❑ Paid helper   _____

❑ not needed   ❑ Volunteer   _____

    ❑ Other   _____

Yard work, such as mowing the lawn, raking leaves, snow removal

❑ a definite need now
❑ might be helpful
❑ possibly in the future
❑ not needed

❑ Family or friend
❑ Senior services agency
❑ Paid helper
❑ Volunteer
❑ Other

Notes: _____
_____
_____
_____
_____

Minor home repairs, such as fixing a leaky faucet, changing light bulbs

❑ a definite need now
❑ might be helpful
❑ possibly in the future
❑ not needed

❑ Family or friend
❑ Senior services agency
❑ Paid helper
❑ Volunteer
❑ Other

Notes: _____
_____
_____
_____
_____

Organizing and paying bills

❑ a definite need now
❑ might be helpful
❑ possibly in the future
❑ not needed

❑ Family or friend
❑ Senior services agency
❑ Paid helper
❑ Volunteer
❑ Other

Notes: _____
_____
_____
_____
_____

Companionship—reassurance check-in

❑ a definite need now
❑ might be helpful
❑ possibly in the future
❑ not needed

❑ Family or friend
❑ Senior services agency
❑ Paid helper
❑ Volunteer
❑ Other

Notes: _____
_____
_____
_____
_____

Other

❑ a definite need now
❑ might be helpful
❑ possibly in the future
❑ not needed

❑ Family or friend
❑ Senior services agency
❑ Paid helper
❑ Volunteer
❑ Other

Notes: _____
_____
_____
_____
_____

Worksheet for Hiring a Home Helper

Part I: Basic Information

Person's name: _____

Agency name (if applicable): _____

Address: _____

Phone and E-mail: _____

Supervisor's name (if applicable): _____

Notes on the person's background: _____

_____

_____

_____

_____

Part II: What services will this person/agency provide?

❑ Transportation   ❑ Yard work

❑ House cleaning   ❑ Home repairs

❑ Meal preparation   ❑ Companionship

❑ Doing laundry   ❑ Other: _____

❑ Shopping   ❑ Other: _____

❑ Personal care needs   ❑ Other: _____

   (bathing, dressing, grooming, etc.)   ❑ Other: _____

Part III: Budget

$_____/hour X _____ hours per week = $ _____/week

Other notes on fees and other financial terms: _____

_____

_____

_____

_____

Part IV: Worksheet for checking references

Name (reference #1): _____

Relationship: ❏ current client   ❏ former client   ❏ other: _____

Phone or e-mail: _____

Services provided?   _____

Over what period?   _____

Quality of work?	❏ outstanding	❏ satisfactory	❏ less than satisfactory
Reliable and on time?	❏ outstanding	❏ satisfactory	❏ less than satisfactory
Honest and respectful?	❏ outstanding	❏ satisfactory	❏ less than satisfactory
Would you hire again?	❏ definitely	❏ probably	❏ probably not

Other information?   _____

_____

Name (reference #2): _____

Relationship: ❏ current client   ❏ former client   ❏ other: _____

Phone or e-mail: _____

Services provided?   _____

Over what period?   _____

Quality of work?	❏ outstanding	❏ satisfactory	❏ less than satisfactory
Reliable and on time?	❏ outstanding	❏ satisfactory	❏ less than satisfactory
Honest and respectful?	❏ outstanding	❏ satisfactory	❏ less than satisfactory
Would you hire again?	❏ definitely	❏ probably	❏ probably not

Other information?   _____

_____

Name (reference #3): _____

Relationship: ❏ current client   ❏ former client   ❏ other: _____

Phone or e-mail: _____

Services provided?   _____

Over what period?   _____

Quality of work?	❏ outstanding	❏ satisfactory	❏ less than satisfactory
Reliable and on time?	❏ outstanding	❏ satisfactory	❏ less than satisfactory
Honest and respectful?	❏ outstanding	❏ satisfactory	❏ less than satisfactory
Would you hire again?	❏ definitely	❏ probably	❏ probably not

Other information?   _____

_____

Checklist for Choosing a Home Health Agency

Part I: Questions to Ask Before Making Your Selection

Agency name: _____

Address: _____

_____

Phone and e-mail: _____

Licensure/accreditation: Is this agency properly licensed and accredited?
❑ yes   ❑ no   ❑ not sure

Services and skills: Does this provider offer the specific care and services I need?
❑ yes   ❑ no   ❑ not sure

Service coverage: Does this provider offer the service coverage (for example, 24-hour on-call nurse) I need?
❑ yes   ❑ no   ❑ not sure

References: Is this a home health provider my doctor recommends?
❑ yes   ❑ no   ❑ not sure

Do others recommend this agency?
❑ yes   ❑ no   ❑ not sure

Have I asked for references and followed up by calling them?
❑ yes   ❑ no   ❑ not sure

Fees and billing: How will fees and billing be handled? Do I understand what charges I will be responsible for? _____

_____

_____

_____

_____

Care planning and care team: How are care planning and care conferences handled? Will a family member be part of the care team? _____

_____

_____

_____

_____

Supervision: Will the person(s) actually providing services be actively supervised? Will a supervisor be available to discuss any concerns we have? _____

_____

_____

_____

_____

_____

Part II: Questions for Evaluating Performance and Giving Feedback

Skills as a caregiver:	❏ outstanding	❏ satisfactory	❏ needs improvement
Works as a team; family feels included:	❏ outstanding	❏ satisfactory	❏ needs improvement
Good communications skills; instructions are easy to understand:	❏ outstanding	❏ satisfactory	❏ needs improvement
Keeps patient and family informed:	❏ outstanding	❏ satisfactory	❏ needs improvement
Patient's and family's privacy is protected:	❏ outstanding	❏ satisfactory	❏ needs improvement
Patient is treated with dignity and respect:	❏ outstanding	❏ satisfactory	❏ needs improvement
Friendly and helpful:	❏ outstanding	❏ satisfactory	❏ needs improvement

Notes: _____

_____

_____

_____

_____

_____

_____

"Is It Time to Move?"
Retirement Housing Planning Sheet

Weighing the pros and cons of moving from where you are now to a retirement living community can be a challenge. Use the following list to help you organize your thoughts.

Decide how each separate consideration might influence your answer to the question, "Is it time to move?" Put a check mark in the appropriate column, based on the importance of each topic.

	Big Reason to Move	Small Reason to Move	Doesn't Matter	Small Reason NOT to Move	Big Reason NOT to Move
• My current needs, and how well they are being met?					
• Staying physically active?					
• Staying connected to other people?					
• Eating right?					
• Help with personal care and health needs?					
• Being prepared, in case my needs increase?					
• The cost of moving?					
• The up-front cost and monthly fees of a new situation, after taking into account any savings or sales proceeds from my current living situation?					
• The cost—in time, energy, and money—involved in planning and actually doing a move?					

	Big Reason to Move	Small Reason to Move	Doesn't Matter	Small Reason NOT to Move	Big Reason NOT to Move
• What it's costing me to maintain the home I'm in now?					
• The challenge it will be to leave one neighborhood or community and move to another?					
• Location?					
• Would a move allow me to move to a community I would prefer in terms of climate, amenities, etc.?					
• Would a move make it easier to visit family and friends and for them to visit me?					
• How does a move at this time fit with my personal goals and priorities?					
• Considering the experience of friends and relatives, does a move at this point in my life seem to make good sense?					

Notes: _____

_____

_____

_____

_____

_____

_____

Worksheet for Evaluating a Senior Living Community

Facility or Community: _____

Location: _____

Type of unit: ❑ Studio ❑ 1-Bedroom ❑ 2-Bedroom ❑ Other

Contact Person: _____

Phone/E-mail: _____

Location

❑ Surrounding neighborhood is safe, attractive?

❑ Access to transportation, amenities, etc., is good?

❑ Location is convenient for family and friends?

Evaluation: ❑ Excellent ❑ Good ❑ Acceptable ❑ Unacceptable

Notes: _____

Cost

❑ "Buy-in" investment, if any, is affordable?

❑ Monthly costs are within my/our budget?

❑ Things not included in the monthly rate have been taken into account?

Evaluation: ❑ Excellent ❑ Good ❑ Acceptable ❑ Unacceptable

Notes: _____

Terms and Conditions

❑ Lease or rental agreement (including attachments) has been read and looks fair?

❑ Resident rules are OK, including rules on . . .

  ❑ Pets?

  ❑ Smoking?

  ❑ Alcohol?

  ❑ Visitors?

  ❑ Absences due to hospitalization?

  ❑ Other: _____

Evaluation: ❑ Excellent ❑ Good ❑ Acceptable ❑ Unacceptable

Notes: _____

Building(s) and grounds...

❑ appear to be clean and well maintained?
❑ are senior-friendly and easy to get around in?
❑ have adequate parking?
❑ include amenities, such as:
    ❑ exercise facility?
    ❑ rooms for private meals and get-togethers?
    ❑ computer center?
    ❑ other: _____

Notes: _____

Evaluation: ❑ Excellent ❑ Good ❑ Acceptable ❑ Unacceptable

Services and support include...

❑ housekeeping and laundry?
❑ dining room or meal plan?
❑ active social and recreation program?
❑ transportation?
❑ personal care and help with ADLs?
❑ health care services?
❑ other: _____

Notes: _____

Evaluation: ❑ Excellent ❑ Good ❑ Acceptable ❑ Unacceptable

The employees appear...

❑ courteous, friendly, eager to help?
❑ neat, clean, well-groomed?
❑ adequately trained, good at what they do?
❑ above all, respectful of the residents?

Notes: _____

Evaluation: ❑ Excellent ❑ Good ❑ Acceptable ❑ Unacceptable

The residents say...

❑ they are kept well informed?
❑ staffing is adequate to meet their needs?
❑ issues, if they arise, are dealt with fairly?
❑ resident decision-making is encouraged?
❑ they would make the same choice again?

Notes: _____

Evaluation: ❑ Excellent ❑ Good ❑ Acceptable ❑ Unacceptable

Retirement Living Move-in Guide

Use this three-part checklist to help you make a smooth transition to your new retirement living home.

Part I: Leading up to the move   *Notes:* _____

- ❑ Understand your new space limitations.
- ❑ Decide what you can and cannot take.
- ❑ Dispose of surplus furniture, clothing, etc.
    - ❑ Gifts to family/friends.
    - ❑ Garage sale, consignment shop, eBay, other sale.
    - ❑ Goodwill, Salvation Army, other charity.
    - ❑ Storage unit.
    - ❑ Other: _____

- ❑ Discontinue old/sign up for new...
    - ❑ Phone service.
    - ❑ Cable service.
    - ❑ Utilities.
    - ❑ Newspaper.
    - ❑ Other: _____

- ❑ Give change of address notice to...
    - ❑ Magazine subscriptions.
    - ❑ Church and clubs.
    - ❑ Bank, investments, insurance, etc.
    - ❑ Post Office.
    - ❑ Family and friends.
    - ❑ Other: _____

- ❑ Arrange for moving company or helpers.
- ❑ Pack whatever the movers won't be packing.
- ❑ Label each item or box with contents and its room location in the new unit.

Part II: Moving in

❑ Supervise arrangement of furniture and other larger items.

❑ Unpack kitchen and arrange new drawers and cupboards.

❑ Unpack clothing and set up new closets.

❑ Hang pictures/arrange personal items.

❑ Set up books and bookcases.

❑ Present a friendly first impression to onlookers.

❑ If you have helpers, don't forget treats!

Part III: Settling in after the move

❑ Introduce yourself to new neighbors, and take advantage of "new resident" resources.

❑ Sign up for upcoming social and recreation opportunities.

❑ Learn about and join groups, clubs, or classes that interest you.

❑ Learn about and begin using exercise facilities, programs, or classes.

❑ Introduce yourself to the administrator, resident services director, and workers you meet.

❑ Check out your new surrounding community for ...

    ❑ Convenient shops, pharmacy, grocery store, etc.

    ❑ Upcoming cultural events.

    ❑ Museums, libraries, etc.

    ❑ Parks and places of interest.

❑ Select a new primary care physician, if necessary.

❑ Select a new faith community, if appropriate.

❑ Switch your voter registration.

Notes: _____

Checklist for Communicating Clearly With Your Doctor

My Name: _____

Date: _____

Appointment With: _____

Part I: Information I want to give my doctor:

My health care goals and priorities (especially any changes since my last visit): _____

_____

_____

_____

My advance directives (especially any changes since my last visit): _____

_____

_____

_____

	I would want	I would not want	I'm not certain
✔ CPR (Emergency steps to restart my heart and breathing if they stop)			
✔ Forms of treatment if I were terminally ill or in a permanent coma			
• chemotherapy/radiation			
• blood transfusions			
• kidney dialysis			
• respirator/ventilator			
• tube or IV feeding, water			
• antibiotics			
• other			
✔ Organ donation			
✔ Hospice care if I had a terminal illness			

Part II: Questions I want to ask; concerns I want to discuss:

1:_____

_____

_____

2:_____

_____

_____

3:_____

_____

_____

4:_____

_____

_____

Part III: Information my doctor is giving me:

1:_____

_____

_____

2:_____

_____

_____

3:_____

_____

_____

4:_____

_____

_____

List of Current Medications

Prescription Medications I am Taking Regularly or as Needed:

Name/Usage/Dose	Prescribing Physician	Date Began

Over-the-Counter Medications I am Taking Regularly or as Needed (Be Sure to Include Herbs, Vitamins, and Supplements):

Name/Usage/Dose   Date Began

_____

_____

_____

_____

_____

_____

_____

_____

_____

_____

_____

_____

_____

_____

_____

_____

_____

_____

_____

_____

Medications Check-off List

Week of: _____

			✔ Each Day a Dose is Taken						
Medication	Amount	Time	**Sun**	**Mon**	**Tues**	**Wed**	**Thur**	**Fri**	**Sat**
Morning									
Noon/Afternoon									
Evening/Dinnertime									
Bedtime/Night									

THIS FORM IS FROM THE BOOK *AGING IN STRIDE* • TO ORDER: CALL 800-448-5213 OR VISIT WWW.AGINGINSTRIDE.ORG

Medications Check-off List

Week of: _____

✔ Each Day a Dose is Taken

Medication	Amount	Time	Sun	Mon	Tues	Wed	Thur	Fri	Sat
Morning									
Noon/Afternoon									
Evening/Dinnertime									
Bedtime/Night									

Personal Values Statement

What is a Values Statement?

A values statement is simply a description in your own words of how you feel about certain health care issues.

You may create a values statement in writing, on a computer, audiotape, or videotape. You can even explain your thoughts to a friend, who then writes them down for you. There are no special requirements, such as witnesses. But if you fill out a values statement, you should be sure to sign and date it. Then, give copies to your doctor and to your health care representative, if you have one.

A values statement is NOT the same as an advance directive, and it does not take the place of an advance directive. But it can help your care team—your health care representative, doctor and other care providers, and family—know where you stand on issues that could affect your care. Then, whether you have an advance directive or not, they can use this information if they ever have to make a difficult care decision on your behalf.

Using This Form

This form is a worksheet you may find convenient in organizing and writing down your wishes. If you find you need more space, just attach extra pages. (If you do add pages, it's a good idea to number and sign or initial each extra sheet and staple everything together.)

If you would like more help, ask for it. There are many resources available to you: social workers, chaplains, and patient advocates, to name just a few.

One last note: the words and phrases marked with footnote numbers are defined on page 4 of this form.

Personal Values Statement of: _____

When you first fill out this form, enter the date below. Then as you update information, enter those dates as well.

Date written or last reviewed: [_____] [_____] [_____] [_____]

To my care team:

If the time ever comes when I do not understand my situation and cannot act for myself, please take the following information into account in making care decisions for me. Here, in my own words, is where I stand:

My priorities and goals for my future health care are: _____

_____

_____

_____

My views concerning use of life-saving measures, such as CPR[1], are: _____

_____

_____

_____

My thoughts about medical treatment if I were either terminally ill or in a permanent coma:

Chemotherapy or radiation[2]: _____

_____

_____

_____

_____

Blood transfusions[3]: _____

_____

_____

Dialysis[4]: _____

_____

_____

Ventilator[5]: _____

_____

_____

Artificial nutrition and hydration[6]: _____

_____

_____

Antibiotics[7]: _____

_____

_____

My thoughts on being an organ donor: _____

_____

_____

_____

My thoughts about use of comfort measures, such as medications that reduce pain and hospice care[8]: _____

_____

_____

_____

_____

_____

Other thoughts I would like to include: _____

_____

_____

_____

_____

_____

_____

_____

_____

Definitions

1. CPR stands for "cardiopulmonary resuscitation." That means emergency steps to restart a person's heart and breathing after they have already stopped. If a person does not want CPR, he or she can ask the doctor to write a DNR ("do-not-resuscitate") Order in the medical chart. (In a few states, a person can wear a bracelet that says to emergency response people, "Don't start CPR." But, normally, the 911 team will start CPR first, and sort out advance directive status later.)

2. Chemotherapy and radiation are two forms of cancer treatment. They often cause side effects, such as nausea.

3. Sometimes a person, especially someone with advanced cancer, may be bleeding on the inside. This would normally cause death, but blood transfusions may delay death for a time.

4. If a person's kidneys shut down, death will follow. Dialysis is using a machine to clean the person's blood artificially.

5. A ventilator is a breathing machine. It forces air in and out of the lungs.

6. Some people lose the ability to swallow. Artificial nutrition and hydration refers to food and water taken through a tube or IV (intravenous) line.

7. A person who is dying, for example from cancer, might get an infection, and the infection might actually be the immediate cause of death. Under these circumstances, using antibiotics to fight infection might actually prolong the person's dying.

8. Hospice care is care for persons who are living with a terminal illness. The focus is on the person's comfort.

Worksheet for Evaluating a Nursing Facility

Facility or Community: _____

Location: _____

Level of care needed: ❑ Subacute care or rehabilitation after hospital stay
❑ Long-term skilled nursing care
❑ Long-term care for Alzheimer's or other dementia
❑ Other: _____

Contact person: _____

Phone/E-mail: _____

Part I: Preliminary considerations

Location is convenient for...   *Notes:* _____

❑ trips to doctor's office or hospital?   _____
❑ visits by family and friends?   _____
Evaluation: ❑ Excellent ❑ Good ❑ Acceptable ❑ Unacceptable

This facility is well regarded by...   *Notes:* _____

❑ primary care doctor?   _____
❑ hospital discharge planner?   _____
❑ others:_____   _____
Evaluation: ❑ Excellent ❑ Good ❑ Acceptable ❑ Unacceptable

Part II: Points to discuss; questions to ask

Who will pay...   *Notes:* _____

❑ Medicare?   _____
❑ Medicaid?   _____
❑ long-term care insurance?   _____
❑ resident will be responsible
   for:_____   _____
Evaluation: ❑ Excellent ❑ Good ❑ Acceptable ❑ Unacceptable

Is this facility a good fit...

❑ for meeting the person's immediate and future nursing and rehabilitative care needs?

❑ in light of other factors, such as social and emotional needs and the availability or non-availability of other alternatives?

Evaluation: ❑ Excellent   ❑ Good   ❑ Acceptable   ❑ Unacceptable

Notes: _____
_____
_____
_____
_____
_____

Part III: Things to watch for during a visit

Building and grounds...

❑ appear to be clean and well maintained?

❑ include amenities, such as:

   ❑ rooms for private meals and get-togethers?

   ❑ computer access to send and receive e-mail?

   ❑ patio or walkways for outdoor time when weather permits?

Evaluation: ❑ Excellent   ❑ Good   ❑ Acceptable   ❑ Unacceptable

Notes: _____
_____
_____
_____
_____

The employees are...

❑ courteous, friendly, eager to help?

❑ neat, clean, well-groomed?

❑ adequately trained, good at what they do?

❑ respectful of the residents?

Evaluation: ❑ Excellent   ❑ Good   ❑ Acceptable   ❑ Unacceptable

Notes: _____
_____
_____
_____

The residents are...

❑ dressed and groomed appropriately?

❑ engaged in activities?

Evaluation: ❑ Excellent   ❑ Good   ❑ Acceptable   ❑ Unacceptable

Notes: _____
_____

Nursing Facility Move-in Checklist

Use this three-part checklist to help you or your loved one make a smooth transition to living and receiving care in a nursing facility.

Part I: Before the move

Notes: _____

❑ Decide which clothing and personal items will make the move.

❑ Mark these items with a laundry-safe form of personal identification.

❑ Put together a written inventory of the items you or your loved one will be taking.

❑ Make arrangements, as needed, for:

  ❑ taking care of a pet

  ❑ organizing and paying bills

  ❑ managing property

  ❑ other: _____

Part II: On moving day

❑ Unpack clothing and set up new closet.

❑ Hang pictures/arrange personal items.

❑ Get acquainted with staff and nearby residents.

❑ Share a meal.

❑ Plan an upcoming visit or outing.

❑ Take a tour and spend some time exploring the building and grounds; look for amenities such as:

  ❑ Patio or outdoor walks

  ❑ Rooms for private meals or get-togethers

  ❑ Library

  ❑ Chapel

  ❑ Activities room

Part III: Settling in after the move

☐ Learn about and take part in social and recreation activities.

☐ Learn about and join groups that interest you.

☐ Attend a meeting of the resident council.

☐ Select a new primary care physician, if you need to.

☐ Get acquainted with the facility's:

  ☐ Caregivers.

  ☐ Social work staff.

  ☐ Chaplain.

  ☐ Administrator.

☐ Switch your voter registration.

Notes: _____

_____

_____

_____

_____

_____

_____

_____

_____

_____

_____

Additional Notes: _____

_____

_____

_____

_____

_____

_____

_____

_____

_____

_____

_____

_____

_____

_____

Resident/Family Care Conference Worksheet

My Name: _____

Resident's Name (if different): _____

Facility: _____

Part I: Before The Care Conference—Preparation Notes
Next Care Conference Scheduled for:

Date: _____ Time: _____ Location: _____

Information and Questions I Want to Discuss:

✓ Resident's Personal History: _____
_____
_____
_____

✓ Resident's Medical/Health Status: _____
_____
_____
_____

✓ Resident's Social/Emotional Status: _____
_____
_____
_____

✓ Questions about Resident's Care Plan: _____
_____
_____
_____

✓ Possible Concerns/Complaint Issues: _____
_____
_____
_____

✓ Opportunities for Family Support and
Involvement: _____
_____
_____
_____

Part II: At the Care Conference—Participation Notes

Date Held: _____

Location: _____

Who Was There: _____

What We Discussed:

✓ Resident's Personal History: _____
_____
_____
_____

✓ Resident's Medical/Health Status: _____
_____
_____
_____

✓ Resident's Social/Emotional Status: _____
_____
_____
_____

✓ Resident's Care Plan: _____
_____
_____
_____

✓ Possible Concerns/Complaint Issues: _____
_____
_____
_____

✓ Family Support and Involvement Issues: _____
_____
_____
_____

Next Care Conference Scheduled for:

Date: _____ Time: _____ Location: _____

Worksheet for Questions, Concerns, and Complaints

To*: _____

Name of resident: _____

My name, if different: _____

How to reach me: _____

Today's date: _____

    *   Usually, the best place to start is the facility's administrator or the nurse in charge of your care or your loved one's care. Complaints may also be directed to the state's Long Term Care Ombudsman or to its Medicare and Medicaid survey and certification agency.

The following is . . .

    ❑   Feedback or an observation I think you should be aware of.

    ❑   A question or concern I have.

    ❑   A complaint I am asking you to do something about.

    ❑   Other: _____

My concern or question is (please be as specific as possible in describing the "what," "where," "when," and "who" involved in this situation): _____

_____

_____

_____

_____

_____

_____

The outcome or change I am seeking is: _____

_____

_____

_____

_____

Please use the back of this sheet if you need more space

Confidential Personal Information

Use this form to create a road map of your most important relationships, service providers, records, and investments. When you first fill out this form, enter the date below. Then as you update information, enter those dates as well.

Remember, much of this information is confidential. Keep this information in your safe deposit box or other secure location, and don't forget to let a close family member or friend know where they can find it, if they need it.

Date prepared or last updated: [_____] [_____] [_____] [_____]

Personal Information

Name _____

Address _____

Phone _____

Social Security No. _____

Driver License No. _____

Medicare No. _____

Medicaid No. _____

Armed Forces No. _____

Religious Affiliation/Minister _____

Children *(names, addresses and telephone numbers)*

_____

_____

_____

_____

Other Close Relatives/Friends *(names, addresses and telephone numbers)*

_____

_____

_____

_____

Household Support *(include name, contact person and telephone number)*

Chore service agency _____

_____

Personal care provider _____

_____

House cleaning _____

_____

Other (security? transportation? meals?) _____

_____

_____

_____

Health Care Providers *(name and telephone number)*

Primary care physician _____

Physician specialists _____

_____

Eye doctor _____

Dentist _____

Long-term care or assisted living facility _____

_____

Hospital _____

Home health care provider _____

Pharmacist _____

Other care provider(s) _____

_____

_____

_____

_____

Insurance Information *(company, plan, policy number, telephone number)*

Health Insurance/HMO/Managed care _____

_____

Medicare supplement _____

_____

Long-term care insurance _____

_____

Car insurance _____

_____

Homeowners insurance _____

_____

Life insurance _____

_____

_____

Legal and Financial *[Bank/firm name(s), branch(es), account number(s), and signer(s)]*

Attorney _____

Accountant _____

Stock broker or investment advisor _____

Bank _____

Checking accounts _____

_____

Savings accounts _____

_____

Safe deposit box _____

Stocks and bonds _____

_____

_____

Estate Planning Documents *(location, date signed or last updated)*

Will (including trust documents) _____

_____

Living will (health care directive) _____

_____

Appointment of health care representative *(include name, address, and telephone number of person you have appointed)* _____

_____

Financial Records *(where kept)*

Prior tax returns _____

_____

This year's tax information _____

_____

Checkbook and savings passbooks _____

_____

Pension, IRA, Keogh, and other deferred compensation records _____

_____

_____

Real estate documents *(deeds, mortgages, notes)* _____

_____

Insurance policies and premium payment records _____

_____

Health care expense and reimbursement records _____

_____

Prepaid funeral plan, burial plot documents _____

_____

Other notes and instructions _____

_____

Checklist for Selecting Long-Term Care Insurance

My name: _____   Today's date: _____

    Company: _____

    Agent: _____

    Policy Name: _____

Notes: _____

What does this policy cover?

❑ Care in a nursing home?

❑ Care in an assisted living facility?

❑ Care services provided at home?

❑ Care management services?

❑ Other:_____

What are the limits of coverage?

❑ Life-time limit on payment for nursing come care?

❑ Life-time limit on payment for home health care services?

❑ Maximum length of stay in a nursing home?

❑ Maximum duration of home care services?

❑ Waiting period for pre-existing conditions?

❑ Coverage for Alzheimer's or other dementia care?

❑ Waiting period before benefits start?

❑ Other:_____

How does this policy handle rising costs of care due to inflation?

❑ Automatically adjusts for inflation?

❑ Able to buy more coverage?

❑ Other: _____?

What conditions have to be met before benefits begin?

❑ Physician certifies that care is needed?

❑ Prior hospitalization?

❑ Other:_____?

Can the company cancel this policy?

❑ If so, under what circumstances?

How much will this policy cost?

❑ Cost per month? _____

❑ Cost per quarter? _____

❑ Cost per six months? _____

❑ Cost per year? _____

Notes: _____

_____

_____

_____

_____

_____

_____

_____

_____

_____

_____

_____

_____

_____

Additional Notes: _____

_____

_____

_____

_____

_____

_____

_____

_____

_____

_____

_____

_____

_____

_____

Checklist for Selecting a Hospice or Palliative Care Provider

Finding a hospice provider near you is usually not difficult. Ask your doctor, hospital discharge planner, home care staff, or nursing home staff for a referral. You may also search a convenient national database of hospice providers by going to www.nhpco.org.

Before you make your choice, here are some questions you should ask.

License and Affiliations

❑ Most states license hospice organizations. Is this program fully licensed?

❑ Does this agency belong to the National Hospice and Palliative Care Organization?

Payment

❑ Is this hospice program approved to accept the Medicare Hospice Benefit?

❑ If the Medicare Hospice Benefit is not available, what services will be charged for? How will fees be set?

❑ Many hospice services are covered by Medicare or other insurance. What are the covered services? What help will the hospice program offer in processing claims?

❑ If you have limited ability to pay for hospice care, will the provider accept you anyway?

Notes: _____

_____

_____

_____

_____

_____

_____

_____

_____

_____

_____

_____

_____

_____

_____

_____

_____

_____

_____

_____

_____

_____

_____

_____

Services Offered

Notes: _____

❑   Does this hospice offer 24-hour
    nursing coverage? If not, what
    coverage arrangements are available?

❑   Will the same hospice staff generally
    stay with the patient and family
    throughout the course of care?

❑   Does this hospice provide hospital or
    other inpatient care services? If not,
    what transfer arrangements will be
    made, if needed?

❑   What bereavement and other family
    support services does this hospice
    provide?

❑   Does this hospice provide respite care
    for primary caregivers when needed?
    If not, is the agency able to help the
    family arrange for respite care from
    another source?

Funeral or Memorial Service Planner

Name: _____ Date: _____

Type of Service Preferred

❏ Funeral—open casket   ❏ Religious

❏ Funeral—closed casket   ❏ Non-religious

❏ Memorial service   ❏ Family only

❏ Other:_____   ❏ Open

Arrangements

Location of service: _____

Time of service: _____

Do you wish to hold visiting hours before the service? _____

_____

When? _____ Where? _____

Do you wish to have a reception after the service? _____

_____

When? _____ Where? _____

Content of Service

❏ Organ or other instrumental music

❏ Soloist

❏ Hymns or songs for congregational singing

Musical selections: _____

_____

_____

_____

_____

Scripture readings/other readings: _____

_____

_____

Eulogies/personal statements or recollections: _____

_____

_____

Other important elements: _____

_____

_____

Participants

Person(s) officiating: _____

Musicians: _____

_____

Speaker(s): _____

_____

Pallbearers/honorary pallbearers: _____

_____

_____

Ushers: _____

_____

_____

Other notes: _____

_____

_____

_____

_____

_____

Family Meeting Planner

Purpose of meeting:

(*Example: To discuss eldercare needs for Mom and how best to meet them.*)

_____

_____

_____

Suggested ground rules:

- **Be inclusive.** Invite everyone who should be involved or thinks they should be involved; invite the person or people whose care and well-being you plan to discuss.

- **Try to deal in facts and truth.** But remember, people of good faith and good intentions often see things very differently. Building a consensus usually means meeting somewhere in the middle, so try not to be a "hold out." As a group, agree on what you can agree on, and agree to respect each other's views in those areas where you can't agree.

- **Stay focused.** Stick to the purpose of the meeting and the eldercare needs you are there to address. Agree at the beginning that this is not an appropriate time or place for "other stuff," for example, past disagreements, hurts, etc.

- **Be fair.** The whole idea is to tap the full range of resources available in the family. Those involved need to be willing to share the load. It's OK to ask for help. It's also important to ask, "How can I help?"

What are the eldercare issues and needs we should discuss and address?

1. _____

_____

2. _____

_____

3. _____

_____

4. _____

_____

5. _____

_____

What specific steps are we agreeing to take? Who will be responsible for what?

TASK	PERSON RESPONSIBLE	DUE DATE
_____	_____	_____
_____	_____	_____
_____	_____	_____
_____	_____	_____
_____	_____	_____
_____	_____	_____
_____	_____	_____
_____	_____	_____
_____	_____	_____
_____	_____	_____
_____	_____	_____

Where do we go from here? How will we follow up with one another? Circulate copies of what we discussed and decided? Check in with one another by e-mail or phone? Have a second meeting?

_____

_____

_____

_____

_____

_____

_____

_____

_____

Checklist for Selecting and Working
With a Geriatric Care Manager

*This is a three-part form. Use **Part I** to help decide how you might use the services of a geriatric care manager (GCM). Use **Part II** as a guide in choosing a qualified GCM. Use **Part III** to help you work effectively with the GCM you select.*

Part I: Do we need a Geriatric Care Manager?   *Notes:* _____

Do you or does your loved one need . . .

❑ A professional needs assessment on:

    ❑ Medical issues or health concerns.

    ❑ Psychological, emotional, or mental health needs.

    ❑ Housing, personal care, or quality-of-life issues.

❑ Support in finding, arranging, and monitoring support services:

    ❑ Meals and nutrition.

    ❑ Transportation.

    ❑ Help with activities of daily living.

    ❑ Bill paying and similar tasks.

    ❑ In-home health care.

    ❑ Other support for independent living.

❑ An "on the scene" surrogate for family living at a distance.

❑ Someone to help with family communications, meetings.

❑ An advocate in dealings with the health care system, insurance plans, etc.

❑ Other: _____

Part II: Selecting a Geriatric Care Manager

In most states, geriatric care managers are not licensed or regulated. So, it pays to do your homework before making your selection.

❑ What are the person's qualifications, education and experience?

❏ Ask for three or more references. Then, follow up by giving them a call. (Note: for confidentiality reasons, a GCM will probably not be able to give you the names of other clients or families served. Instead, expect to see as references physicians, lawyers who serve mostly older clients, and other similar professionals.)

❏ How long has this person been providing GCM services?

❏ Does this person know the local senior services scene?

❏ How does this person charge for services? Is this a service you can budget for? Who will be paying for these services?

❏ Is this person affiliated with a particular organization or service provider? If so, can he/she be impartial in making recommendations?

❏ Will this person make good communications a priority? How will you exchange information? By meeting in person? By phone? By e-mail?

Part III: Getting the Most Out of Your Relationship

Here are some easy ways to get the most out of your relationship:

❏ Arrange for regular updates; when you receive new information, deal with it promptly.

❏ Give regular feedback to your GCM on how well the arrangement seems to be working; ask for his/her feedback, too.

❏ Ask yourself from time to time whether there is an expanded role your GCM could be playing, or whether there are areas in which you or your loved one no longer needs help.

Notes: _____

_____

_____

_____

_____

_____

_____

_____

_____

_____

_____

_____

_____

_____

_____

_____

_____

_____

_____

_____

_____

_____

_____

_____

_____

_____

_____

_____

_____

Health Care Representative's Discussion Checklist

Acting as another person's health care representative is both an honor and a responsibility. You may never have to step in and make decisions; but if you do, the more you know about the person's values and wishes, the easier your job will be.

Here is a worksheet listing questions you may want to discuss with the person who is asking you to be their health care representative. There is room for additional notes on the second page.

Written Notes, Personal Values Statement

_____ Have you (the person for whom decisions might have to be made) written down your health care wishes? If so, who has copies?

    _____ Living will form

    _____ Health care appointment form

    _____ Personal values statement form

    _____ Other: _____

Life-saving Measures

_____ Have you discussed CPR ("cardiopulmonary resuscitation") and DNR ("do not resuscitate") orders with your doctor? (CPR is emergency treatment to restart a person's heart and breathing after they have stopped. A DNR order is a doctor's written instructions not to start CPR.)

_____ Would you want to have CPR started if your heart or breathing were to stop?

Life-sustaining Measures

_____ Are there some forms of treatment you would or would not want if you were close to dying or in a deep, permanent coma? For example, how do you feel about:

    _____ Ventilator (mechanically-assisted breathing)?

    _____ Dialysis (a machine doing the work of the kidneys)?

    _____ Receiving food and water through a tube or needle?

    _____ Blood transfusions?

    _____ Drug or radiation therapy?

    _____ Antibiotics (drugs to fight a life-threatening infection)?

    _____ Being an organ donor?

    _____ Other? _____

Notes: _____

_____

_____

_____

_____

_____

_____

_____

_____

_____

_____

_____

_____

_____

_____

_____

_____

_____

_____

_____

_____

_____

_____

_____

_____

_____

_____

_____

Glossary

Adult Day Center—Also called *Adult Day Services, Adult Day Care Centers,* or *Adult Day Health Centers,* these facilities provide regular daytime care to older adults for socialization, recreation, help with personal care, safety, and in some cases, health and rehabilitation-related services.

Adult Family Homes—Single-family, private residences that have been licensed to provide room, board, and support services to a small number (usually from four to six) of older adults.

Advance Directive—A legal document that allows you to make statements about your health care in case you are unable to do so at a later time. (See *Durable Power of Attorney; Health Care Directive.*)

Aerobic Exercise—Exercise that strengthens the heart and lungs so that oxygen is more efficiently delivered.

Area Agency on Aging—The local or regional agency established under the Federal Older Americans Act to coordinate and provide a wide variety of services to the elderly.

Assisted Living—Assisted living facilities offer private, homelike living space (for example, an apartment or cottage) with some of the same services a nursing facility can offer, including help with personal care needs and some health care services. Most facilities also include housekeeping, meals, and an activity program.

Care Conferences—Meetings held in a nursing facility or other care setting to devise and carry out a plan of care for the resident. Care conferences are attended by the care team, made up of key provider staff, the resident, and family members (if the resident desires).

Continuing Care Retirement Communities—CCRCs are retirement communities that include various levels of care—from independent living to assisted living to skilled nursing care. Residents typically must move in when they are relatively healthy.

Cycle of Inactivity—A pattern that can develop when an older adult sustains a fall, and develops a fear of falling that leads to a lack of exercise, leading to a decline in physical condition, which in turn makes another fall more likely.

Deductible—The amount of expense that an insured person must incur before an insurance carrier becomes liable for payment.

Dementia—Disorders of the brain (including Alzheimer's disease and other illnesses) that result in a decline in the memory and other intellectual functions.

Discharge Planning—A service provided through hospitals and other health care providers to help place a convalescing patient in an appropriate care setting, or to arrange appropriate services at home or other lesser-care location.

Durable Medical Equipment—Home care equipment that is used over an extended period of time (such as oxygen delivery system, hospital bed, wheelchair, commode).

Durable Power of Attorney—A legal document executed as part of a person's estate planning. In it, the person names an "attorney-in-fact" or "agent" to act on his or her behalf in business and/or health care matters.

Durable Power of Attorney for Health Care—Also called a *Health Care Appointment* or a *Health Care Proxy*. This is a legal document that lets you give someone else the power to make health care decisions for you if a time comes that you can't speak for yourself.

Eldercare Locator—A nationwide toll-free telephone number and online service from the U.S. Administration on Aging (1-800-677-1116 or *www.eldercare.gov*).

Enteral Therapy—Feeding through a tube when a patient cannot receive adequate nutrients by eating.

Geriatric Care Manager—An eldercare professional, usually a nurse or social worker, who can do assessments, give guidance, and help families develop and implement a plan of care for frail older adults.

Guardianship—A legal proceeding in which a person is appointed by the court to control and manage another person's affairs and/or property—most typically when the person is incapacitated and unable to act on his/her own.

Health Care Appointment—See *Durable Power of Attorney for Health Care*.

Health Care Directive—Also called a *Living Will*. This is a document that lets you say what kinds of care you would want and not want if you were nearing the end of your life. Usually deals with life-sustaining measures.

Health Care Representative—Also called an *Agent* or *Surrogate*. A representative designated to make decisions about a person's medical care when the person can't speak for him- or herself.

Home Health Care—Health care services provided in the home. Includes care and support provided by home health aides, certified nursing assistants, registered and licensed nurses, rehabilitation therapists, and social workers.

Home Helper—A person who comes into your home to provide help with personal (non-medical) care needs and household chores (also called *Chore Services*).

Homesharing—An arrangement in which two or more people share the same home. Many communities have formal or informal coordinating services to connect people who are interested in homesharing.

Hospice Care—Care for the terminally ill and their families, emphasizing pain management and controlling symptoms, rather than seeking a cure. Offered by hospitals, long-term care facilities and hospice organizations, on an inpatient basis or at home.

Incontinence—Leaking or loss of control of urine. It can result from a variety of causes, and can often be treated through exercise, medication, or surgery.

Independent Living Retirement Communities—Also called *Congregate Care Communities*. Retirement communities offer independent senior living, serving seniors who are generally in good health and able to live independently. They typically offer services such as housekeeping, transportation, and exercise facilities.

Informed Consent—Your right to be in charge of your own health care by having your medical situation and proposed treatment explained to you in language you understand; and your right to give or refuse consent for medical treatment.

Infusion Therapy—Intravenous (IV) medications, such as antibiotics, pain relief drugs, nutritional infusion, or chemotherapy.

Living Will—See *Health Care Directive*.

Long-Term Care Insurance—Private insurance designed to cover all or part of the cost of care in a nursing facility or (in some cases) home health care.

Meals On Wheels—Community-based meal service that delivers meals to the homes of older adults at a modest charge.

Medicaid—A joint state/federal program which helps pay the medical expenses of low-income individuals who meet the program's qualifying standards.

Medicare—The federal program that provides health insurance for people 65 and over, for people with permanent kidney failure, and those with certain disabilities.

Medicare Supplement ("Medigap") Insurance—Private insurance programs designed primarily to cover Medicare deductibles and co-payments.

Nurse Registry—Employment agency for home care nurses and aides; may or may not be licensed.

Nursing Homes—See *Skilled Nursing Facility*.

Ombudsman—In long-term care and assisted living, the ombudsman program provides advocacy and trouble-shooting support for residents. Open access to the ombudsman is a protected resident right.

Palliative Care—Medical care designed not to cure disease or halt adverse medical conditions, but to minimize symptoms and control pain.

Physiologic Reserve—The ability of the body's systems to function effectively, and to fight off or bounce back from illnesses. Physiologic reserve decreases with age, illness, and inactivity.

Power of Attorney—A legal document that gives another person legal authority to act on one's behalf. (See *Durable Power of Attorney*.)

Proprioception—The ability of the nerves to feel or sense where we are in space.

Respite Care—Temporary care for a person, provided by a home health care agency or other provider, in order to give the person's regular caregiver rest and personal time. Respite care can be in the home, at an adult day center, or in a long-term care facility or hospital.

Reverse Mortgage—A loan against your house that allows you to convert part of your equity into cash; the loan and interest are paid back when the home is sold or the owner dies.

Senior Information and Referral—Also called *Senior Information and Assistance* in many communities. A telephone and/or online referral service operated in each community by the local or regional Area Agency on Aging or an organization designated by it; the primary access point for identifying services and resources for older adults.

Skilled Nursing Facility—Also called *Nursing Homes,* these facilities play two important roles: they provide rehabilitation or "subacute care" for people who have just been discharged from the hospital but are not medically or physically able to return home; and they provide extended long-term care to frail or chronically ill persons who require a higher level of skilled nursing and medical supervision than is available in other settings.

Trust—A form of ownership under which property is held and managed by a person or institution (the trustee) for the benefit of other persons or institutions (the beneficiaries).

Index

assisted living facilities, 91, 93-94
Continuing Care Retirement Communities, 90-91, 94-95
Decision-making, 87-89
homesharing, 89
low-income senior housing, 90, 95
nursing facilities, 92
options, 87-95
Retirement Housing Planning Sheet, 317
retirement living communities, 90, 93
selecting a facility, 97-102
senior housing, 90
Worksheet for Evaluating a Senior Living Community, 319

I

Incontinence (see *Urinary incontinence*)

Incontinence aids, 149

Informed consent, 155-158, 359

Infusion therapy, 75, 359

Intestacy, 194

J

Journal-keeping, 28

K

Kegel exercises, 146, 148

L

Living wills (see *Advance Directives*)

Long distance caregiving, 173, 176, 267, 273-278
communicating in, 275-276

Long-term care (see *Nursing facilities*)

Legal assistance, 64

Long-term care insurance, 168, 218-223, 360
Checklist for Selecting Long-Term Care Insurance, 345

cost, 219
determining need for, 218-219
shopping for, 220-222

M

"Meals On Wheels" (see *Nutritional programs*)

Medicaid, 214-217, 360
and adult day services, 83
applying for, 216-217
and home health care, 77
hospice benefit, 245-246
and nursing facility care, 167-168, 214-216
"spending down" for, 214

Medicare, 205-212, 360
2003 Medicare Reform Act, 208-209
enrolling in, 211
and home health care, 76, 208
hospice care coverage, 207, 245-246
hospital inpatient coverage, 206
and nursing facility care, 167-168, 207
Part A, 205-209
Part B, 209-211
prescription coverage, 208-209

Medicare Supplemental Insurance, 212-213, 360
home health care benefit, 76
selecting, 212-213

Medications
for depression, 137-138
interactions, 122
List of Current Medications Form, 325
managing, 118, 121-126
Medications Check-Off List, 327
overmedication, 122
and pain, 152-153
types, 121

"Medigap" (see *Medicare Supplement Insurance*)

Memorial societies, 250